A House Dividing

Comparing the economic and social development of Virginia and Pennsylvania, John Majewski shows how these two states exemplified the remarkable economic divergence between North and South on the eve of the Civil War. New archival research reveals that a broad spectrum of residents in both states embraced canals, railroads and other commercial projects to hold their communities together in America's mobile society. Virginia's commitment to slavery, however, undercut the state's aggressive efforts to keep pace with its northern neighbors. While Philadelphia capitalists financed trunk railroads that opened new markets for Pennsylvania manufacturers, Virginia's railroads remained a collection of local lines serving market towns and slave plantations. The chains of slavery, Virginians learned to their dismay, also shackled the invisible hand of the market.

John Majewski is Associate Professor of History at the University of California, Santa Barbara. His articles have appeared in a number scholarly journals, including *Journal of Economic History*, *Journal of Interdisciplinary History*, and *Law and Society Review*. His dissertation – which provides the basis for *A House Dividing* – won the Allen Nevins Prize from the Economic History Association.

STUDIES IN ECONOMIC HISTORY AND POLICY

Edited by
Louis Galambos, *The Johns Hopkins University*
Robert Gallman, *University of North Carolina at Chapel Hill*
Naomi Lamoreaux, *University of California, Los Angeles*

Moses Abramovitz, *Thinking About Growth: And Other Essays on Economic Growth and Welfare*

Michael A. Bernstein, *The Great Depression: Delayed Recovery and Economic Change in America, 1929–1939*

W. Bernard Carlson, *Innovation as a Social Process: Elihu Thomson and the Rise of General Electric*

Christopher J. Castaneda and Clarance M. Smith, *Gas Pipelines and the Emergence of America's Regulatory State: A History of Panhandle Eastern Corporation, 1928–1993*

Sally H. Clarke, *Regulation and the Revolution in United States Farm Productivity*

Richard Gillespie, *Manufacturing Knowledge: A History of the Hawthorne Experiments*

Margaret B. W. Graham, *The Business of Research: RCA and the Videodisc*

Michael J. Hogan, *The Marshall Plan: America, Britain, and the Reconstruction of Western Europe, 1947–1952*

David A. Hounshell and John Kenly Smith, Jr., *Science and Corporate Strategy: Du Pont R&D, 1902–1980*

Simon Kuznets, *Economic Development, the Family, and Income Distribution: Selected Essays*

Peter D. McClelland and Alan L. Magdovitz, *Crisis in the Making: The Political Economy of New York State since 1945*

William N. Parker, *Essays on the Economic History of Western Capitalism; Volume 1: Europe and the World Economy; Volume 2: America and the Wider World*

Leonard S. Reich, *The Making of American Industrial Research: Science and Business at GE and Bell, 1876–1926*

Hugh Rockoff, *Drastic Measure: A History of Wage and Price Controls in the United States*

Christopher L. Tomlins, *The State and the Unions: Labor Relations, Law and the Organized Labor Movement in America, 1890–1960*

Richard H. K. Vietor, *Energy Policy in America since 1945: A Study of Business–Government Relations*

A House Dividing

*Economic Development in Pennsylvania
and Virginia Before the Civil War*

John Majewski
*University of California,
Santa Barbara*

CAMBRIDGE
UNIVERSITY PRESS

PUBLISHED BY THE PRESS SYNDICATE OF THE UNIVERSITY OF CAMBRIDGE
The Pitt Building, Trumpington Street, Cambridge, United Kingdom

CAMBRIDGE UNIVERSITY PRESS
The Edinburgh Building, Cambridge CB2 2RU, UK   http:\\www.cup.cam.ac.uk
40 West 20th Street, New York, NY 10011-4211, USA   http:\\www.cup.org
10 Stamford Road, Oakleigh, Melbourne 3166, Australia
Ruiz de Alarcón 13, 28014 Madrid, Spain

First published 2000

Printed in the United States of America

Typeface New Baskerville 10/12 pt.   *System* QuarkXPress   [TW]

A catalog record for this book is available from the British Library.

Library of Congress Cataloging in Publication Data

Majewski, John D., 1965–
A house dividing : economic development in Pennsylvania and
Virginia before the Civil War / John Majewski.
p. cm. – (Studies in economic history and policy)
Includes bibliographical references (p. 184).
ISBN 0-521-59023-X
1. Railroads – Pennsylvania – History – 19th century.   2. Railroads –
Virginia – History – 19th century.   3. Free enterprise – Pennsylvania –
History – 19th century.   4. Slavery – Virginia – History – 19th
century.   5. Pennsylvania – Economic conditions.   6. Virginia –
Economic conditions.   I. Title.   II. Title: Economic development
in Pennsylvania and Virginia before the Civil War.   III. Series.
HE2771.P4M35   2000
330.9748´03–dc21   99-28146
                                              CIP

ISBN 0 521 59023 X   hardback

FOR LISA

Contents

Tables

Appendix Tables

Abbreviations

ACLP   Albemarle County Legislative Petitions, Virginia State Library and Archives

ARBPW *Annual Report of the Board of Public Works* (Richmond, various years)

ABPW   Archives of the Board of Public Works, Virginia State Library and Archives

CCHS   Cumberland County Historical Society

CVRR   Cumberland Valley Railroad

PRR   Pennsylvania Railroad

PSA   Pennsylvania State Archives

UVA   Special Collections, Alderman Library, University of Virginia, Charlottesville

VCRR   Virginia Central Railroad

VSLA   Virginia State Library and Archives, Richmond, Virginia

Acknowledgments

One of the great pleasures of finally finishing this book is the opportunity to thank the many individuals and institutions who have helped me along the way. My interests in this topic began many years ago while an undergraduate at UT Austin. My undergraduate advisors, Bruce Hunt and Dave Bowman, spent hours patiently reading my work and listening to my arguments as I worked on my undergraduate thesis. Points taken from that thesis – somewhat improved, I hope – appear in this book. Dave's own work in comparative history largely inspired my decision to undertake the comparison of Pennsylvania and Virginia. Similarly, the social and quantitative history that appears here can be traced to the influence of Peter Earle and Bill Kennedy of the London School of Economics.

The Ph. D. program at UCLA provided me with the opportunity to interact with a number of first-rate scholars. Eric Monkkonen, Jean Laurent Rosenthal, Bill Summerhill, and Mary Yeager are among the many who generously shared their time with me. Two UCLA mentors deserve special mention. Joyce Appleby oversaw my dissertation (reading every chapter at least twice) and helped me come to grips with the ideological and political implications of my research. Readers familiar with the historiography of the early republic will have little trouble detecting her influence in the pages that follow. Nor will they have much difficulty finding the impact of Ken Sokoloff. At every step of the way, Ken provided training, advice, and support. Even more importantly, he served as a superb exemplar of an innovative and meticulous scholar.

My fellow graduate students at UCLA gave me plenty of help, advice, and argument. I am especially indebted to EATS (Early American Thesis Seminar), whose members prepared delicious meals and provided penetrating insights. Hans Eicholtz, Dave Lehman, Anne Lombard, Jim Pearson, Paula Scott, and Barbara Wallace were particularly supportive. Jonathan Sassi gave especially helpful comments and advice. Graduate school – which has it shares of ups and downs – would have been downright impossible without the support and friendship of Jim and Heather Meriwether.

A number of scholars commented on portions of the manuscript, including Sean Adams, Loren Brandt, John Bezis-Selfa, Charles Dew, Lacy Ford, Sally Griffith, Carl Harris, John Laurent Larson, Maggie Levenstein, Frank Lewis, David Meyer, Ken Moure, and Winifred Rothenberg. Gavin Wright and Richard John gave a particularly close and sympathetic reading to several chapters. I received excellent comments at many conferences, including workshops at the University of Michigan, the University of Toronto, the Philadelphia Center for Early American Studies, and Queens University. I am especially appreciative of the All-UC Economic History Group, who have provided a critical but supportive audience since this project's inception.

I have been fortunate enough to receive generous funding that made this project possible. I want to thank the Philadelphia Center for Early American Studies, the Beveridge Research Grants of the American Historical Association, the John R. Rovensky Foundation, the Philadelphia Center for Early American Studies, and the Virginia Historical Society. I owe an especially large debt to Walter Grinder, John and Christine Blundell, and Greg Rehmke, all formerly of the Institute for Humane Studies. The Institute not only provided much needed financial assistance during the early stages of my graduate career, but also excellent training, sage advice, and tremendous moral support. Perhaps the best thing the Institute did for this book was putting me in touch with Dan Klein, who gave me the opportunity to coauthor several articles on New York turnpikes and plank roads. It would be hard to overstate the influence of Dan's research on my thinking.

Many librarians and archivists provided help in tracking down obscure references. I especially want to thank the staffs at the Alderman Library of the University of Virginia, the Cumberland County Historical Society, the Hagley Museum and Library (especially Christopher Baer), the Pennsylvania Historical Society, the Pennsylvania State Library, the Virginia Historical Society, and the Virginia State Library and Archives.

It has been a pleasure to work with Cambridge University Press. Naomi Lamoreaux was a tremendous help as the series editor. She read the manuscript three times, offering excellent criticism at each stage. The book would have suffered greatly without her comments and support. Frank Smith and Jennifer Carey expertly guided the book through the final stages of production.

My colleagues at UCSB provided a friendly and supportive environment for completing my research and writing. I would especially like to thank Randy Bergstrom, Elliot Brownlee, Mark Elliott, Carl Harris, Fred Logevall, Alice O'Connor, Ken Moure, Ann Plane, Jack Talbot, and Erika Rappaport. Sarah Case and Jay Carlander were superb research assistants who gathered data, proofed chapters, and made excellent comments. I am especially thankful that I had Jay's help during the last stages of preparing the manuscript.

I would also like to thank the *Journal of Interdisciplinary History* and MIT Press for allowing me to reprint portions of an article ("The Political Impact of Great Commercial Cities" 28:1 [Summer, 1997], 1–26) that appears in Chapter 5. The editors of the *Journal of Economic History* have allowed me to reprint portions of "Who Financed the Transportation Revolution? Regional Divergence and Internal Improvements in Pennsylvania and Virginia" 56:4 (December 1996), 763–788.

Writing can be a fairly lonely business, but Barbara and Bob Reilley, James and Verline Majewski, Jeff and Carrie Majewski, Jamey and Lecia Majewski, and their respective families made sure that I experienced plenty of laughter. So, too, did Charles and Vivian Jacobson, Melanie Jacobson and Jim Pearson, and Karen Jacobson and Jerry Schwartz. No words could convey my love and gratitude for Lisa Jacobson and Samuel Jacob Majewski. It will be many years before Sam will read this book, but Lisa had to live with it almost as long as I did. She provided insightful criticism, sound advice, and constant support. She not only made this project possible, but also worthwhile. It is to her that this book is dedicated.

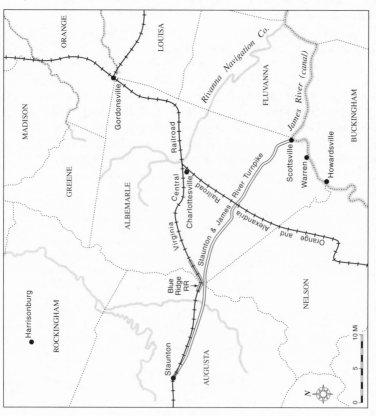

Selected Improvements in Albemarle County, Virginia   In the 1820s, intense town rivalry motivated residents to invest in projects such as the Staunton and James River Turnpike and the Rivanna Navigation Company. Charlottesville landed the deciding blow in 1850, when the Virginia Central extended its line through the town. The Orange and Alexandria, completed in 1860, had a more limited impact.

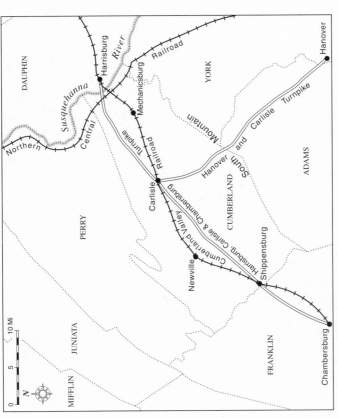

Selected Improvements in Cumberland County, Pennsylvania In the 1810s, local residents financed several turnpikes and the Harrisburg Bridge. Philadelphia capitalists, hoping to capture the county's trade, financed the Cumberland Valley Railroad in the 1830s. Baltimore interests later sponsored the Northern Central, but the company teetered near bankruptcy in the 1850s.

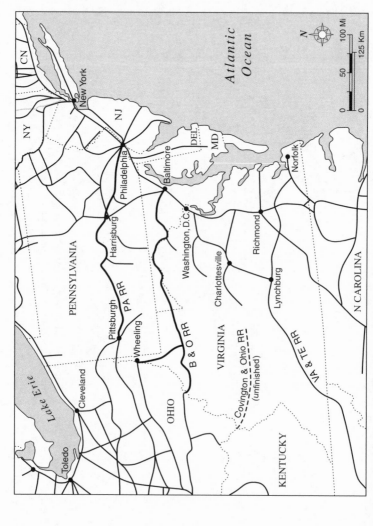

Railroads in the Middle Atlantic States, 1860   Large cities such as Philadelphia and Baltimore built trunk lines such as the Pennsylvania Railroad and the Baltimore and Ohio Railroad across the Appalachians. Virginia's railroad network, on the other hand, never reached the Ohio River before the Civil War.

Introduction

Regional Development in Comparative Perspective

In 1858, Abraham Lincoln proclaimed that America was a "house divided." The political agitation over the extension of slavery into the western territories had convinced Lincoln that America was at a crossroads. "Either the *opponents* of slavery, will arrest the further spread of it, and place it where the public mind shall rest in the belief that it is in course of ultimate extinction; or its *advocates* will push it forward, till it shall become alike lawful in *all* the States, *old* as well as *new – North* as well as *South*."[1]

The latter possibility terrified many Northerners, and not only because of the growing conviction that slavery corrupted republican politics and undermined Christian morals. Many believed that the institution had stripped the South of entrepreneurial vigor and enterprise, leaving in its wake unprofitable plantations, stunted cities, and widespread poverty. When New York politician William Seward visited Virginia, he found nothing but "[a]n exhausted soil, old and decaying towns, wretchedly-neglected roads, and, in every respect, an absence of enterprise and improvement."[2] Seward and other Republican spokesmen contrasted the degradation of the slave South with the well-kept farms, growing cities, and technological advances of the free-labor North.[3] Northern pessimism about the South's economic prospects was so widespread that historian John Ashworth has argued that "the Republicans fought the Civil War primarily because they deplored the economic effects of slavery."[4] Ashworth may overstate the point, but the rapid economic divergence of the North and South undoubtedly provided fertile ground for the ominous predictions and stark dichotomies outlined in Lincoln's "house divided" speech.

We now know that Republicans greatly exaggerated the degree of southern stagnation. Economic historians have conclusively shown

---

[1] Lincoln, "A House Divided," pp. 372–73.
[2] Quoted in Ashworth, *Slavery, Capitalism, and Politics*, p. 80.
[3] Important works on the Republican critique of the South include Foner, *Free Soil, Free Labor, Free Men*, pp. 40–72 and Fogel, *Without Consent or Contract*, pp. 344–54. For a nuanced analysis of free labor ideology, see Glickstein, *Concepts of Free Labor*.
[4] Ashworth, *Slavery, Capitalism, and Politics*, p. 80.

that the South was remarkably prosperous on the eve of the Civil War. Southern incomes – at least those for whites – rose rapidly between 1840 and 1860. High crop prices for southern staples such as cotton and tobacco accounted for much of this prosperity, but white southerners were hardly passive recipients of good fortune. They built thousands of miles of railroad tracks, improved the productivity of farms and plantations, and established a small but growing industrial base. By international standards, at least, the South was an economic powerhouse.[5]

International comparisons, however, mattered little during the sectional controversies of the 1840s and the 1850s. Even a brief perusal of the 1850 or 1860 census suggested that the Republican economic critique rang true. The South had fallen dramatically behind the North (especially the Northeast) in manufacturing output, population growth, urbanization rates, inventive activity, and almost every other measure of development.[6] Slaveholders living in older southern states such as Virginia and South Carolina had special reason to be concerned with the growing developmental divide. The failure of their states to industrialize created a pattern in which the oldest southern states were among the poorest in the nation, while the oldest northern states were among the richest.[7] As the historian Joseph Persky has observed, Southerners perceived themselves as carrying "the burden of dependency" which left them vulnerable to the North's growing economic and political power.[8] No wonder many slaveholders believed that territorial expansion was critical to maintaining their regional independence and peculiar institution. Unable to augment their political influence through development, Southerners had to expand through space.

This study seeks to understand the roots of regional divergence through a comparison of economic development in Pennsylvania and Virginia. The study contains two separate but related comparisons. The first traces how residents of Cumberland County, Pennsylvania and Albemarle County, Virginia financed and built the turnpikes, toll bridges, canals, railroads, and banks that transformed their local economies. The second examines the Old Dominion and the Keystone

---

[5] Fogel and Engerman, *Time on the Cross*, pp. 59–78, 191–223, 247–57; Fogel, *Without Consent or Contract*, pp. 81–113; Engerman, "A Reconsideration of Southern Economic Growth"; Engerman, "The Antebellum South"; Bateman and Weiss, *A Deplorable Scarcity*, pp. 1–23; and Tchakerian, "Productivity, Extent of Markets, and Manufacturing."

[6] Civil War historians, undoubtedly reflecting the crucial importance of regional comparisons, have focused especially on the relative backwardness of the South. See, for example, Ransom, *Conflict and Compromise*, pp. 41–81; McPherson, *Battle Cry of Freedom*, pp. 91–103; and McPherson, *Ordeal by Fire*, pp. 26–34.

[7] Fischbaum and Rubin, "Slavery and Economic Development," p. 123.

[8] Persky, *The Burden of Dependency*, pp. 61–96.

State as a whole, focusing on state economic policy and urban development. The focus on economic growth will disappoint readers looking for more general comparisons of family life, religious experiences, and reform movements. Concentrating on economic issues, however, allows coverage of the entire period from 1800 to 1860 rather than a snapshot of the 1840s and 1850s. The longer time frame provides a dynamic account of how changing regional economies constituted a "house dividing" rather than a static portrait of a "house divided."

Virginia and Pennsylvania, I conclude, became a house divided because of the Old Dominion's failure to develop a large commercial city. Virginians worked feverishly to modernize their economy through large investments in canals, railroads, and banks. Such efforts, however, largely failed. Virginia's transportation network remained highly localized with little integration; no intersectional trunk lines connected Virginia's cities to midwestern markets; and the manufacturing base remained small, especially in relation to northern states. The central problem was that Virginia's slave economy discouraged the development of a large commercial city that could provide investors, traffic, and passengers for major transportation projects. The situation was very different in Pennsylvania. Beginning in the 1830s, Philadelphia's financiers controlled railroads throughout the state, which they increasingly integrated into a trunk line system that reached deep into the Midwest. The Pennsylvania Railroad and other trunk lines gave Philadelphia entrepreneurs access to new markets that accelerated the city's industrial growth. A major aim of this book is to explain how Philadelphia launched itself into a cycle of self-reinforcing growth.

Comparing Apples and Oranges

Before outlining these arguments in more detail, the question that bedevils most who practice comparative history must first be answered: Aren't you comparing apples and oranges? The main issue boils down to whether the two counties and states were alike enough to justify a sustained comparison, but different enough to reveal something historically relevant.

Although hardly "representative" in the statistical sense of the word, Albemarle and Cumberland had enough in common geographically to help isolate the impact of slavery. Both were settled at approximately the same time. Both contained large pockets of fertile land that supported thriving agricultural economies. Both were located near major marketing centers to encourage commercial agriculture, but were far enough away to demand transportation improvements ranging from turnpikes to railroads. Slavery was the major difference between these two counties. Whereas slaves were virtually absent in Cumberland, about half of Albemarle's population lived in bondage until 1865. My hope is that the similarities, general as they are, will help untangle slavery's impact on local development and economic attitudes.

The same logic of isolating the impact of slavery motivates the more general comparison of Virginia and Pennsylvania. One of the most obvious similarities between these states is that both numbered among the original thirteen colonies. The common colonial experience is admittedly not much of a similarity, but it would make little sense to compare Virginia (settled by whites in the 1600s) with Illinois or Iowa (settled by whites in the 1800s). Although Virginia and Pennsylvania had significantly different climates, the Old Dominion supported a mixed regime of tobacco, wheat, and livestock that at least vaguely resembled the output of Pennsylvania's grain farms. Again, the justification for the Virginia and Pennsylvania comparison is best put in negative terms. Comparing Pennsylvania to Georgia, South Carolina, and other semitropical cotton states would make it difficult to disentangle the effects of climate from the effects of slavery.[9] In terms of geography, the comparison is stronger because both states faced the daunting task of connecting Atlantic ports to western markets. Unlike New York, which had a less imposing pathway to the West, Pennsylvania and Virginia had to build canals and railroads over the rugged Appalachians.[10] The Keystone State and the Old Dominion spent considerable resources to accomplish this task, which makes their respective efforts a fruitful test of slavery's developmental impact.

Holding constant geography, climate, and timing of settlement, if only in the most general terms, isolates the local economic impact of slavery, thereby adding a new dimension to the large comparative literature on northern and southern development. A large literature comparing northern and southern economies – including the seminal work of Robert Fogel, Stanley Engerman, and Gavin Wright – has made essential contributions to our understanding of the antebellum era. Yet these econometric studies have used mostly aggregated regional data, usually derived from the 1850 and 1860 censuses.[11] A rich and

[9] Julius Rubin has perceptively analyzed the crucial importance of the Lower South's distinctive climate in "The Limits of Agricultural Progress."
[10] Chapter 5 analyzes the differing geography of New York, Pennsylvania, and Virginia in more detail.
[11] Historians focusing on regional economic comparisons include the works of Fogel, Engerman, and Bateman and Weiss cited above, as well Gavin Wright, *Political Economy*; Genovese, *Political Economy of Slavery*; and Pessen, "How Different from Each Other."

provocative literature has also developed along international lines, comparing southern slavery with unfree labor in Latin America and Europe.[12] Again, these studies have made crucial contributions to historical scholarship, but it still remains difficult to isolate the developmental impact of southern slavery within the context of widely divergent geography and cultural systems.

The comparative literature has frequently focused on the concept of capitalism. Capitalism has been such a favorite topic that the question of "Why did the North and South develop differently?" has been overshadowed with the question of "Was the South capitalist?" The question "Was the South capitalist?" owes its remarkable staying power, in part, to the provocative work of Eugene Genovese, who argued in his 1964 *Political Economy of Slavery* that southern planters held "an aristocratic, antibourgeois spirit with values and mores emphasizing family and status, a strong code of honor, and aspirations to luxury, ease, and accomplishment."[13] Genovese's contention that the planters embraced fundamentally anticapitalist values spawned a contentious debate that has yet to run its course, but even Genovese's most steadfast critics have framed their refutations within the capitalist versus anticapitalist dichotomy. The resulting research agendas encouraged either the broad regional and international comparisons noted above, or comparisons of southern development with an "ideal type" of what capitalism was supposed to resemble. The very scope of the capitalism question, in other words, encouraged scholars to think in the broadest possible terms.[14]

If capitalism has provided scholars with a standard for comparison, the term itself has no agreed-upon meaning. Scholars following Genovese often define capitalism as the widespread presence of wage labor, leading them to categorize slaveholders as anticapitalists or at least noncapitalists.[15] Economists, on the other hand, usually associate capitalism with the growth of regional, national, and international markets. The efficient production of highly profitable staple crops led economic historians Robert Fogel and Stanley Engerman to label

---

[12] The international comparisons include Elkins, *Slavery*; Kolchin, *Unfree Labor*; Fredrickson, *Comparative Imagination*; Bowman, *Masters and Lords*; Degler, *Neither Black Nor White*; and Genovese, *From Rebellion to Revolution*.

[13] Genovese, *Political Economy*, p. 28. Some historians who do not completely agree with Genovese's formulation of capitalism nevertheless stress traditional characteristics of southern ideology (such as a concern for honor) that clashed with bourgeois attitudes of the modernizing North. See, for example, Wyatt-Brown, *Honor and Violence*.

[14] More detailed comparative studies are now starting to appear. See, for example, Bezis-Selfa, "Planter Industrialists," and Adams, "Different Charters, Different Paths."

[15] Recent examples of these interpretations include Reidy, *From Slavery to Agrarian Capitalism*, pp. 31–57; Egerton, "Markets Without a Market Revolution," pp. 207–21; and Kulikoff, "Transition to Capitalism."

planters as "agricultural capitalists."[16] Scholars influenced by the world-systems framework of Immanuel Wallerstein take a similar position, equating participation in world markets for cotton, tobacco, and other staple crops with participation in capitalism.[17] Still other historians agree with economists that planters were indeed capitalistic, but stress that southern yeoman farmers remained hostile to commerce and speculation, leading to the formation of a "dual economy."[18] With all of these competing interpretations of capitalism showing considerable vigor, the literature remains in a state of flux.[19]

Scholars attempting to put northern economic development within a capitalism framework have suffered similar disagreements. At the risk of grave simplicity, the controversy can be boiled down to this question: Did rural Northerners embrace capitalism from an early date, or did they oppose capitalism until population growth, land shortages, and government policies left them with no other alternative? Once again, the answer often depends on whether one defines capitalism as a system of wage labor, a system of commercial markets, or a system of economic values.[20] Many social historians emphasize that northern farm families formed tight-knit communities antithetical to capitalist values such as individualism and commercialism. That extensive archival research shows that northern farm families participated in regional and international markets as early as the 1750s has not dissuaded these historians.[21] When northern farm families participated in commercial markets, they claim it was only to raise money to buy necessities or pay taxes, not to accumulate capital and wealth. Here, though, the evidence becomes impossibly murky, involving inferences from contradictory behavior open to a wide range of possible interpretations.[22]

---

[16] Fogel and Engerman, *Time on the Cross*, p. 232. Other neoclassical economists have come to much less optimistic conclusions about the long-run efficiency of slave labor, but still agree that planters displayed attitudes that were more or less capitalist.

[17] The most sophisticated statement of the world-systems perspective is Bowman, *Masters and Lords*, pp. 79–111.

[18] The best article-length summaries of the "dual economy" thesis include Watson, "Slavery and Development"; Hahn, "Yeomanry of the Nonplantation South"; and Oakes, "Politics of Economic Development."

[19] One indication of the continuing controversies over the South's slave economy is the very different conclusions reached by three recent synthetic works. Compare Kolchin, *American Slavery*, pp. 169–99; Fogel, *Without Consent or Contract*, pp. 81–113; and Ashworth, *Slavery, Capitalism, and Politics*, pp. 80–121.

[20] Key statements of the anticapitalist position include Kulikoff, *Agrarian Origins*; Henretta, *Origins of American Capitalism*, 71–120; Merrill, "Anticapitalist Origins"; Merrill, "Cash is Good to Eat"; and Clark, "Household Economy."

[21] The divide between neoclassical economic historians and Marxist historians is most evident in Rothenberg, "The Market and Massachusetts Farmers"; Weiss, "The Market and Massuchusetts Farmers"; and Rothenberg, *From Market-Places to a Market Economy*, pp. 25–55.

[22] Historians such as Daniel Vickers have downplayed the capitalism framework, preferring instead more historically-grounded terms such as "competency" to describe

Perhaps to correct some of the defects of the capitalism standard, a new term to describe nineteenth-century economic change is now in vogue: the market revolution. The market revolution metaphor correctly emphasizes that the expansion of markets in the first half of the nineteenth century led to the acceleration of economic growth. Unfortunately, equating economic change with revolution creates its own problems. A revolution implies a sudden, violent transformation.[23] Historians using the market revolution metaphor, not surprisingly, often stress dramatic social and economic conflict. Charles Sellers, one of the leading proponents of the market revolution thesis, argues that the extension of markets led to nothing less than a "*Kulturkampf* that would decide American destiny on the private battlegrounds of every human relationship."[24] Such portraits of economic change as destructive and divisive, more than one critic has noted, invariably underplay the degree to which many Americans supported economic expansion and the considerable material benefits it entailed.

Rather than engage in the capitalism and market revolution debates head-on, I attempt to use explicit comparisons to outflank them. The comparative method makes concepts such as capitalism and the market revolution less important. The story of Albemarle and Virginia gives meaning to events in Cumberland and Pennsylvania, and vice versa. Instead of using the terms "capitalism" and "market revolution," I use the phrase "market development" to describe economic change of the nineteenth century. Hopefully, this term captures the notion that the remarkable economic expansion from 1800 to 1860 was built upon foundations established in the colonial and early national periods. Critics will surely object that "market development" implies a moral judgment that economic change was natural and consensual. To the extent that this charge is true, it reflects the biases of the actual historical participants. Many Virginians and Pennsylvanians who wrote about economic matters, as we shall see, often associated the extension of markets with the inevitable march of progress.

eighteenth and nineteenth century economic culture. See Vickers, "Competency and Competition."

[23] Historians who use the metaphor of revolution to synthesize the economic and political history of the Jacksonian period include Sellers, *The Market Revolution*; Watson, *Liberty and Power*; and Wilentz, "Society, Politics, and the Market Revolution." See also the articles in "Symposium on Charles Sellers" appearing in the Winter 1992 issue of the *Journal of the Early Republic*, as well as the essays in Stokes and Conway, eds., *The Market Revolution in America*.

[24] Sellers, *The Market Revolution*, p. 31. For more detailed critiques of the concept of the market revolution, see Majewski, "A Revolution Too Many?"; Feller, "The Market Revolution Ate My Homework"; and Howe, "The Market Revolution and the Shaping of Identity."

The Social Origins of Market Expansion
in Albemarle and Cumberland

In establishing that such a consensus existed, my starting points are stockholder lists and other corporate records that show what social and economic groups financed economic change. Virginians and Pennsylvanians organized most of their turnpikes, river improvements, toll bridges, railroads, and banks as corporations that sold shares to investors. My method is to link these investors to census and tax records, thereby revealing the groups responsible for market development. Although analytically simple – it is the economic historian's equivalent to what spy novelists call "following the money trail" – this method allows historians to uncover the social origins of America's economic expansion.[25] When put in a comparative context, the method also allows historians to understand how slavery influenced investment decisions.

Linking shareholders to census and tax records reveals an important similarity between Albemarle and Cumberland during the first third of the nineteenth century. As outlined in Chapters 1 and 2, hundreds of investors funded early turnpikes, navigation companies, toll bridges, and canals. The vast majority of shareholders were local residents, not outside financiers. What made the widespread local participation especially remarkable was the poor financial performance of the transportation corporations. The companies paid little in the way of dividends, and the shares quickly plummeted to less than ten percent of their original value. The motivations of shareholders centered on indirect benefits, such as raising land values and improving access to markets for their localities. I call these companies "developmental corporations" to highlight that their aim was not quick profit, but long-term community development.

Most of the investors in developmental corporations owned far more wealth than average, but evidence from legislative petitions and newspaper correspondence suggests that the corporations received widespread local support. The strong support for developmental corporations has important implications for understanding the relationship between communities and development. Scholars have frequently viewed market development as marching hand-in-hand with individualism, competition, and a decline of communitarian values. Individualism and competition were not absent in Albemarle and Cumberland,

---

[25] The classic work on transportation improvements, George Rogers Taylor's *The Transportation Revolution*, gives surprisingly little consideration to the issue of who financed improvements. Monographs that have devoted attention to the social origins of the transportation revolution include Siegel, *Roots of Southern Distinctiveness*, pp. 106–19; Ford, *Origins of Southern Radicalism*, pp. 219–43.

but residents realized that long-term cooperation was essential if they were to achieve their individual aims. Reciprocity, civic participation, and public spirit allowed developmental corporations to succeed where individualistic profit taking would have failed. Not only were community ties compatible with development, but they were downright essential for its success.[26]

This community orientation, as we shall see in Chapter 4, helped circumscribe political conflict surrounding developmental corporations. Corporations in Albemarle and Cumberland became involved in heated political and legal battles over their right to take property through eminent domain proceedings and other corporate privileges. The debates over corporate power show that many residents feared that the companies in question might corrupt America's republican institutions.[27] Few residents in either county, however, questioned the importance of economic development. Given the concrete economic benefits these corporations produced, the widespread political support that many residents gave developmental corporations was not surprising. The companies succeeded in raising land values and creating town growth. However much Jeffersonians and Jacksonians railed against corporate power, they could not oppose the substantial benefits that a local turnpike or river improvement could bring.

The Railroad and Regional Divergence

The railroad's voracious appetite for capital dramatically changed the impetus of market development, especially within Cumberland County. As documented in Chapter 3, Philadelphia financiers such as Nicholas Biddle provided much of the capital for the Cumberland Valley Railroad (CVRR) in the late 1830s. Statewide data suggest that the CVRR typified a wider trend in which Philadelphia capitalists financed most of Pennsylvania's railroad network. Virginians, however, remained firmly wedded to local investment. Almost all of the 500 investors in Albemarle's primary railroad, the Virginia Central, lived within five miles of the road. The investors represented a diverse array of occupations and social classes, including wealthy planters, substantial yeomen, shopkeepers, merchants, and professionals. Yet even a wealthy rural county such as Albemarle could hardly afford to finance a railroad alone, leading the state government to purchase more than

[26] For a similar take on the importance of community to developmental efforts, see Innes, *Creating the Commonwealth*, pp. 181–223.
[27] The same political dynamic occurred in New York, where the state heavily regulated turnpike corporations to favor local users. See Klein and Majewski, "Economy, Community, and Law."

60 percent of the Virginia Central's stock. Fears that Virginians were falling behind their northern rivals gave special impetus to state spending in the Old Dominion, especially on projects that promised to capture western trade. Sectional rivalry, combined with a good dose of local boosterism, produced a strong consensus for railroad construction. During the 1850s, Virginians invested in more miles of railroad per capita than did Pennsylvanians.

It was one thing to wish for improvements that would capture western trade; it was another to build them. As Chapter 5 demonstrates, local financing made coherent networks cumbersome to organize, especially with no fewer than four cities seeking to build *the* central trunk line. The state legislature, an institution that might have transcended local interests, never overcame the state's commercial rivalries. Pitting Richmond, Norfolk, Petersburg, and Lynchburg in a battle for mercantile supremacy, these commercial rivalries prevented the legislature from focusing resources on a single trunk line. By 1860, a collection of uncompleted and unprofitable railroads and canals littered Virginia's landscape. Competition, which did so much to stimulate growth and innovation in the private sector, had disastrous consequences when expressed through a fractious state legislature. In Pennsylvania, on the other hand, large corporations such as the Pennsylvania Railroad (PRR) began to integrate systems around large trunk lines that reached Chicago and beyond. Because the PRR received its capital from either Philadelphia capitalists or city governments, it avoided the intrigue in the state legislature that did so much to damage Virginia's railroad system. The greater centralization of Pennsylvania's economy within a few dominant urban centers, in other words, promoted economic efficiency.

Chapter 6 tackles the question of why Virginia never managed to develop a city with the wealth and population of Philadelphia. The issue is particularly important in the first three decades of the nineteenth century, when cities such as Richmond and Lynchburg stagnated while Philadelphia began its industrial ascent. I argue that a multiplicity of factors hindered the early growth of Virginia's cities. In the colonial period, Virginians focused on tobacco, which had such light processing requirements that it did little to encourage urban growth. The Navigation Acts, which forced Virginians to ship tobacco to Britain first, made it logical to locate the mercantile and financial services connected to the tobacco trade in Glasgow and London, where tobacco would then be re-exported to the Continent. Already far behind Philadelphia at the beginning of the nineteenth century, Virginia's cities faced another barrier to growth: sparsely settled hinterlands that limited the market for manufactured goods. The market for consumer goods in Virginia's slave economy, as we shall see, was much smaller than similar markets in Pennsylvania. Philadelphia's densely populated countryside, in fact, spurred industrialization well before the arrival of interregional railroads. The head start allowed Philadelphia to attract specialized firms and skilled workers that made the city's manufacturers even more productive in the 1840s and 1850s.

Virginia's failure to develop a large city and an accompanying interregional railroad network highlighted the long-term economic consequences of slavery. Slavery, by increasing farm size and discouraging the growth of small towns, prevented the emergence of densely populated hinterlands. Without sufficient market demand to spur industrialization, Virginians failed to develop thriving urban centers. The Old Dominion's lackluster urban growth, in turn, left the state without the concentration of capital and traffic necessary to build an adequate interregional railroad network. This self-reinforcing cycle left many Virginians nervous and worried. For all of their blustering sectional pride, Virginians could not quite dispel their nagging doubts that Lincoln, Seward, and other northern critics were indeed correct. A slave society, no matter how much wealth it produced, could not compete against a northern economy that harnessed the power of ordinary households left free to invent, to improve, to invest, and to consume.

1

Developmental Corporations
in a Slave-Labor Society

The Rivanna was hardly the most impressive of Virginia's many rivers, nor the most commercially viable. In the heat of the summer the Rivanna sometimes became little more than a trickle; in spring and fall heavy rains often caused floods that damaged mills and inundated fields. However great these obstacles, residents of central and northern Albemarle perceived the river in terms of commercial promise: a source of power for local mills and a means of cheap transportation for tobacco and other crops. Thomas Jefferson, whose Monticello estate was a stone's throw from the Rivanna's banks, organized the first of many attempts to tap the river's economic potential. After surveying the Rivanna in 1765, Jefferson concluded that clearing a series of small obstructions could convert the stream into a navigable waterway. The young planter secured an act from the colonial assembly that authorized a trusteeship to undertake the "laudable and useful" enterprise. Jefferson and other prominent gentlemen became trustees, collecting voluntary subscriptions and then paying local contractors to remove the obstructions.[1] The trusteeship was not a complete success – a series of navigation and canal companies would attempt to build more permanent improvements over the next 100 years – but Jefferson took considerable pride in his public-spirited efforts. Thirty-five years after the trusteeship had been formed, president-elect Jefferson asked "whether my country was the better for my having lived at all?" Listing his public service chronologically, Jefferson put his efforts to improve the Rivanna at the top of his list:

The Rivanna had never been used for navigation; scarcely an empty canoe had ever passed down it. Soon after I came of age, I examined its obstructions, set on foot a subscription for removing them, got an Act of Assembly passed, and the thing effected, so as to be used completely and fully for carrying down all our produce.[2]

---

[1] Jefferson's early efforts to improve the Rivanna are briefly summarized in Malone, *Jefferson the Virginian*, p. 115.
[2] "A Memorandum (Services to My Country)" in *Jefferson*, p. 376

Jefferson's attempts to improve the Rivanna set the tone for Albemarle's later transportation projects. Trusteeships gave way to better-organized corporations that could sell shares of stock, collect tolls, and issue dividends. These turnpikes, toll bridges, navigation companies, and river improvements, however, had much in common with Jefferson's non-profit trusteeship. Stockholders hoped to reap rewards for their investment not so much through direct returns (such as dividends and stock appreciation), but from indirect benefits (increased commerce and higher land values). The financial performance of these transportation corporations, in fact, ranged from merely bad to completely catastrophic: Revenues were low, dividends were rare, and shares often became worthless. For this reason, it is best to think of most transportation enterprises of the early nineteenth century as "developmental corporations" that promised to enrich stockholders less through dividends than by bringing the fruits of market development to local communities.[3]

The developmental corporation's emphasis on community improvement, combined with the high losses that stockholders sustained, presents an economic puzzle. Consider the following scenario: Farmer Smith, after patiently listening to boosters discuss the great benefits of a turnpike, decides that the project would raise the value of his land by $500. Farmer Smith also knows that any initial investment in the turnpike company would be lost – a share purchased for $100 would quickly become worth only a few dollars. While $400 is undoubtedly a tidy profit on a single share, Farmer Smith knew how to get an even bigger return: Let Farmer Jones or another neighbor invest in the turnpike. According to public goods theory, every farmer in the neighborhood should have thought like Farmer Smith, and the turnpike should never have been built.[4] Economic logic, ironically enough, demonstrates the inadequacy of theories of development built around "profit maximization." At some point Albemarle residents had to transcend their own narrow, short-term interests to improve the county's commercial infrastructure.

This chapter shows how local boosterism, kinship ties, honor, and simple friendship provided the glue that held Albemarle's developmental corporations together when the epoxy of direct profits failed. The presence of these nonpecuniary motivations did not mean that self-interest was absent. As we will see in the following sections, the indirect benefits of the developmental corporations were large and substantial. What made developmental corporations viable was the

---

[3] This view of early transportation companies is hardly new. See, for example, Handlin and Handlin, *Commonwealth*, pp. 106–33, and Goodrich, "Public Spirit," pp. 305–09.

[4] For an extended analysis of the freerider problem and its social consequences, see Olson, *Logic of Collective Action*.

congruence of the economic goals of individuals and the general interests of the community that formed what Alexis de Tocqueville called "self-interest rightly understood." According to de Tocqueville, nineteenth-century Americans took pride "in how an enlightened regard for themselves constantly prompts them to assist one another and inclines them willingly to sacrifice a portion of their time and property to the welfare of the state."[5] If one substitutes "local community" for "state," de Tocqueville's observation accurately describes the attitudes that made it possible to fund developmental corporations.

A deep-seated fear of community decline added to the power of "self-interest rightly understood." Without improved transportation, Albemarle's planters and farmers realized competition from newly-settled areas would lower land values and limit economic opportunity. Families would be forced to move to the frontier and sunder the ties of kinship and reciprocity. A prosperous and thriving local economy, on the other hand, would allow sons to farm, trade, or manufacture close to home. The fear of large-scale out-migration, as we will see, became tied to the wider concerns of the declining economic and political fortunes of the Old Dominion. Improved transportation, many Virginians thought, would spur farmers and planters to be more productive while expanding the Old Dominion's fledgling mercantile and manufacturing sectors. Without such steps, many feared that Virginia's influence in national politics would continue to wane. The widespread presence of these concerns suggests that the origins of market development lay not in the actions of rugged individualists and lone entrepreneurs, but in cooperative efforts that enriched local residents so that their community and state would remain strong.

"The Ligaments of Community": Planters and Power in a Slave Society

For mid-eighteenth-century planters looking to replace failing Tidewater estates or to acquire fresh lands for future generations, few places could have been more attractive than Albemarle County. Blessed with viable (if hardly perfect) transportation down the James River, rich soils, and a temperate climate, Albemarle was a prime location for tobacco growers. Tobacco prices began to rise in the 1740s, and remained high until the Revolution. Simultaneously, planters in the Tidewater area, with their land exhausted from years of heavy tobacco cultivation, switched to wheat and other grains. The shift to grains in the Tidewater area meant that newly settled counties such

---

[5] Alexis de Tocqueville, *Democracy in America*, p. 416.

as Albemarle would dominate the tobacco market, especially since Scottish merchants eagerly provided credit and marketing services for newly settled areas. Population statistics paint the general picture of the Piedmont boom. In 1729, 8 percent of Virginia's tithables (the number of taxable inhabitants) lived in the Piedmont; in 1773, 44 percent of the colony's tithables resided there.[6]

Although the unoccupied lands of the Piedmont beckoned many small planters and farmers, Albemarle and other counties of the region replicated the inequality inherent in Tidewater society. Families from the Tidewater elite, often allied with less prominent but nevertheless well-to-do men, claimed the most fertile Albemarle land in the 1730s and 1740s.[7] The head start that these wealthy men enjoyed – often as a result of superior political connections and inside information within the colonial government – translated into substantial inequality in the distribution of real estate. The top 10 percent of property owners held about 70 percent of the value of the county's real estate in the late eighteenth century. Those at the top of Albemarle's economic hierarchy managed to slightly expand this proportion in the nineteenth century.[8]

The planters who owned most of the real estate in the county quickly introduced slavery. Prominent families, in fact, often sent slaves and overseers to clear land before moving themselves. About half of Albemarle's colonial population were slaves, a proportion that would hold more or less steady as the nineteenth century advanced. By 1787, as the period of the initial settlement was coming to a close, the top 10 percent of the county's households owned 61 percent of the taxable slaves. This percentage would decrease somewhat over time, but the top 10 percent of white households still held between

---

[6] Kulikoff, *Tobacco and Slaves*, pp. 122–57; Nicholls, "Piedmont Plantations," pp. 4–7; Morgan and Nicholls, "Slaves," pp. 215–16 (especially Table 1).

[7] One indication of Albemarle's prosperity was the growth of Richmond as a tobacco inspection and warehouse center. The planters and farmers of Albemarle sent most of their crop down the James River, where it would then be inspected and warehoused in Richmond. By the 1760s and 1770s, about one-sixth of the state's tobacco crop (representing 10,000 hogsheads) was inspected in Richmond. See Kulikoff, *Tobacco and Slaves*, p. 124.

[8] Based upon samples drawn from Albemarle Real Property Tax Lists, microfilm, VSLA. Please see appendix on methods for precise details about calculations. The ability of a relatively small number of families to dominate the county's real estate holdings was apparent in the initial distribution of the colonial patent system. The top 5 percent of land patentees, 24 individuals in all, patented almost two-thirds of the county's land before the Revolution. In contrast, those in the bottom 80 percent of the distribution patented less than a quarter of the land. The wealthy planters who speculated in the Piedmont frontier patented their land in 1730s and 1740s, thereby having first choice of the prime locations. Watts, "Colonial Albemarle," pp. 34–49; Watts, "Land Grants," pp. 20–21; and Moore, *Jefferson's County*, pp. 19–29.

50 and 55 percent of Albemarle's slaves during the first half of the nineteenth century.[9]

These dry statistics underscore a social reality in which a few powerful families dominated Albemarle politics and society. The illustrious Thomas Jefferson was a case in point. Jefferson's father Peter was a member of the Tidewater gentry who aggressively used his connections to patent new lands in the Piedmont, leaving his son a rich inheritance of land and slaves. Jefferson increased his inheritance through marriage to make himself one of the richest men of the Old Dominion.[10] Jefferson was hardly the most typical Albemarle resident, but then again he was not entirely unexceptional. Other prominent Tidewater families – the Carters, the Meriwethers, the Nicholases, the Lewises – had branches and connections that settled in Albemarle.

Control of land and slaves gave Albemarle's planters considerable political power. Most of Albemarle's important politicians – Thomas Jefferson, Thomas Jefferson Randolph, Thomas Mann Randolph, Alexander Rives, and Samuel Carr — came from slave-holding families with deep roots in the county or neighboring localities. Wealthy slaveowners, for example, dominated Albemarle's representation in the state assembly, which was perhaps the most important political body in the state. Albemarle's state assemblymen owned, on average, 20 slaves during the period 1800 to 1860. Voters occasionally elected men with relatively small slave holdings to the Assembly, but they tended to be lawyers belonging to successful planter families.[11]

Anecdotal evidence suggests that the political power of the planters often evolved out of the close economic relationships they had with small farmers and tradesmen. In 1805, Bezaleel Brown (whose namesake would be elected three times to the state legislature in the 1840s) received a letter from Robert Branham profusely apologizing for not paying a debt. After explaining that one of his children was seriously ill with the mumps, Branham pleadingly wrote, "You may rest satisfied that you shall never be forgotten in weighting [sic] so long as you have." He even offered to sell his home and lot, for Branham "would make a sacrifice in any property" rather than see Brown "suffer on my account."[12] We do not know the conclusion to Branham's sad story,

---

[9] The distribution of slaves and land was calculated from samples drawn from Albermarle Personal Property Tax Lists, microfilm, VSLA. Please see appendix on methods for a precise description of my procedures.

[10] Malone, *Jefferson the Virginian*, pp. 21–48; Sloan, *Principle and Interest*, pp. 14–15.

[11] Between 1800 and 1820, those elected to the state assembly owned an average of 23 slaves; between 1820 and 1840, the figure was 22 slaves, and for 1840–1860 it was 18 slaves. The declining average probably reflects the increasing importance of Charlottesville's lawyers and other professionals in county politics. These statistics calculated from Albermarle Personal Property Tax Lists, microfilm, VSLA, and Woods, *Albermarle County*, pp. 384–85.

[12] Robert Branham to Bezaleel Brown, May 5, 1805, Brown Family Papers, UVA.

but it is reasonable to assume that Brown would expect to see the same deference at the polls, especially since voting in nineteenth-century Virginia was a public act. Benjamin H. Magruder may have had similar expectations when he asked planter John H. Cocke whether he could loan "Mr. Thomas Burton, an industrious mechanic of this town [of Scottsville]," $1,500.[13] Cocke and Magruder were strong Whigs – did they expect Burton to vote accordingly? Such economic relationships hint at what historian J. William Harris has called "the ligaments of community"; ligaments that helped prominent planters maintain their political dominance.[14]

Kinship was perhaps an even more important ligament of the community. Because travel within the county was often slow and expensive, potential marriage partners for most residents lived in one's local neighborhood. Constant intermingling of the same families in the same neighborhoods produced increasingly large kinship groups. Albemarle tax records, which give rough coordinates for each piece of property, hint at these neighborhood kinship groups. In 1830 the property tax records list six members of the Wood family who owned small farms within a five-mile radius of each other; similarly, four members of the Dowell family owned property within a four mile radius. These families were not unusual: Samples from tax records show that 81 percent of Albemarle's households shared their surname with at least one other Albemarle family.[15] These kinship groups formed reciprocal networks that provided credit and emergency assistance, shared farm tools and animals, and mobilized political support.[16] As we will see, kinship groups would also help encourage investment in developmental corporations.

"Worn Out, Washed, and Gullied": Relative Decline in the Virginia Piedmont

Kinship groups, however close, could be split apart because of migration. Migration became a more likely prospect for many Albemarle residents in the early nineteenth century, when the county felt the first signs of relative decline. Population growth leveled off significantly after 1800 (Table 1.1). Slow population growth meant a slow growth in land values. Land assessments in 1819 and 1838 showed that, in real terms, land values within the Virginia Piedmont increased at an

[13] Benjamin H. Magruder to John H. Cocke, November 21, 1833, Box 76, UVA.
[14] Harris, *Plain Folk*, pp. 94–122.
[15] These examples are taken from the 1830 Albemarle County Property Tax Records, microfilm, VSLA.
[16] Recent research on southern kinship networks includes Kulikoff, *Tobacco and Slaves*, pp. 205–60; Cashin, *Family Venture*, pp. 9–31; and Kenzer, *Kinship and Neighborhood*, pp. 6–51.

Table 1.1. *The First Sign of Relative Decline: Albemarle's Slow Population Growth*

Census Year	Total Population	Percent Increase	Percent Slave
1790	12,585	—	44
1800	16,439	31	45
1810	18,268	11	51
1820	19,750	8	54
1830	22,618	15	51
1840	22,924	1	52
1850	25,800	11	52
1860	26,625	3	52

Notes and Sources: Moore, *Jefferson's County,* p. 115; Androit, *Population Abstract,* p. 821.

annual rate of less than 1 percent.[17] Compared to the high returns that the new cotton planters of the Southwest could reap, Albemarle's planters and farmers seemed mired in a stagnating economy. The reminiscences of planter Edmund Ruffin about his own county of Prince George probably applied to Albemarle as well: "There was scarcely a proprietor ... who did not desire to sell his land, and who was prevented only by the impossibility of finding a purchaser, unless at half of the then very low estimated value. All wished to sell, none to buy."[18]

Planters often blamed tobacco, which had a notorious reputation for depleting the soil, for stagnant land values. In 1799, John H. Craven reported that Albemarle's land was "worn out, washed and gullied, so that scarcely an acre could be found in a place fit for cultivation."[19] When tobacco prices entered a long-run period of decline in the early nineteenth century, many planters and farmers eagerly switched to wheat.[20] Perhaps wheat and grains, they reasoned, would reverse the long-term decline in Albemarle's soil fertility. Growing wheat proved no guarantee of success, however, as weevils and wheat rust frequently beset Albemarle's grain farmers. As the eighteenth century came to a close, Thomas Jefferson wrote that "The unprofitable condition of Virginia estates in general leaves it now next to impossible for the holder of one to avoid ruin."[21] Jefferson's own

---

[17] These figures taken from "Virginia Statistics," *Southern Planter* 27 (August 1857), pp. 486–87. Rates of deflation calculated from *Historical Statistics,* p. 115.

[18] Quoted in Craven, *Edmund Ruffin,* pp. 52–53. For an excellent overview of the end of the frontier in the Virginia Piedmont, see Kulikoff, *Tobacco and Slaves,* pp.157–61.

[19] Quoted in Merrill, *Jefferson's Nephews,* p. 45.

[20] Moore reports that this shift began as early as the Revolution, when international tobacco markets were increasingly difficult to reach and the demand for grain (spurred in part from an influx of prisoners of war into Albemarle) surged. See *Jefferson's Albemarle,* pp. 56–58.

[21] Quoted in Merrill, *Jefferson's Nephews,* p. 47.

financial predicament of accumulating debt undoubtedly led him to exaggerate the hardship that planters often faced, but he nevertheless accurately captured the perception that Albemarle's economy was headed for further decline.

For young men eager to establish their independence, declining fortunes and exhausted soils created an atmosphere of intense insecurity. Consider the case of nineteen-year-old George Carr, who in 1821 wrote an unpublished short story outlining the courtship, marriage, and early life of a fictional "James" and "Elizabeth." At the beginning of the story, James is so smitten by Elizabeth's beauty that he can no longer concentrate on his studies and drops out of medical school.[22] Here the story is largely autobiographical, for Carr himself fell head over heals in love while studying at the University of Virginia. His close friend Thomas W. Gilmer discouraged Carr from marrying too rashly, warning that "no body swims on this sea without a good fortune."[23] Yet a good fortune was precisely what Carr lacked. His father had been a successful Albemarle planter, but even his large plantation could not provide a secure head start for all of his five sons and five daughters. Like the characters in his story, George would have to make his way in the world without significant family assistance.[24]

Carr's story revealed profound pessimism about his prospects. The ill-fated couple fell in love, but James despaired of marriage. Elizabeth's wealthy merchant father had experienced an unfortunate "accident" and lost his fortune. James found himself "indigent, immersed in love, [and] engaged to a lady in similar circumstances." Love, however, won out, and James and Elizabeth were soon married. The sudden death of Elizabeth's father, who had been straining to help the newlyweds, spelled disaster. The couple was forced to "attend" a small grocery for a disagreeable old man, a station in life that was "little preferable to death to Elizabeth." Within a few years, James and Elizabeth had saved enough money to enter into a formal partnership. Almost on the verge of acquiring their own independence, economic misfortune struck again: The old man went bankrupt, leaving the couple destitute once again.[25]

What ultimately happened to James and Elizabeth? Carr simply states that "they removed. I know not where they are or what they are doing at this time."[26] The declining fortunes of Albemarle led many

---

[22] George Carr, unpublished composition, George Carr papers, Alderman Library, UVA. Quote found on p. 1.
[23] T. W. Gilmer to George Carr, February 7, 1821, George Carr papers, UVA.
[24] Cashin, *Family Venture*, p. 131. Cashin reports that George Carr was the son of Micajah Carr, a planter with 20 slaves and father of 5 daughters and 5 sons.
[25] George Carr, unpublished composition, George Carr papers, UVA. Quotes found on pp. 3–4.
[26] George Carr, unpublished composition, George Carr papers, UVA, p. 7.

planters and farmers "to remove" to more fertile western soils. The siren call of fresh lands (Kentucky and Tennessee in the 1790s and early 1800s; Missouri and the Southwest later in the century) led to the exodus of thousands of Albemarle residents. One historian has traced more than 300 Albemarle households who moved to Kentucky in the late eighteenth and early nineteenth centuries.[27] How many left Albemarle over the entire nineteenth century is hard to determine, but Albemarle's slow population growth over the antebellum period suggests that many young men and women moved elsewhere. Albemarle, of course, was hardly unique among Virginia counties. By 1850, almost 400,000 Virginia natives lived in other states.[28]

To leave for the West, however popular, was not an easy decision. For many families, the tightly-spun web of kinship networks and social ties offered a powerful inducement to stay. Kin could provide needed credit to expand a farm, emergency labor during the harvest, or financial assistance during hard times. Even young men who resented the smothering constraints of community had to think twice about leaving these reciprocal networks. Gilmer, for example, had few nice things to say about "such toads and lizards as the Charlottesvillians," and he informed his friend Carr that he intended "to take advantage of the first very favorable wind that blows and drift myself out to the deserts of Missouri, there to flourish among owls, bears, and panthers, to the infinite satisfaction of soul and body."[29] Yet Gilmer, like Carr, would spend a good part of his adult life in Albemarle.[30]

Many members of Albemarle's wealthiest families made the same decision to stay. To get some sense of the economic and social positions of those who left the county and those who stayed, I calculated "persistence rates" – the percentage of households that "survived" from one census year to the next – for the 1830s and the 1840s. As one might expect during a period of high migration, persistence rates were low in Albemarle. In the 1830s, only 46 percent of residents "persisted" in Albemarle; in the 1840s, about 50 percent stayed in the county.[31] The

---

[27] Merrill, *Jefferson's Nephews*, pp. 84–96.

[28] Craven, *Edmund Ruffin*, p. 52.

[29] T. W. Gilmer to George Carr, February 17, 1821, George Carr Papers, UVA.

[30] Cashin (*Family Venture*, p. 131) documents that Carr achieved planter status by the 1860 census, while 1840 property tax records show that Gilmer owned two Charlottesville lots collectively valued at $4,000. For an excellent discussion of planter migration, see Cashin, *Family Venture*, pp. 32–52.

[31] Calculated from Personal and Real Property Tax Lists, microfilm, VSLA. Please see appendix for precise methods of calculation. Persistence rates are flawed measures of migration rates because a family might fail to show up on a tax or census record because of death or marriage. Nevertheless, they give historians at least an approximation of those who left and those who stayed behind. The findings for Albemarle County fit well; see Steckel, "Household Migration," p. 198 and Shaeffer, "Statistical Profile," p. 567. Both of these studies find that owning land and slaves often deterred migration.

wealthiest slaveholders, however, were much more likely to stay. Households owning more than 15 slaves, in fact, had persistence rates of 70
percent in the 1830s and 1840s. These wealthy households who developed a long-term stake in Albemarle could provide the capital and
leadership to revive the economic fortunes of their neighborhoods.[32]

Agricultural Reform in Albemarle

For the planters and farmers who decided to stay, restoring vitality to
their declining plantations and farms often hinged upon agricultural
reform. "Agricultural reform" was a catchall phrase that summarized a
new attitude toward farming that stressed scientific experimentation
and rigorous cost-benefit analysis. Reformers frequently charged that
Virginians traditionally performed "slovenly and incomplete execution of farming operations," while displaying "a want of careful attention and accurate observation."[33] Scathingly denouncing the "slash
and burn" practices of past generations as economically irrational and
aesthetically unappealing, reformers envisioned a new landscape of
tidy, well-kept farms that utilized the best implements, rotations, and
fertilizers.

Although agricultural reformers frequently wrangled over the merits of this fertilizer and that crop rotation, they almost always agreed
on the benefits of intensive farming – reaping more output from fewer
acres. One prominent Albemarle planter, Dr. John R. Woods, chas-
tised his neighbors in 1858 for "the imperfect and hurried manner
which all our farming operations are performed." Growing less
tobacco and cultivating less land, Woods asserted, would allow
planters to apply more manure to their corn crop, give more attention
to fattening livestock, and allow them to erect more permanent farm
buildings.[34] Woods was repeating a familiar argument among Albemarle's agricultural reformers. Twelve years earlier Franklin Minor
had declared "The land is the farmer's capital, the crops are the
annual interest from it; and his must be a losing business who has consumed a part of his capital each year in the form of interest."[35] William
G. Rives, one of the most prominent slaveholders in Albemarle
county, similarly argued in 1842 that "[T]he best application I could
make of money derived from the land, was to return it back to the land
in the shape of improvement. There is no investment of capital which

---

[32] Please see Table 4 in the statistical appendix for precise calculations.

[33] Frank Carr [Constitution of "The Albemarle Hole and Corner Club, No. 1"], *Southern Planter* 2 (July 1842), p. 153.

[34] Dr. John R. Woods, "Defects of Agricultural Productions of Albemarle County," *Southern Planter* 18 (July 1858), p. 432.

[35] Franklin Minor, "Agricultural Address," *Southern Planter* 5 (April 1846), p. 88.

could be more safe, and in ninety-nine out of a hundred cases, none half so profitable."[36]

The emphasis on rational land use, increasing productivity, and detailed accounting procedures gave the agricultural reform effort a clear orientation toward markets and commerce. The glorification of the calculating economic man, however, was only one side of this complex movement. Above all else, reformers desired to create new associations that would bring together scattered, isolated farmers into a community of sharing and cooperative experimenters. Reformers sponsored periodicals, agricultural societies, public speakers, and agricultural fairs to encourage the dissemination of new knowledge. While private profit might encourage a farmer to take up a successful experiment, it was the approbation of the community that would lead him to share it with others. As the editor of the *Southern Planter* put it in 1841, "Individual and isolated action needs the stimulant of public exhibition. The gratification of an honest pride, the applause of friends, are nobler, and we believe stronger incentives than pecuniary interest."[37]

Agricultural reformers in Albemarle spread their doctrines with missionary zeal, forming societies and clubs to lure potential converts to their cause. Their organizational mainstay was the Albemarle Agricultural Society, formed in 1817. Although the Society's stiff membership requirements ($5 to join, plus the recommendation of two current members) gave the organization the feel of a gentlemen's club, it nevertheless sponsored speakers (usually local luminaries), held an annual agricultural fair, encouraged experimentation through premiums, and communicated with other societies for the latest developments. The Baltimore-based *American Farmer*, America's first agricultural reform periodical, gave the Society national recognition through the publications of the group's proceedings and lectures.[38]

The Albemarle Hole and Corner Club added an even more local element. The club's quaint name, taken from a Scottish predecessor, aptly captured the group's scope: The organization encompassed no more than a small corner of the county. Its 1842 constitution mandated that "this Club shall not embrace more than twelve farms" within

---

[36] Mr. Rives Speech [delivered to the Agricultural Society of Albemarle], *Southern Planter* 2 (December 1842), p. 277.

[37] "Association," *Southern Planter* 1 (October 1841), p. 189.

[38] "Rules and Regulations of the Agricultural Society of Albemarle," *American Farmer* 1 (12 November 1819), pp. 262–63; "Premiums offered by the Agricultural Society of Albemarle," *American Farmer* 1 (19 November 1819), p. 272; and Jas. Barbour, "Cultivation of Wheat," *American Farmer* 1 (17 December 1819), pp. 300–01. For the early history of the *American Farmer* and the agricultural reform press, see Demaree, *American Agricultural Press*, pp. 23–38.

a defined geographic area "twelve miles from the forks of the Rivanna River." Once every three weeks club members would meet at the farm of a member to evaluate its operation. Members would then dine with the owner of the farm "to discuss, in an orderly and temperate manner by conversation and not by speeches" agricultural matters. All other topics of conversation that might lead the club astray were expressly prohibited: "No subject shall be introduced into the conversations of the Club unless it be of kin to agriculture; and politics shall especially be excluded."[39] Perhaps because the *Southern Planter* published the proceedings of the Hole and Corner Club, other chapters were formed throughout Virginia, including at least one other club in Albemarle.[40]

Gentleman planters dominated the early agricultural societies and clubs. They frequently denounced the resistance to "book farming" that their less wealthy counterparts sometimes displayed, interpreting hesitation to adopt reforms as inveterate and irrational traditionalism.[41] Traditionalism aside, the hesitation among ordinary farmers was understandable: They could little afford the expense of adopting unproven fertilizers and implements. As reform proved its worth in actual practice, more farmers became converts. If a few enterprising farmers adopted a successful new method, wrote James Fife in 1849, then "his neighbors[,] becoming eyewitnesses of its powerful effects[,] will certainly adopt it."[42] Success, in other words, bred imitation. When the statewide Virginia Agricultural Society was organized in the early 1850s, almost 500 Albemarle residents (representing close to half of the county's farmers) joined the organization.[43]

For those reformers who actively recruited members of the Virginia Agricultural Society, something more was at stake than great profits and higher land values. Reformers hoped that better returns from farming would help stem the tide of emigration, thus keeping together

[39] Frank Carr [Constitition of "The Albemarle Hole and Corner Club, No. 1"], *Southern Planter* 2 (July 1842), p. 154.
[40] "Another Hole and Corner Club," *Southern Planter* 5 (February 1845), p. 47, and "Report of the Upper Hole and Corner Club of Mecklenburg," *Southern Planter* 4 (February 1844), p. 31.
[41] Rural historians have sometimes interpreted the lack of interest of ordinary farmers in agricultural reform as part of a general hostility to the commercialization of agriculture and market imperatives. A more straightforward economic explanation is that wealthy planters had the time, money, and education to experiment with expensive and untried fertilizers, crop rotations, and livestock breeds; they could well afford to make mistakes that might mean bankruptcy for a smaller farmer. In many ways, the farmer who steadfastly ignored the "book farming" was more rational than the enthusiastic reformer. While the reformer spent time and money on experiments that often failed, the skeptic watched and waited, implementing only those reforms that had proven themselves through trial and error.
[42] James Fife, "Guano," *Southern Planter* 9 (April 1849), p. 113.
[43] "Number of Members of the State Agricultural Society in the Several Counties and Towns in Virginia," *Southern Planter* 14 (June 1856), p. 189.

settled communities. Editorialists and correspondents to the *Southern Planter* glorified the benefits of staying at home (and practicing scientific agriculture, of course) over moving to the rugged and unsettled West. Dr. Daniel Archer, in the inaugural address of the Agricultural Society of Elizabeth City (a county in the Tidewater region) declared in 1841 that "Our farmers have at last discovered the golden secret, that it is easier to improve a field, naturally fertile, but exhausted by bad cultivation, than to open a new one." It was the advent of agricultural reform, Archer argued, that "will tend more to arrest the tide of emigration than any one circumstance that could possibly have happened."[44] A Dr. Philips made a more sentimental appeal. Why would anyone want to "sever every tender tie that binds him to 'home, sweet, home?'" Philips asked in 1844. Instead of uprooting their families, farmers should instead "study the economy of manures, improved agricultural implements, stock, seeds, the best rotations, and management of crops."[45]

The desire to stop the flow of emigrants had a strong political element as well. Virginians connected the stagnation of their economy with the decline of their political fortunes. Once the most powerful state in the Union, slow population growth had eroded Virginia's political clout. Many observers connected this decline to too much political talk and not enough economic action. The Richmond *Enquirer* warned in 1852 that "As other States accumulate the means of material greatness, and glide past us on the road to wealth and empire, we slight the warnings of dull statistics, and drive lazily along the field of ancient customs, or stop the *plough*, to speed the politician."[46] What better way to get the plough going again than systematic improvement in Virginia's agriculture? Reform would stop emigration and help Virginians keep pace with the rapidly advancing North, thus restoring to greatness what Andrew Stevenson, in a speech before the Agricultural Society of Albemarle, called "this glorious and renowned Old Commonwealth."[47]

Many reformers were keenly aware that preventing emigration, preserving rural communities, and restoring Virginia's political influence would take more than better agricultural practices. They realized that the Old Dominion's planters and farmers needed better transportation, a point that they never failed to emphasize. Better transportation would allow more farmers to sell more surpluses, thus stimulating the incentive to reform backward agricultural practices. Better transportation would stimulate urban growth, thus creating new markets for dairy products, garden produce, and other profitable

---

[44] "Dr. Archer's Address," *Southern Planter* 2 (July 1841), p. 110.
[45] "Emigration," *Southern Planter* 4 (June 1844), pp. 124–25.
[46] Quoted in Goldfield, *Urban Growth*, p. 6.
[47] "Agricultural Address," *Southern Planter* 8 (January 1848), p. 5.

commodities. Better transportation would lower the cost of importing fertilizers, thus encouraging farmers to use guano and lime to replenish their lands. The editor of the *Southern Planter* summarized the prevailing wisdom with the assertion that "all property upon or adjacent to a good railroad or canal rises in value, perhaps even more than to balance the amount of outlay for the improvement."[48]

Albemarle's flourishing agricultural reform movement provides a counterexample to arguments that slavery lessened the incentive for Southerners to improve their lands. Planters who could take their slaves (which was their principle form of capital) to the fresh lands of the West, some historians have argued, had little incentive to renew the fertility of their land or finance internal improvements. Slave prices, after all, rose or fell regardless of the condition of local infrastructure, reducing the incentive of slaveholders to invest in better fertilizers, improved roads, or new railroads.[49] Yet rising slave prices were small consolation for Albemarle reformers if depleted lands and poor transportation forced them to migrate. Families who had spent generations in the Piedmont viewed western migration as an evil to avoid, not an opportunity to embrace. Such attitudes led Albemarle's wealthiest residents to embrace a new creed of economic rejuvenation. With the prospect of increased land values and renewed political power firing their imaginations, residents of Albemarle worked hard to build turnpikes, river improvements, and canals.

Town Rivalry and Albemarle's Developmental Corporations

To improve transportation, however, was a task easier said than done. Residents of Albemarle soon found that the quest to raise land values would require a peculiar combination of cooperation and competition. Cooperation was the lifeblood of the developmental corporation, whether it came to securing approval from the state legislature or financing companies that paid meager dividends. What got this lifeblood circulating, however, was the impetus of town competition. The indirect benefits of a new turnpike or canal were extremely local – those who lived near the improvement would benefit the most from rising land values and increased trade. As people and trade began to gravitate toward the improvement, population growth and land values in other parts of the county might fall. Albemarle's residents perceived the effort to revitalize their economy as a zero-sum game in which one town's gain was another town's loss. The result was a vigorous town rivalry that powerfully influenced state and local politics.

[48] "The Value of Canals and Railroads to Farmers," *Southern Planter* 10 (December 1850), p. 364.
[49] See, for example, Wright, *Old South, New South*, pp. 19–31.

Town rivalry was apparent in Albemarle's initial creation. When the county was first formed in 1744, the county court awarded Samuel Scott the right "to Build a Court House, Prison, Stocks, and pillory, (at his Own proper cost) ... on condition that he may Build them on his own Land," which was near the present site of Scottsville.[50] Scott owned a tavern and ferry near the county seat, both of which would be especially busy on court days. Locating the courthouse on Scott's property also made geographical sense – it was near the center of the county. But when the colonial legislature reduced Albemarle's size, Scott's courthouse suddenly stood at Albemarle's southern periphery. In 1761, residents of the central part of the county persuaded the legislature to move the courthouse to Charlottesville, creating an issue that remained a sore point for decades. In 1835, Carter Harrison advised Thomas Jefferson Randolph that citizens of Scottsville had decided to postpone a petition that called for moving the courthouse back to Scottsville. Harrison noted that "The location of a Ct. house seemed already to have been a bone of contention, and I imagine will always be."[51]

As the first signs of economic stagnation appeared in the late eighteenth century, several new towns were founded. The boom in town building led one local historian to write that "an eager ambition was manifested to build up towns in the county."[52] The state legislature chartered Milton in 1789, followed by North Milton (across the Rivanna from Milton), Warren (on the James), and at least six others.[53] Most of the new towns were little more than a country store at a crossroads, but a few became viable commercial centers. Two main rivalries developed in the late eighteenth century: one between Charlottesville and Milton in the central portion of the county, the other between Warren and Scottsville in the southern part.

Despite the heated competition, the more established towns of Charlottesville and Scottsville won their respective contests. Although Milton was located at the head of navigation for the Rivanna River, planters and farmers west of the town had to traverse a series of difficult hills to reach its warehouses and mills. They successfully petitioned the legislature in 1806 for a canal around the falls. When completed in 1812, the canal made Charlottesville the head of navigation, giving it a decisive advantage over its neighbor. Milton quickly declined; by 1820, the town was little more than unimproved lots.[54]

[50] Rawlings (ed.), "Albemarle County Court," p.16.
[51] Peyton Harrison to Thomas Jefferson Randolph, Jan. 19, 1835, Thomas Jefferson Randolph Papers, UVA. See also Moore, *Jefferson's County*, p. 8.
[52] Woods, *Albemarle County*, p. 57.
[53] Woods, *Albemarle County*, pp. 57–63.
[54] Dabney, "Jefferson's Albermarle" (Ph.D. diss.), pp. 140–46; Albemarle County Real Property Lists, 1820, microfilm, VSLA.

Geography and improvements also allowed Scottsville to triumph over Warren, but the competition was more protracted. Wilson Carey Nicholas, a prominent planter of distinguished lineage and even more distinguished political connections, founded Warren near his plantation in 1790. Nicholas used his political muscle to keep Scottsville from receiving legislative permission to build a tobacco inspection station or to establish a formal town government, thus giving Warren a decided advantage. When Nicholas, financially strapped because of unprofitable speculations in frontier land, sold his mills, distillery, tavern, and other Warren property in 1803, the town lost its political influence. As one historian concluded, Warren's "demise was assured."[55] Scottsville's families finagled an inspection station and a formal town charter, and then secured a legislative charter for a turnpike road in 1824 over the vociferous objections of Warren's residents. Warren soon ceased to be a serious competitor.

With their local rivals out of the way, Charlottesville and Scottsville battled for commercial supremacy of Albemarle County. Scottsville struck the first blow when its residents helped finance the Staunton and James River Turnpike in 1824. The turnpike, which created an improved road in exchange for the right to collect tolls, helped Scottsville capture a significant portion of the trade of the Shenandoah Valley. Since the end of the Revolution, farmers in the Valley had been exporting large quantities of wheat, creating an opportunity for Albemarle towns to act as middlemen between the Valley farmers and Richmond. With the turnpike finished, farmers could take their wheat by wagon from Augusta county to Scottsville, and then along the James River to Richmond. If legislative petitions from Scottsville are to be believed, in 1831 more than 35,000 barrels of flour and 600 hogshead of tobacco passed through the town every year.[56]

Charlottesville residents grew concerned. The *Central Gazette* (published in Charlottesville) expressed surprise in 1825 that "no active and energetic attempts have been made to effect an object so desirable" as improvement of the Rivanna River. "We must be up and doing," the newspaper warned, "or we shall soon be left out at a sightless distance behind those whom it is in our power to surpass."[57] In 1827 planters and merchants along the river secured a charter for the Rivanna Navigation Company. Although previous attempts had been made to improve the river, the companies had been undercapitalized and constantly wrangled with local millowners. The residents of Charlottesville hoped that the new company, capitalized at

---

[55] Golladay, "Nicholas Family," (Ph.D. diss.), pp. 299–302; quote on p. 302.
[56] Young, *Brief History*, pp. 1–5; ACLP, December 19, 1831.
[57] *Central Gazette*, 10 Sept. 1825, p. 2.

$80,000, would finally build permanent improvements that would induce farmers from the Valley to send their products to Charlottesville, and then down the Rivanna to the town of Columbia on the James.[58]

Both sections of the county had a clear interest promoting the James River and Kanawha Company. Incorporated in 1832 and organized in 1835, the company was to build a canal that would connect Richmond to the Ohio River. Although the project never came close to fulfilling its larger aims, residents of Albemarle nevertheless benefited from the project. When the first division of the canal (connecting Richmond to Lynchburg) opened in 1840, Scottsville's importance as a marketing center increased, and business on the Staunton and James River Turnpike rose accordingly.[59] The canal also made it easier to send goods along the improved Rivanna River to Richmond. In 1842, the navigation company wanted to dig a complete canal (as opposed to merely improving the Rivanna) to the James. After more than $117,000 was spent on the project during the 1850s, the ill-fated attempt was abandoned without reaching Charlottesville.[60]

Indirect Benefits of Albemarle's Developmental Corporations

As the 1830s ended, Charlottesville and Scottsville appeared deadlocked: Charlottesville served as the commercial hub for the central portion of the county, including the nearby University of Virginia, and undoubtedly benefited from its position as county seat. Scottsville, meanwhile, depended upon the nearby plantations in the James River Valley as well as the trade from Augusta County. The stalemate would not be broken until 1847, when Charlottesville secured the Virginia Central Railroad. Deadlock did not mean stagnation. Both towns enjoyed a brisk prosperity during the 1830s and 1840s, a remarkable accomplishment given the lackluster state of Virginia's economy. In 1839 residents of Charlottesville proudly recounted, in excruciating detail, the accomplishments of their "enterprising" town: its rapidly growing population (now at 2,000 people); its thriving retail sector (22 dry good stores, 9 groceries, 2 drug stores, 2 book stores, and

[58] For an overview of the navigation company, see McGehee, "Rivanna Navigation Company," pp. 1–20. I am indebted to Edward Perkins for sending me this article. To complement the river improvements, Charlottesville interests also sponsored the Rivanna and Rockfish Gap Turnpike, which they hoped would divert trade away from Scottsville. The turnpike left little documentation behind, and never became the important improvement that Charlottesville residents hoped that it would be. The lack of records prevents full analysis of investment in the turnpike.
[59] According to the *ARBPW*, tolls on the turnpike increased from an average of $2,500 before 1840 to more than $4,200 after 1840.
[60] McGehee, "Rivanna Navigation Company," pp. 10–13. See also *ARBPW* (1842), pp. 398–400.

Table 1.2. *The Indirect Benefits of Developmental Corporations:*
Property Values in Charlottesville and Scottsville, 1820–1840

Town (Year)	Charlottesville 1820 ($)	Charlottesville 1840 ($)	Scottsville 1820 ($)	Scottsville 1840 ($)
Average Value Per Lot	733	1,337	109	647
Average Value of Buildings	582	954	49	517
"Intrinsic Value" of Average Lot	151	383	50	130
Average Annual Rent Per Lot	54	110	12	44

Notes and Sources: The "intrinsic value" of a lot is defined as the lot's total value minus the value of its buildings. Calculated from Albemarle County Real Property Tax Lists, 1820 and 1840, microfilm, VSLA.

4 taverns) and its prosperous artisans and manufacturers (3 tanneries, 2 jewelers, 2 saddlers, 3 wheel wrights, and 9 merchant mills).[61] Scottsville was somewhat smaller than Charlottesville, but its residents never tired of boasting about its growth and prospects. An 1835 legislative petition asking for a bank touted Scottsville's "extensive Ware Houses and other neat buildings," its "population of about Three hundred Inhabitants," and its trade of "nearly half a Million of Dollars annually."[62]

We should not take these glowing self-assessments (the staple crop of American boosterism) at face value, but tax valuations tell a similar story. Although rural property values generally stagnated from 1820 to 1840, the value of Albemarle's urban property increased significantly (Table 1.2). In Charlottesville, the value of a town lot increased about 82 percent over this period. The increase was fueled, in part, because there were more buildings – vacant or undeveloped lots were replaced with stores, workshops, and other businesses. Even if one takes into account the greater number of buildings, the "intrinsic value" of lots (total value minus the value of buildings) more than doubled. The performance of Scottsville real estate was even more impressive. The value of the average lot increased more than fivefold and the average annual rent more than threefold.

Developmental corporations, to a lesser degree, also raised rural land values. The Rivanna Navigation Company serves as the best example. The value of property lying on the Rivanna River within a

[61] ACLP, February 4, 1839.
[62] ACLP, December 21, 1835.

seven mile radius of Charlottesville (thus benefiting from both the growth of the town and direct improvements on the river), increased 6 percent in absolute terms and almost 10 percent in real terms between 1820 and 1840. Although this increase sounds modest, owners of large plantations often found that even a small rise in land values more than justified their investments in developmental corporations. A 5 percent increase in the value of Thomas Jefferson Randolph's $57,000 plantation – which came to a hefty $2,850 – represented an excellent return on his $1,000 investment in the Rivanna Navigation Company.[63]

In contrast to these high indirect returns (increased commerce and higher land values) the direct returns of Albemarle's developmental corporations were exceedingly low. The ill-fated James River and Kanawha Company (whose many problems will be discussed in greater length in Chapter 5) did not issue a single dividend. The Rivanna Navigation Company averaged dividend payments of just over one percent from 1830 to 1850, when competition with the Virginia Central Railroad put the improvement on the edge of bankruptcy.[64] The Staunton and James River Turnpike did better, but its 2.8 percent average annual return between 1827 and 1848 hardly constituted a great success.[65]

Because of these low direct returns, most investment came from those who could best benefit from the increase in land values. For the Staunton and James River Turnpike and the Rivanna Navigation Company, 95 and 88 percent of investors lived in Albemarle or another county through which the respective improvement passed.[66] More precise linkages of Albemarle investors show that investment was even more localized. The vast majority of the Albemarle stockholders in the Rivanna Navigation Company, for example, owned real estate in or around Charlottesville or along some other point near the river. Only four Albemarle stockholders, with an aggregate investment of a meager $550, owned real estate further than six miles from the river. Notably absent were investors from the southern and western sections of the county, who received few if any indirect benefits from the project.[67]

[63] Calculated from Albemarle Real Property Tax Lists, microfilm, VSLA.
[64] Compiled from annual reports in *ARBPW*.
[65] Calculated from Hunter, "Turnpike Movement," p. 345, and various annual reports found in *ARBPW*.
[66] The figures apply to only those investors who could be linked to census and tax records. Please see the appendix for precise methods of calculation.
[67] Location of investors in the Rivanna Navigation Company calculated from stock lists found in ABPW and Albemarle County Real Property Tax Lists, microfilm, VSLA. The four Albemarle investors living far from the river may be added to the six investors who lived outside of Albemarle and Fluvanna Counties altogether. Thus out of a total of 121 investors linked to census and tax records, only 10 (8 percent) were not in position to reap indirect benefits.

Wealthy slaveholders provided the bulk of the capital for the developmental corporations. Albemarle residents who owned 15 or more slaves provided 90 percent of the capital for the Staunton and James River Turnpike, 52 percent for the Rivanna Navigation Company, and 49 percent for the James River and Kanawha Company. Large slaveholders, who owned much of the land in the county, would have the most to gain from improvements that raised property values. Nor were Albemarle's planters passive investors, for they also provided much of the political, organizational, and engineering skills necessary to run the transportation companies. They lobbied the state legislature for charters, lent their names and prestige to petition drives, chaired the town meetings that organized the enterprises, and served as corporate officers. William H. Meriwether, for example, invested $1,000 in the Rivanna Navigation Company. As a board member of the company, he frequently surveyed and oversaw the works, eventually becoming president in 1836. Meriwether, like many area planters, had a special interest in a work that promised to raise the value of his 1,150 acre plantation.[68]

Planters who promoted canals and turnpikes were often the same ones championing agricultural reform. In 1826 the Agricultural Society of Albemarle sponsored a petition supporting incorporation of the Rivanna Navigation Company, noting that there was "nothing more dependent for its [Albemarle's] prosperity than the provision of safe, cheap, and practical channels of transportation."[69] Some reformers did much more than sign a petition. "A Member" of the Agricultural Society wrote to the Charlottesville *Virginia Advocate* suggesting that the club invest its funds in the Rivanna Navigation Company. There could be no doubt, "Member" declared, that "its accomplishment would of itself confer a benefit on the Agriculture of the county that no other conceivable scheme could effect." Believing that "no plausible objection even can be made to the measure," the writer requested a full meeting to appropriate the suitable funds.[70] The Society itself apparently did not invest in the company, but many individual members did so enthusiastically. Of the 29 people who attended a meeting endorsing the company, 22 became stockholders, collectively investing $11,200.[71]

The public arm twisting that "Member" applied suggests a model of entrepreneurship that can be applied to developmental corporations

---

[68] The activities of Meriwether in the company are outlined in "Minute or Record Book of the Rivanna Navigation Co. from 1828 to 1851," UVA, pp. 228–29, 236.
[69] ACLP, December 20, 1826.
[70] *The Virginia Advocate*, 3 May 1828, p. 3.
[71] The members attending the meeting were found in the "Proceedings of the Agricultural Society of Albemarle," UVA. The meeting was held December 17, 1826.

more generally. Entrepreneurs such as "Member" effectively used
local newspapers and agricultural societies to overcome the freerider
problem associated with indirect benefits. The property owners in
and around Charlottesville and Scottsville, after all, enjoyed higher
property values whether or not they made an investment in the developmental corporations. To make sure that developmental corporations got built, individual boosters had to convince kin, friends, and
associates to invest in the enterprises.

John H. Cocke's Web of Influence and the James River and Kanawha Company

John H. Cocke, a rich planter living on Albermarle's border in neighboring Fluvanna County, exemplifies the efforts of such organizers.
Born of a wealthy Tidewater family but a long-term resident of the
Piedmont, Cocke passionately promoted both agricultural reform
and developmental corporations. Widely recognized as one of central
Virginia's best farmers, he was elected an officer of the Albemarle
Agricultural Society and frequently corresponded with reformers and
societies across Virginia. Cocke's "Bremo" estates became a model of
enlightened management, sometimes achieving wheat yields three to
four times larger per acre than more typical Albemarle plantations.
He also invested heavily in several internal improvements, including
the James River and Kanawha Company ($5,000) and the Staunton
and James River Turnpike Company ($300). Cocke undoubtedly
knew that these improvements would increase the value of his large
James River holdings.

Economic interest, however, was only one of Cocke's many motivations. He wanted nothing less than the rejuvenation of the Old
Dominion founded upon new respect for work, discipline, and science. In 1836, Cocke lectured his son John Jr. that "System and order
are the grand secrets of using our little span of time to best account.
Besides there is a beautiful consistency in it which makes the nearest
approach we are capable of to our Divine Master – the maker of the
Universe."[72] No wonder that Cocke tirelessly advocated scientific agriculture, which would bring order and enterprise to Virginia's faltering
plantation economy. His belief in agricultural reform dovetailed with
his unquestioning faith in the power of applied science. Cocke advised
John Jr. that "mathematics, or Nat. philosophy," was infinitely superior
to writing "the most profound metaphysical treatise that has ever
bewilder'd the World."[73] He later encouraged John Jr. to develop a

---

[72] John Hartwell Cocke to John, Jr., January 2, 1836, Cocke Papers, Box 84, UVA.
[73] Quoted in Coyner, "John Hartwell Cocke" (Ph. D. diss.), p. 19.

road based on science, not tradition. "A well located & faithfully made Road on scientific principles," he wrote in 1836, "is one of the few Monuments of our day and generation in the way of individual enterprise which may be expected to go down to posterity."[74]

Cocke's strong faith in engineering expertise and economic progress all came together in his support of internal improvements. The Erie Canal became Cocke's symbol of how transportation enterprises spurred commercial greatness and economic vigor. He held the New York improvements to be his generation's greatest accomplishment, and esteemed DeWitt Clinton as its most deserving hero. Cocke frequently wrote Clinton, asking advice about a "northern college" where his son could study engineering and mineralogy in order to build canals in Virginia. (John Jr. eventually attended Yale after visiting Clinton and touring the New York canal.) Cocke's letters expressed nothing but gratitude and admiration. He told Clinton that New York would "spread its benignant & salutary influence to the remotest confines of the Union . . . and we too of the Ancient Dominion will follow the wake of your glorious example." As for Clinton himself, Cocke thought that the New York governor would rightfully "receive the gratitude of a Nation which . . . will be repeated loud & long by future generations."[75]

To help Virginia follow New York's example, Cocke became an outspoken advocate of the James River and Kanawha Company. Cocke predicted that the canal would not only open up the produce of the West to Richmond and Norfolk, but it would also create new attitudes and values among the Old Dominion's planters and farmers. Cocke dreamed that the enterprise would result in new interest in engineering and internal improvements, ultimately producing "a corps of *scientific working* Gentlemen – each *one* of whom will be worth to the Community six Doctors & as many Lawyers – & at least a Cowpen full of our Jimmy-Jessimy Gentlemen at large."[76]

To insure that his beloved canal was built, the James River planter became the center of a web of friends and contacts designed to catch potential investors. His extensive correspondence suggests that among economic motivations, the quest for higher land values was the most important. In 1835, Abraham Shepard, Jr. wrote to congratulate Cocke on the passage of the canal's charter. Shepard reported that he had been contemplating buying a farm, and now looked "upon this farm, as worth 12 per centum more now than immediately before the passage of the Bill securing the charter of the J&K

[74] John Hartwell Cocke to John, Jr., January 2, 1836, Cocke Papers, Box 84, UVA.
[75] Cocke to DeWitt Clinton, July 30, 1825, Cocke Papers, Box 44, UVA. Cocke to DeWitt Clinton, July 2, 1824 (draft), Cocke Papers, Box 41, UVA.
[76] Quoted in Coyner, "John Hartwell Cocke" (Ph. D. diss.), p. 19.

company."[77] John Timberlake, Jr. gave even more convincing testimony on the importance of indirect benefits. Timberlake had been trying to induce subscriptions from his neighbors in Fluvanna County, but had been decidedly unsuccessful. He attributed his difficulties to his location away from the canal, "where the least interest seems to be felt in relation to the Improvement." Although he hoped that "additional subscription might be obtained if the subject was again fully brought before the people at their hustings," he remained pessimistic about his chances.[78]

Timberlake's reference to bringing the James River and Kanawha Company "before the people" speaks to the armtwisting that canal supporters employed. Tucker Coles, a prominent planter living near Scottsville, wrote Cocke in 1834 that some of the subscribers in his area had withdrawn their support. "I have had a laborious duty to perform, to restore the deficiency," he reported. Coles did not reveal the details of his methods, but his letter suggested that he made many personal visits. "The proper exertion," he wrote, would "bring back to the fold some of the herd [who] strayed in their wantonness."[79] The exertion Coles applied was proper indeed, at least in terms of his own family. Tucker, John, and Isaac Coles ranked among the top five of Albemarle stockholders, collectively investing $10,000 in the project.

The personal relationships that encouraged investment were evident in a lengthy letter written to Cocke by William Bolling. Bolling tried to explain why he sold his stock in the canal, an action that apparently offended his good friend Cocke. Bolling emphasized that he always believed that the stock itself was a poor investment, yet he purchased shares anyway because the work "would be highly advantageous to the state, & that as a citizen thereof I should in that way be benefited." Significantly, Bolling not only purchased shares, but worked with the president of the James River and Kanawha Company "in inducing others to do the same." Bolling felt that once the company had been chartered and organized, he could sell his stock in good conscience. Bolling's letter attested to how important investing in developmental corporations was to some Virginia planters – nothing less than his long friendship with Cocke was on the line. "I am not of making *professions* of friendship" he reminded Cocke, "yet I have always estimated you as one among the few friends that I have most highly valued."[80]

[77] Abraham Shepard, Jr. to John Hartwell Cocke, February 11, 1835, Cocke Papers, Box 81, UVA.
[78] John Timberlake, Jr. to John Hartwell Cocke, January 11, 1834, Cocke Papers, Box 76, UVA.
[79] Tucker Coles to John Hartwell Cocke, January 17, 1835, Cocke Papers, Box 80, UVA.
[80] William Bolling to General John H. Cocke, October 8, 1836, Cocke Papers, Box 86, UVA.

Much like Bolling, other correspondents cited their patriotism to the Old Dominion when buying shares. The canal's promise to raise land values and invigorate commerce would not only benefit individual investors, but halt the state's general decline. "[I]f the friends of the James River improvements fail to avail themselves the opportunity offered them by our Legislature," warned Abraham Shepard, Jr. in 1835, "in a few years she will be stripped of nearly all that is worth preserving, and will continue, deservedly too, to retrograde."[81] Similarly, Martin Tutwiler predicted in 1835 that if the canal failed, "Richd. will go like old Wmsburg and Eastern VA will lose all her former grandeur and her most enterprising citizens."[82]

The flip side of Tutwiler's remark was that those who did not participate might be called unpatriotic, a fear boosters could use to encourage investment. An example of this sort of social pressure, found outside of Cocke's correspondence, was a letter written in 1850 to Tucker Coles. The letter, signed by 19 men, noted that the legislature had just approved a new charter for the Staunton and James River Turnpike Company that allowed the company to cover its road with a stone or plank surfacing. All that was needed now, the writers stated, was "some gentleman of known ability and of practiced business habits" who would represent "the incomparable benefits that might result to the community in its completion." The writers then appealed to Coles' sense of obligation, "hoping that considerations of personal inconvenience, will serve as *little* to *deter* him from engaging in it, as considerations of personal benefit would *induce* him to do so."[83] Coles' plantations near Scottsville – his "considerations of personal benefit" – would surely appreciate in value if the road was a success. It would be unjust, the writers implied, for Coles to do nothing while others built a road that benefited his interests.

On the other hand, association with a road destined to become a "second to none in the state" would undoubtedly bring recognition to Coles. In this respect, the letter shows how participation in transportation projects fit a particular brand of southern honor. "In a rural, slaveholding society steeped in the old traditions of 'honor,'" Kenneth S. Greenberg has written, "election to political office was one of the major ways in which a man's status and reputation could be publicly confirmed for all to see."[84] The same could be said of active participation in transportation corporations. What better way to show concern for the "public good" than selflessly organizing a petition drive or

---

[81] Abraham Shepard, Jr. to John Hartwell Cocke, February 11, 1835, Cocke Papers, Box 81, UVA.
[82] M. Tutwiler to John Hartwell Cocke, January 17, 1835, Cocke Papers, Box 80, UVA.
[83] Letter to Tucker Coles, March 28, 1847, Coles Family Collection, MSS2C678b, VHS.
[84] Greenberg, *Masters and Statesmen*, p. 12.

virtuously serving as a company officer? Such activities put politically ambitious planters before the public eye and helped solidify community support. Here the lack of direct profits reinforced the "patriotism" associated with transportation enterprises, for their absence confirmed that the participating planter was a truly disinterested public servant. No wonder that many of Albemarle's prominent politicians also played an active role in transportation corporations.[85]

Self-interest and the Community

Honor and political prestige helped developmental corporations successfully acquire the capital they needed to build commercial infrastructure. Self-interest was not absent; those who lived closest to an improvement (and hence received the greatest economic benefit) provided most of the financing for the projects. Yet one should not ignore the lessen from public goods theory that individuals with too much self-interest would have let "suckers" finance improvements that benefited all property owners. Albemarle residents, especially wealthy planters with long-term connections to the county, pooled their knowledge to promote agricultural reform and their capital to build transportation improvements. A vigorous local boosterism emanating from the county's small towns gave added impetus to the construction of turnpikes, river improvements, and canals. These local boosters always gave an optimistic appraisal of their town's future, but a sense of desperation lurked in the background. Facing depleted soils, falling tobacco prices, and rapid out-migration, the planters and businessmen connected to Albemarle's various towns resembled a shipwrecked crew facing the open ocean on a frail lifeboat. All had to row together to avoid a most unhappy fate.

---

[85] Nor were Albemarle politicians atypical. Siegel's study of Pittsylvania County concludes that "regardless of their occupation, residence, or political affiliation, they [Pittsylvania's elected representatives] were strong promoters of internal improvements and economic growth." *Roots of Southern Distinctiveness*, p. 112.

2

Developmental Corporations in a Free-Labor Society

The Susquehanna, lying on Cumberland County's eastern border, was clearly a river of major importance. Although shallow and filled with rapids, it was a major thoroughfare in the colonial period, and would later become an important weapon in the trade war between Philadelphia and Baltimore.[1] Yet even with such high stakes, the early efforts to improve the river strongly resembled Jefferson's trusteeship that had improved the Rivanna River in colonial Albemarle. Carlisle merchant Robert Whitehill, Jr., received two circulars in 1795 that asked for contributions to improve the river to Pennsylvania's state line. The circulars outlined the important commercial advantages of improving the river, but its authors also appealed to public spirit as well. "Let *all* give to what *all* will be greatly benefited by," the circular declared. "We *see* and *feel* that our *interest* is *one* – Let *each* consider it as his own."[2] As was the case with Jefferson's Rivanna River project 30 years earlier, the project's promoters expected prominent gentlemen to contribute. At the bottom of one circular a handwritten note instructed Whitehill to "direct and forward the enclosed Copies to such respectable & influential Characters of your neighborhood as you think most likely to assist with us in opening the River."[3]

The circular addressed to Whitehill foreshadowed the essential similarities between Cumberland's developmental corporations and those in Albemarle. Many of Cumberland's developmental corporations performed even worse than those of Albemarle, often failing to pay a cent in dividends. Most investment, therefore, came from local property owners interested in reaping the benefits of higher property values and increased commerce. Buying stock in Cumberland's developmental corporations was perceived as investment in the local community that would benefit farmers, merchants, and artisans alike.

---

1 The competition between Baltimore and Philadelphia for the trade of the Susquehanna is summarized in Livingood, *Philadelphia-Baltimore Trade Rivalry*, pp. 27–41.
2 "To all those interested in the Navigation of the River Susquehannah," circulars dated May 29, 1795 and August 13, 1795, Robert Whitehill, Jr. papers, 7-1, CCHS. Hereafter cited as "Susquehannah Circulars."
3 "Susquehannah Circular," May 29, 1795.

Developmental corporations in Albemarle and Cumberland, to be sure, reflected the very different social worlds of these two localities. No great slave-holding planters dominated Cumberland's transportation improvements. Investors tended to be more numerous and more diverse, representing a wider range of occupations. Investment in Cumberland was also somewhat more equal, as the top stockholders owned a smaller percentage of shares than the top stockholders in Albemarle. Perhaps the most important difference was one of timing. Cumberland residents, reflecting the advantage of a more densely populated county, organized and built their developmental projects a decade or more before their Albemarle counterparts. During the first third of the century, however, it was essential similarities – communities mobilizing local capital to finance unprofitable improvements – that characterized market development in Cumberland and Albemarle.

"One of the Richest And Finest Countries I Ever Saw"

Beginning in the 1720s, Scotch-Irish and German farm families settled in the Cumberland Valley. Despite the lack of legal title to the land and the threat of Indian attack, they found the fertile soils of the Cumberland Valley almost irresistible, especially since cheap land was increasingly hard to find in more settled parts of the colony. As part of the Pennsylvania extension of the "Great Valley" running from Alabama to New York, the Cumberland Valley was bordered by South Mountain (also known as the Blue Ridge) and North Mountain. Although these mountains prevented the easy movement of goods to southeastern destinations such as Baltimore, the valley itself formed a natural connection between eastern Pennsylvania and the colonial interior. More importantly, the southern and central portions of the valley contained some of the best soils in Pennsylvania, which allowed family farms to produce surpluses of grains, hay, and dairy products. The valley's fertility varied greatly – the hilly landscape and slate soils of the northern valley were far less productive than the limestone lands of the southeastern portion. Cumberland county nevertheless held great promise for newly arriving settlers.[4]

Once Thomas Penn, the colony's main proprietor, secured title to the Cumberland Valley in 1736, settlement increased dramatically. Penn encouraged this migration. More settlers meant higher land values, which translated into great profits for the land that Penn owned and developed. The rising price of grain undoubtedly helped his cause. Beginning in the mid-eighteenth century, rapid population growth in Europe and a series of poor European harvests led to an

---

[4] Ridner, "Handsomely Improved Place" (Ph. D. diss.), pp. 8–24.

upsurge in international grain prices that made the rich lands of southeastern and south-central Pennsylvania even more valuable. The resulting prosperity, one scholar has written, made the Pennsylvania countryside a "land of opportunity that many immigrants hoped to find."[5] Immigrants certainly had little problem finding Cumberland – the county's population grew from approximately 5,000 in 1750 to more than 24,000 in 1779.[6]

At this stage of its development, Cumberland had much in common with Albemarle. Both counties had been rapidly settled in the late colonial and revolutionary periods; both counties, despite high transportation costs, had significant commercial links with the Atlantic world; and both counties benefited from the rising prices of staple crops (wheat in Cumberland, tobacco in Albemarle). These similarities, however important, could not hide a crucial difference: slavery. Slavery was not completely absent in the Pennsylvania locality, but in 1790 slaves constituted only 1.2 percent of Cumberland's population, a far cry from the thousands of slaves working Albemarle's farms and plantations. Individual households – not large plantations – became the central unit of production.

Because of the different labor regimes, Cumberland's early settlers established small farms that paled in comparison to Albemarle's imposing plantations. In Middleton township – one of Cumberland's most well-developed areas – the average farm was only 189 acres in 1787 (the median was somewhat smaller, at 169 acres). Only 12 percent of the county's farms exceeded 300 acres.[7] As Cumberland's population grew and farmers subdivided their lands among heirs, the county's farms became even smaller. By 1850, average farm size was 130 acres; in contrast, the average Albemarle farm contained 417 acres. Cumberland residents undoubtedly would have been amazed at the size of William G. Rives's 2,122 acre plantation, Thomas Jefferson Randolph's 2,482 acre estate, and other large Albemarle holdings.[8]

Albemarle planters could cultivate such sprawling plantations as long as they could afford the slaves to work them. Labor in Cumberland, on the other hand, came from the farm families themselves, effectively reducing the number of acres that could be cultivated. Laborers might be hired, but high wage rates put this outside the

[5] Tully, "Economic Opportunity," p. 128. For a similar analysis of economic opportunity in Pennsylvania, see Lemon, *Best Poor Man's Country*, pp. 42–70.

[6] Wing, *History of Cumberland County*, p. 14; Sutherland, *Population Distribution*, p. 132.

[7] Calculated from Cumberland County Tax Lists, 1787, microfilm, PSA. A large tract of 5,494 acres was excluded from these calculations, because it provided fuel for an ironworks.

[8] The size of these Albemarle plantations were found in the 1850 Albermarle Real Property Tax Lists, VSLA. For a classic analysis of how slave labor removed constraints on plantation size, see Fleisig, "Slavery," pp. 572–95.

means of most families. Wage rates were especially high in the colonial and revolutionary periods, when the frontier character of Cumberland created particularly acute labor shortages. As historian Daniel Vickers has noted, frontier areas needed labor to help clear the land, yet could rarely afford it since newly established farms usually had few cash crops to sell. Cumberland also contained plenty of unsettled land, which made wage work unappealing for the many settlers who placed a premium on propertied independence. With labor in short supply, Cumberland households mobilized every member of the family. Husbands and sons cleared fields, plowed land, and performed other heavy work; wives and daughters spun cloth, made candles, kept poultry, planted gardens, and churned butter.[9]

As Cumberland's population grew and links with outside markets improved, wage labor became more common. Documenting precisely how fast it grew is a difficult task. Cumberland's tax lists did not consistently record occupations until the late 1830s, and even then assessors sometimes failed to report them. Nor did having a taxable occupation necessarily mean that a person avoided wage work on a farm – a weaver or carpenter or even a schoolteacher might well find it worth his or her while to labor during the harvest, when wages were particularly high. The tax lists do show, however, that the number of landless households in the rural townships, which might be taken as the maximum number of farm laborers, increased substantially in the early 1800s. As early as 1787, 32 percent of households in rural townships did not own land, increasing to 50 percent in 1820 and 1838.[10]

The presence of a landless rural population, however, did not necessarily create a large pool of easily exploitable labor. Rural artisans headed perhaps half of the households without land, which gave them a status closer to an independent proprietor than a dependent wage laborer. Even those workers clearly specified as "laborers" on the tax lists enjoyed considerable autonomy. They were most often paid for specific work – harvesting wheat, hauling hay, building fences – that might be performed on a wide variety of farms. Consider the several jobs that laborer John Lefever recorded in his diary for the week of June 25–July 1, 1826:

---

[9] For a general overview of family farming and wage labor in the colonial North, see Vickers, "Northern Colonies," pp. 223–29. The specifics for Pennsylvania are analyzed in Schweitzer, *Custom and Contract*, pp. 49–56; Lemon, *Best Poor Man's Country*, pp. 10–13; and Clemens and Simler, "Rural Labor," pp. 106–43.

[10] Calculated from the samples described in the appendix. Some residents taxed for land may well have been tenants and hence landless, but still counted as owners in my calculations. There is no easy way to correct this bias, but given that the purpose of the calculations is to give a rough estimate of the number of potential wage laborers, the error appears inconsequential. A tenant working his own farm would be less likely to work for somebody else during the harvest season.

June 25: Came to Isaacs to cut wheat[.] [H]ad a heavy shower or rain.
[Sunday] June 26: Staid at home.
June 27: Cradled for Brother Isaac.
June 28, 29, 30th: Cut grain for A Skiles. [H]ad a shower on the 30th.
July 1: [B]roke my scythe. [P]rice of reaping 62½ cents[.] Cradleing $1.00.[11]

These entries suggest why a growing force of wage laborers did not lead to larger farms. Lefever's constant movement – working on two different farms in one week – suggests farmers hired laborers for particular tasks that household members could not perform. A family dramatically expanding its operations through more permanent arrangements with wage workers risked having the laborers depart at a critical moment, leaving precious crops (and the family fortune) to rot in the fields. Instead of increasing farm size, the hiring of rural laborers for specific tasks led households to diversify their output. Wage laborers who cleaned stalls and helped build barns, for example, allowed a family to increase dairy production without giving up wheat or hay or poultry or gardening. The small family farm, albeit extremely diversified and commercially-oriented, thus remained the foundation of Cumberland's economy into the antebellum decades.[12]

The relatively small size of Cumberland's farms led to what might be called a "less unequal" distribution of wealth. Cumberland, like other northern farm counties, was not an egalitarian paradise. Some farm laborers would own land only after years of hard work, or perhaps never at all. John Lefever, for example, eventually managed to acquire his own owned parcel of Cumberland's soil only after years of toil.[13] On the other end of the spectrum, a small number of entrepreneurs owned numerous farms, mills, tanneries, and other rural enterprises. The degree of inequality, at least on the countryside, was nevertheless much less than in Albemarle's slave society. The wealthiest 10 percent of Albemarle residents owned about 70 percent of the rural real

---

[11] "John Lefever Diary," edited and transcribed by Robert J. Smith, CCHS, pp. 15–16. Hereafter cited as "Lefever Diary."

[12] For excellent discussions of the relationship between wage labor and the development of the northern farm economy, see Wright, *Political Economy*, pp. 44–55; Atack and Bateman, *To Their Own Soil*, pp. 186–88; and Rothenberg, *From Market-Places to a Market Economy*, pp. 181–212. Rothenberg argues that a dual labor market developed in antebellum Massachusetts, with some agricultural workers having labor contracts and others doing day work for particular tasks (similar to the work described in the Lefever diary). The incidence of contract workers for Cumberland is unknown, but falling farm sizes in the county suggests that however prevalent they may have been, they did not allow Cumberland farmers to escape the county's binding labor constraints.

[13] Data on Lefever's property holdings are taken from the 1840 Cumberland County Tax Lists, microfilm, PSA.

Table 2.1. *Free Labor's Crucial Advantage:*
Population Density in Albemarle and Cumberland, 1830–1860

Year	Albermarle Population Per Square Mile (total)	Albermarle Population Per Square Mile (free only)	Cumberland Population Per Square Mile
1830	32	16	53
1840	33	16	56
1850	37	18	62
1860	38	18	73

Notes and Sources: Androit, *Population Abstract*, pp. 672, 821; Moore, *Jefferson's County*, p. 115; Martin, *Gazetteer*, p. 700; and Burrowes, *State-Book*, p. 160.

estate; the wealthiest 10 percent in Cumberland owned about 50 percent of rural real estate.[14]

Smaller farms also created a denser population. In 1820, Cumberland contained about 42 people per square mile, while Albemarle had less than 26. During the antebellum decades, the Pennsylvania county steadily expanded its lead. By 1860, Cumberland's population density doubled that of Albemarle's; if the Virginia county's slaves are discounted, the ratio jumps to a five to one advantage (Table 2.1). Part of Cumberland's greater population resulted from its greater urban growth. The hundreds of small farms that dotted Cumberland's landscape demanded the services of mills and artisans to collect, process, and market wheat and other grains. Cumberland's thick network of farms also generated a far greater concentration of consumers who demanded more goods and services than Albemarle's slave-labor plantations.[15] More stores, merchants, and retailers meant more town growth. No wonder that while Charlottesville's population probably hovered around 3,000 before the Civil War, the 1860 census counted about 5,500 people living in Carlisle. Cumberland's total town population of 10,304 in 1860 was almost as large as Albemarle's *total* white population.[16]

The differences in urbanization reflected parallel differences in manufacturing, for Cumberland was well ahead of its Virginia counterpart. In 1810, residents of Cumberland produced almost $782,000

[14] Calculated from samples drawn from Cumberland County Tax Lists, various years, microfilm, PSA. Please see the appendix for precise methods of calculation.
[15] Consumer demand in Cumberland is discussed in Chapter 3.
[16] The population of Charlottesville is not listed in the 1860 census, but an 1853 gazetteer estimated it to be 2,600. No other town had a population greater than 600. The 1860 census listed the population of Carlisle at 5,664, Mechanicsburg at 1,939, Shippensburg at 1,843, and Newville at 858. See Coleman, "Story of the Virginia Central" (Ph. D. diss.), and *Population of the United States* (1860 Census), pp. 421–22.

worth of manufactured goods, or about $29 per person. Although the county contained some significant ironworks, most of Cumberland's manufacturing was the by-product of a rural economy: flour and meal ($324,850), leather goods ($207,365), and distilled drink ($62,544) accounted for most of the early industrial output. Residents of Albemarle, on the other hand, produced manufactured goods in 1810 valued at only $9.70 per person.[17] Although Albemarle closed the gap somewhat, the county was still well behind as the Civil War approached. According to the 1860 census, residents of Cumberland produced $59 worth of manufactured goods per person, several times greater than the $22 worth of manufactured goods produced per person in Albemarle.[18]

Cumberland's economy possessed one further advantage that would have profound consequences: its strategic proximity to both Philadelphia (1860 population of 565,529) and Baltimore (212,418).[19] These large and growing urban markets allowed Cumberland farmers to diversify into dairy products, garden and orchard produce, and livestock. Virginia's slave economy, on the other hand, locked Albemarle out of such interactive growth. The closest "big city" was Richmond, with an 1860 population of less than 40,000. Despite repeated calls from reformers for greater diversification, Albemarle's farmers and planters found dairy production and market gardening unprofitable in the absence of a major urban market.[20]

Fertile soils, dense networks of family farms, thriving towns, and close proximity to booming urban markets all helped make Cumberland a showcase for northern agriculture. Travelers frequently commented on the beauty of the small, neat farms and well-kept countryside. In 1807, Fortescue Cuming wrote that the "houses and farms [were] good, and the face of the country pleasant."[21] Joshua Gilpin, who visited the county a few years later, found "the country beautifully cultivated in fine farms." Gilpin exclaimed that the land southwest of Carlisle was "one of the richest and finest countries I ever saw, meadows of great expanse being most agreeably mixed with fine corn land, & beautifully wooded."[22] In 1827 Ann Newport Royall declared that the Cumberland Valley was "the finest country, as to scenery, fertility, and situation, in the United States.[23] The travelers' accounts offer a striking contrast to the self-assessment of Albemarle

[17] These statistics were calculated from Coxe, *A Statement of the Arts and Manufacturers.*
[18] Calculated from *Manufacturers of the United States* (1860 Census), pp. 505, 604.
[19] Blumin, *Urban Threshold*, pp. 223–26.
[20] As we will see in Chapter 3, both census records and the observations of Albemarle planters reveal little in the way of surplus dairy production or market gardening.
[21] Cuming, "Sketches of a Tour," p. 46.
[22] Gilpin, "Traveller in the County," pp. 116–17.
[23] Quoted in Ridner, "Handsomely Improved Place," (Ph. D. diss.), p. 11.

planters, who frequently wrote about the declining fertility and deso-
late fields of their own locality.

Imprecise terms such as "neat," "beautiful," and "fine" that frequently appeared in descriptions of Cumberland captured an important element of the county's development: high land values. Land
values in the North were generally higher than those in the South, a
fact that the Cumberland and Albemarle comparison drives home. In
1845, a special tax equalization commission valued Cumberland land
at $23.31 per acre, while in 1850 tax assessors valued Albemarle's land
at an average of $13.82 per acre.[24] Comparing tax assessments across
states is hardly definitive, but the 1850 federal census – presumably a
more consistent and reliable measure of land values – showed an even
larger differential. The value of the average improved (i.e., cultivated)
acre in Cumberland was $46.54; the value of the average improved
acre in Albemarle was only $24.41.[25] The difference in land values
reflects how farm families of Cumberland, attempting to satisfy the
demands of Philadelphia and Baltimore, squeezed every dollar of
productive capacity out of their small farms. Statistics regarding farm
implements bolster that impression. In 1850, Cumberland residents
owned $1.61 of "farm implements and machinery" per improved acre,
three times greater than the comparable figure for Albemarle county.[26]

The high land values in Cumberland, ironically, deterred the development of a vigorous agricultural reform movement. Cumberland's
agricultural regime was precisely the model that Albemarle's agricultural reformers enthusiastically promoted. When the editor of the
Southern Planter, for instance, wrote that "A farm that is neatly kept,
with the dwelling house and ground about nicely ordered, gains a
reputation that will cause it to command a purchaser at a higher
price," he had in mind landscapes such as those of Cumberland
county.[27] To tout the merits of agricultural reform in Cumberland,
was, in essence, to preach to the converted. Unlike the farm press of
Albemarle, few speeches or editorials or pamphlets lectured Cumberland's farmers about the benefits of smaller farms, better implements,
and diversified agriculture. Cumberland residents practiced the tenets
of agricultural reform without having to be told how to do so.[28]

---

[24] Cumberland calculations based upon data in *Journal of the Senate*, Doc. No. 54 (Harrisburg, 1845), pp. 321–26. I used the column "Aggregate Amount" on p. 322.
Albemarle data based upon "Virginia Statistics," *Southern Planter* 17 (August 1857),
pp. 486–87. The *Southern Planter* article did not include the total number of acres,
which I took from the 1850 census.

[25] Calculated from *Seventh Census* (1850), pp. 194, 273.

[26] Calculated from *Ibid*.

[27] *Southern Planter* 2 (January 1842), p. 4.

[28] This is not to say that there was absolutely no agricultural reform in Cumberland. An
agricultural society was formed in the early nineteenth century, but I have not been
able to locate much documentation about its activities in either local archives or

Vigorous competition among towns, which had done so much to stimulate Albemarle's developmental corporations, was also less important in Cumberland. The most significant competition among Cumberland towns occurred in 1750 when Thomas Penn, son of William Penn and owner of three-quarters of the colony's proprietary rights, selected the county seat. Penn had no lack of choices. Edward Shippen offered Penn 300 acres if his namesake of Shippensburg was chosen, while Benjamin Chambers vigorously lobbied for his own town of Chambersburg. Penn decided upon Carlisle because of its excellent access to water and good land, while its eastern location promised to facilitate trade between the new county and Penn's own city of Philadelphia. Recurrent warfare after 1750, which made Carlisle an important staging ground for troops and supplies, enlarged the town's mercantile and administrative importance.[29] Once Carlisle became entrenched as Cumberland's administrative and mercantile center, no transportation project could afford to bypass its central location.

Turnpikes and Toll Bridges in Cumberland County

The important geographical and social differences between the two counties notwithstanding, residents in Albemarle and Cumberland shared the same desire to improve transportation. John Lefever's diary points to the importance of roads to even the most modest of Cumberland's farmers. Verbs such as "haul," "sled," "came," and "went" appear on every page. Most of this movement – selling crops, hauling wood, attending sales, marketing butter – had a commercial connotation, suggesting that the man on the go was, to a certain extent, a man on the make. The degree of the entrepreneurial zeal should not be exaggerated, for it often took place within the context of neighbors, friends, and relatives. These community attachments, however, rarely impinged on Lefever's commercial endeavors. Consider, for example, these entries recorded in October of 1825:

Came to market also to Newville with flaxseed & potatoes.
Made cider[.] [B]oiled applebutter[.] Came to Market[.]
Hauled cornfodder assisted by S. McKeehan[.]
Came to Market also to Newville[.]
Came to market. [W]rought on the roads this afternoon.[30]

northern agricultural periodicals. Indeed, a search of *Farmers' Cabinet* (published in Philadelphia) and the *American Farmer* (published in Baltimore) reveals no evidence of an active reform movement within Cumberland. Frederick Watts, a Carlisle lawyer whom we will meet in the next chapter, engaged in statewide agricultural reform, but most of his many accomplishments occurred after the Civil War.

[29] For an excellent analysis of the early development of Carlisle, see Ridner, "Handsomely Improved Place," (Ph. D. diss.), pp. 38–47, 77–154.

[30] "Lefever Diary," p. 17.

Perhaps no other entry conveys the importance of travel and movement more than the diary's first jarring lines: "On the 15th of November [1817] my mother died. I returned from Baltimore a few days
earlier. Had wet weather muddy Roads and my flour condemned."[31]

Lefever's diary suggests how important good roads were to Cumberland's farm economy. The county, despite its numerous attractions,
had only limited access to water transportation. The largest waterway
to cut through its interior was Conedoguinet Creek, which was too
winding and shallow for navigation. The Susquehanna formed the
county's eastern border, but political barriers blocked improvements
until the 1830s. Philadelphia interests, working through the Pennsylvania state legislature, hindered improvements on the Susquehanna
to deter Pennsylvanians from sending crops and goods south to Baltimore. Although Pennsylvania declared the Susquehanna a public
highway and allowed river improvements in 1803, Philadelphia interests blocked the construction of a canal until 1840. As historian James
Weston Livingood writes, the Susquehanna proved risky and dangerous in the meantime:

Arks and rafts could descend the shallow river only at time of high water,
which rarely occurred except in the spring. The consequence was that nearly
the whole trade in the valley descended at about the same time. The market,
which was at all times uncertain, became glutted ... Many [farmers] were
wrecked by the swift currents of the floods and were forced to abandon their
products ... Then too, perhaps there was no spring freshet sufficient for
descending navigation and the producer lost heavily since he had no other
means of reaching market with his products which deteriorated over the
summer months.[32]

Crossing the Susquehanna was undoubtedly easier than navigating
down it, but the river still presented a formidable barrier for overland
routes heading east toward Philadelphia. Building a bridge over the
wide river was a costly proposition that local governments could not
afford. Slow and undependable flatboat ferries provided the only
means of crossing the river. The 1807 travel diary of Fortescue Cuming, for example, tells of waiting most of a morning while the ferries
readied for a winter crossing.[33] Traveler Margaret Van Horn Dwight
recorded a similar experience in 1810, writing that she waited "some
time at the ferry house, [and then] cross'd the Susquehanna with
considerable difficulty. The river is a mile wide & so shallow that the

---

[31] "Lefever Diary," p. 1.
[32] Livingood, *Baltimore-Philadelphia Trade Rivalry*, p. 38.
[33] Cuming, "Sketches of a Tour," p. 42.

boat would scrape across the large stones so as almost to prevent it from proceeding."[34] The ferry crossings must have been even more inconvenient for teamsters laden with large loads of wheat and hay bound for Philadelphia.

Without effective water transportation, Cumberland farmers and merchants attempted to improve the county's roads. The detailed research of Judith Ridner demonstrates how residents creatively used the county government to build roads and bridges that enabled the county's inhabitants to travel "'to meeting[,] to Market[,] and to Mill.'"[35] Although these local road-building efforts solidified connections within the county – especially between area farmers and Carlisle merchants – they did little to improve links to Baltimore and Philadelphia. Localities such as Cumberland built and maintained public roads with a labor tax that forced residents to work on the roads. This system proved disastrous for long-distance routes. Coordination among numerous localities was often difficult to achieve, harvest schedules, not road damage, frequently determined when repairs were undertaken, and supervisors in charge of roads usually had little engineering experience. The haphazard nature of the system prompted historian Joseph Durrenberger to declare that "the labor and money devoted to highways were largely thrown away."[36]

Turnpike corporations, which improved roads for the right to collect tolls, overcame the worst problems of public roads. Instead of depending upon the uncertain and uncoordinated action among townships and counties, a single entity managed an entire route. Moreover, the collection of tolls meant that the company, at least in theory, could afford to grade the road, hire skilled engineers, and pay for repairs as needed.[37] The great success of a few early turnpikes, especially the famed Lancaster Pike, set off a boom throughout Pennsylvania and the rest of the Northeast. By 1821, the Pennsylvania state legislature had chartered 146 turnpikes (about half of which were actually built), resulting in 1,800 miles of improved roads.[38]

Cumberland residents participated in the boom in the 1810s when the legislature chartered two turnpikes that ran through their county. The Harrisburg, Carlisle, and Chambersburg Turnpike, 43 miles in length and capitalized at $150,000, ran along the entire length of the Cumberland Valley. It connected Cumberland's major

[34] Dwight, "Traveller," p. 115.
[35] Ridner, "Handsomely Improved Place," (Ph. D. diss.), p. 268.
[36] Durrenberger, *Turnpikes*, p. 29.
[37] The organizational advantages of turnpikes are discussed in Klein and Majewski, "Economy, Community, and Law," pp. 479–81.
[38] Plummer, "The Road Policy of Pennsylvania," (Ph.D. diss.), p. 53.

towns with Harrisburg, where travelers could then either risk the per-
ilous trip down the Susquehanna, or take a series of improved roads to
Lancaster and then Philadelphia. The Harrisburg, Carlisle, and
Chambersburg Company belonged to a network of toll roads known
as the Pittsburgh Pike, which provided a continuous improved road
between Philadelphia and Pittsburgh. Carlisle and other Cumberland
towns became convenient stops on Pennsylvania's most important
east–west route. The Harrisburg Bridge, a toll bridge over the Susquehanna, strengthened the turnpike network between Cumberland and
Philadelphia; no longer would travelers have to wait for a slow ferry to
cross the river.

   The Hanover and Carlisle Turnpike, which ran in an approximate
north–south direction to improve connections between Cumberland
and Baltimore, provided an alternative to the east–west route. Baltimore merchants had long cultivated commercial ties with Cumberland's residents. Account books and mercantile correspondence, in
fact, suggest that Baltimore may well have had the upper hand in
securing most of Cumberland's trade. Not only did Baltimore benefit
from navigation along the Susquehanna – even a shallow and treacherous river was better than no river at all – but the overland route to the
Maryland city was thirty miles shorter than the Carlisle-to-Philadelphia
trip. Travelers going to Baltimore, however, had to endure the steep
grades of the formidable South Mountain.[39]

   Their different routes notwithstanding, both turnpikes rivaled the
financial ineptitude of Albemarle's developmental corporations.
Higher than expected construction costs, coupled with travelers who
cleverly took shunpike trails around tollgates, prevented the two companies from paying a single dividend. The struggles of the Harrisburg,
Carlisle, and Chambersburg Turnpike to complete its road left the
company with a debt of $55,000.[40] To save the company from bank-
ruptcy, the state legislature mandated that the company allocate any
excess revenues to its creditors. The company's stock, of course, plummeted in value. When Thomas P. Barley put his $300 worth of shares
up for auction, they fetched a grand total of $1.26.[41] The Hanover and
Carlisle Turnpike did little better. According to an 1824 petition, "the
affairs of the company are embarrassed. It is involved in debt. No
resources are within the control of the managers to meet these embar-
rassments, and to keep the road in repair, other than what may arise

---

[39] Carlisle is about 110 miles from Philadelphia as the crow flies, with the actual route
   through Lancaster slightly longer. The distance from Carlisle to Baltimore via
   Hanover is around 80 miles.
[40] 31 *House Journal* (1820–1821), pp. 142–44.
[41] Bailey's plight is recorded in the Ledgers of the Harrisburg, Carlisle, and Chambersburg Turnpike, MG-2, PSA.

from the rates of toll."[42] In 1843, shares in the road, originally worth $100, sold for $4.90.[43]

The Harrisburg Bridge did much better, paying dividends averaging nearly 5 percent per year between 1812 and 1845. The bridge undoubtedly benefited from the dramatic growth of Harrisburg, which became Pennsylvania's state capital the same year the company was organized.[44] The bridge also benefited from the absence of shunpikes – not even the craftiest traveler could avoid the gates of a toll bridge. Still, the company had to work long and hard to sell its stock, suggesting that the poor performance of the turnpikes had soured profit-minded investors on all transportation corporations. In 1845, Joseph Wallace, the company's secretary, recalled that "there were not a few [people] who considered the project and its advocates nearly allied with insanity." According to Wallace, a number of stockholders "felt confident that their money might as well have been cast into the sea, for all the good that would ever come of it."[45]

Investors hoped that their money, even if cast into the sea for the short run, would eventually result in higher land values, increased local commerce, and greater ability to market crops. Gazetteer Thomas F. Gordon aptly summarized the relationship between indirect benefits and investment in developmental corporations: "None [of the turnpikes] have yielded profitable returns to the stockholders, but everyone feels that he has been repaid for his expenditures in the improved value of lands, and the economy of business."[46] Some years later a farmer's advice book argued that transportation corporations were usually poor investments, but still recommended that farmers vigorously support them. "To a community, good roads, good bridges, and railroads or canals, are the same as good fences and fertile fields are to a single farm."[47]

If indirect benefits primarily motivated Cumberland's investors, we

[42] "Memorial of the Subscribers, Stockholders, of the Hanover and Carlisle Turnpike Road," October 6, 1824, John Bear Papers, microfilm, PSA. The turnpike had contracted its large debts as it struggled to finish the road over a series of steep hills. In 1819, a committee of the turnpike's officers warned that "any further attempts to progress with the Road on the crippled means of the company would be utterly unavailing; and in fact unjust to the creditors of the Institution." The report advocated that stockholders subscribe to an additional $12,000 to finish the project. It is unknown how the drive for additional subscription fared. Untitled Report of the Hanover and Carlisle Turnpike Company, April 2, 1819, John Bear Papers, microfilm, PSA.

[43] Hartz, *Economic Policy*, p. 323.

[44] The legislation making Harrisburg the capital was passed in 1810, so that the organizers and investors in the bridge company knew that the importance and prestige of Harrisburg was rising. See Higginbotham, *The Keystone in the Democratic Arch*, p. 334.

[45] Quoted in Rupp, *History and Topography*, p. 271.

[46] Gordon, *A Gazetteer*, p. 35.

[47] Blake, *The Farmer's Every-Day Book*, pp. 95–96.

would expect the organizers to employ armtwisting, to exploit kinship ties, and to appeal to the public spirit of the local citizenry. Unfortunately, there is no smoking gun that confirms the motivations of Cumberland's investors as John Hartwell Cocke's voluminous correspondence did for Albemarle stockholders. Of the meager evidence outlining investor motivation, the most direct comes from a legislature report. Hoping to convince the state to assume the debts of the Harrisburg, Carlisle, and Chambersburg Turnpike, the 1837 report emphasized the importance of public spirit. After noting that the turnpike had "conferred upon the State eminent advantages," the committee reported that stockholders received nothing for their investment except the pride of public service:

It is observed that stockholders who advanced their money to aid in the construction of this work, and who have never received one dollar in return, do not complain; they have the magnanimity to suffer in silence, conscious no doubt, that they have largely contributed to promote the public good, and deriving from that source, the high satisfaction which generous and patriotic conduct always confer.[48]

Political and economic self-interest tainted the committee's report, but other evidence suggests that direct profits motivated few investors. As was the case with Albemarle's developmental corporations, most investors lived or owned property close to the improvement in which they owned shares. The Cumberland tax lists, alas, do not allow us to locate investors with the same degree of precision as the Albemarle records, but one can still link Cumberland stockholders to indexes of the 1810 and 1820 federal census. For those investors that could be linked with a fair degree of certainty, 65 to 90 percent lived in one of the counties through which an improvement passed.[49] As for the outside investors, they usually lived in neighboring counties, and might well have owned land or a mill near the turnpikes or bridge. Conspicuously lacking was any significant investment from residents of Philadelphia, arguably the financial capital of the nation.

We also get a sense of investor motivation by comparing the distribution of shares in the Cumberland transportation corporations with two local banks chartered at the same time (Table 2.2). Because the Pennsylvania state government carefully regulated the number of

[48] "Mr. Fullerton's Report" (Legislative Committee Report), *Carlisle Republican*, 16 March 1837, p. 3.
[49] To avoid the problem of repeating names – there were scores of Henry Millers, John Smiths, and George Whites scattered throughout Pennsylvania – I linked only those investors whose names appeared once or twice in the index. Please see appendix on sources for full details.

Table 2.2. *The Widespread Distribution of Shares in Cumberland's Developmental Corporations*

Enterprise (capital stock held by private investors)	Number of Investors	Average Investment	Median Investment
Cumberland's Developmental Corporations (Wide Distribution of Shares)			
Harrisburg, Carlisle, and Chambersburg Turnpike ($86,500)	580	$149	$100
Hanover and Carlisle Turnpike ($51,500)	368	$139	$100
Harrisburg Toll Bridge ($40,600)	397	$102	$100
Cumberland's Banks (Nondevelopmental Motives for Investment)			
Carlisle Bank ($150,000)	321	$467	$275
Pennsylvania Agricultural & Manufacturing Bank ($152,825)	343	$445	$125
Albemarle's Developmental Corporations (Influence of Wealthy Planters)			
Staunton & James River Turnpike ($30,000)	107	$280	$200
Rivanna Navigation Company ($45,000)	148	$303	$250
James R. & Kanawha Company ($45,000)	104	$631	$500

Notes and Sources: "Stock Ledger of Harrisburg, Carlisle, and Chambersburg Turnpike," MG-2, PSA. Statistics for all other Cumberland corporations derived from stockholder lists found in Mackinney (ed.), *Pennsylvania Archives*, pp. 3144–54, 3211–21, 3543–54, 3878–88. Figures for Albemarle corporations compiled from stockholder lists in the papers of the ABPW. All figures are for private investment only. The James River and Kanawha Company statistics refer only to stock purchased by Albemarle's investors.

banks – thereby providing high profits for those financiers lucky enough to receive a state charter – investors thought of them as low-risk, high-return investments.[50] Not surprisingly, the transportation companies and the banks had strikingly different share distributions. The smaller holdings and the relatively even distribution of shares among stockholders suggest that investors in transportation projects

[50] Lamoreaux, *Insider Lending*, pp. 52–83.

spread the risk of their unprofitable ventures. In the Hanover and
Carlisle Turnpike, for example, the largest investors held only 5 shares
apiece; only 30 investors (8 percent of all stockholders) held more
than 3. Similarly, only 21 of almost 400 investors (5 percent) owned
more than $280 of stock of the Harrisburg Toll Bridge. The Harris-
burg, Carlisle, and Chambersburg Turnpike had a more unequal distribution of investment, but more than two-thirds of investors owned
only a share or two. Investors in banks, on the other hand, took a bigger plunge in the expectation of high dividends. The largest investors
therefore owned a substantially higher proportion of shares.

The distribution of investment in Cumberland's developmental
corporations also differed greatly from Albemarle's early transportation companies. Whereas the average shareholder in an Albemarle
enterprise owned $391 in stock, the typical Cumberland shareholder
purchased stock worth only $132. The Cumberland corporations
made up this difference through sheer numbers – 1,345 investors purchased shares in the county's 2 turnpikes and 1 toll bridge while only
359 investors owned shares in Albemarle's 3 developmental corporations. Perhaps the large number of small investors accounts for why
organizers of Cumberland corporations mobilized their efforts more
quickly than those in Albemarle. The average year of organization
(defined as the year in which the initial stockholders purchased their
shares) for the Cumberland companies was 1813; the average year of
organization for Albemarle corporations was 1828.[51]

Cumberland's significant head start shows the advantages of its
larger population. With a bigger pool of investors to draw upon, individual stockholders needed only to take a share or two to provide
companies with needed capital. The broad distribution of shares, in
turn, allowed less wealthy residents to participate in the projects. The
companies themselves made purchasing stock as easy as possible – a
small payment of $5 or $10 was required up front. Stockholders grad-
ually paid the rest of the purchase price of the share as the company
needed new funds.[52] The county's farm families – not wealthy merchants or professionals – owned most of the shares in developmental
corporations (Table 2.3). Although much better off than the average

---

[51] For the Cumberland corporations, I used the year when the governor approved the
initial list of subscribers as provided in the *Pennsylvania Archives* series. For the Albemarle corporations, no such systematic source exists. For the James River and
Kanawha Company, most shares were sold in 1835 and 1836; for the Staunton and
James River Turnpike and the Rivanna Navigation Company, the initial lists of shareholders do not exist. Instead, I used the date of incorporation (1824 for the turnpike
and 1827 for the river company).

[52] According to reports that companies submitted to the governor's office, stockholders only had to put $10 down for each share they purchased. Mackinney (ed.), *Penn-
sylvania Archives*, 9th Series, pp. 3144, 3211, 3543, 3878.

Table 2.3. *Occupations and Taxable Wealth of*
Cumberland Investors in Developmental Corporations

Occupation	Number of Investors in Sample	Total Capital Invested (percent of total)		Average Investment	Average Assessed Wealth
Farmers	74	$11,760	(42)	$159	$7,052
Artisans	20	$7,400	(26)	$370	$3,480
Merchants	23	$3,950	(14)	$172	$6,416
Professionals	10	$1,550	(5)	$155	$4,502
Unknown	29	$3,660	(13)	$126	$465

Notes and Sources: Investors with names appearing once or twice in census indices were linked to Cumberland County Tax Lists for 1810, 1817, and 1820. Please see the appendix for precise methods of calculation. Assessed wealth included real estate, horses, cattle, mills, stills, and shops.

Cumberland resident, investors possessed neither the wealth nor social standing of Albemarle's planter families. The relatively low average property holdings of the Cumberland shareholders, in fact, indicate that most capital came from the "middling sort" rather than the rich and the powerful.

Did Cumberland's residents benefit from the turnpikes and toll bridges that many had helped finance? The evidence is inconclusive because the Pennsylvania tax records do not allow us to pinpoint land values. Instead, we have to rely on estimates of traffic flows. The logic here is that if traffic utilized the new improvements, then farmers, merchants, and other travelers must have considered them superior to the public roads and ferries. A good case can be made for the Harrisburg Bridge on these grounds – its unexpected financial success suggests that it made travel easier for the thousands of travelers who crossed the bridge every year. As for the turnpikes, the best available data is for the Harrisburg, Carlisle, and Chambersburg Turnpike. Gross revenue for the turnpike often exceeded $9,000 before falling in 1837, when the Cumberland Valley Railroad was built. Translated into actual usage, the toll revenues implied that 18,000 wagons traveled the turnpike's 40-mile length every year.[53] Although many of these wagons constituted through traffic between Philadelphia and Pittsburgh – providing their own brand of indirect benefits to Cumberland's inns and stables – they nevertheless indicated that travelers found the turnpike significantly better than public roads.

[53] Calculated with the prevailing rate of 12.5 cents per 10 miles per wagon.

Predictions of Profitability and Government Investment

One puzzling problem regarding developmental corporations remains unanswered. The location of stockholders and the distribution of shares indicates that indirect benefits motivated investors, but the corporations themselves promised generous direct dividends. Moreover, the companies promised great profits when even the most gullible investor knew that the company was in deep trouble. An 1819 report of the Hanover and Carlisle Turnpike predicted that "the stock will yield a handsome Interest to the subscribers," though the same report dourly noted that the road was unfinished and heavily indebted.[54] Similarly, a report of the Harrisburg, Carlisle, and Chambersburg Turnpike admitted that "the company are [sic] doubtful of their capacity to finish the road and pay the contracts" and that "the company have [sic] labored under immense difficulties." A few paragraphs later the report confidently predicted that "there can be no doubt that the tolls of this road will, when finished, yield a dividend of more than six per cent on the capital expended."[55]

Predictions of profitability also appeared in the reports and promotional literature related to Albemarle's developmental corporations. The Rivanna Navigation Company provides an excellent example. In March of 1828, when the Rivanna Navigation Company was trying to raise funds, the *Virginia Advocate* published a long letter by state engineer Claudius Crozet. Crozet compared rival plans, one to make the river depth 3 feet, which would have cost $132,500, and the other raising it to a more modest depth of 1.5 feet, which he estimated would cost $68,500. Using remarkably precise estimates of construction costs and river traffic, Crozet concluded that *either* plan would pay annual dividends of 9 to 10 percent.[56] Experience proved him dead wrong – dividends averaged a little over 1 percent from 1830 to 1850 – but the company never tired of forecasting large profits just around the corner. In 1833, the company's board hoped "that when the improvement is completed, that stock will yield a profit of six percent"; in 1834, the board was still "sanguine in the belief, that when the improvement is completed, the investment will yield a good per cent to the stockholders"; in 1837, the board promised "to manage the concerns of the company as to make to the stockholders some substantial return of their outlay, in the form of dividends."[57]

---

54 Untitled Report of the Hanover and Carlisle Turnpike Company, April 2, 1819, John Bear Papers, microfilm, PSA.
55 29 *House Journal* (1818–1819), p. 337.
56 *Virginia Advocate*, 22 March 1828, p. 2.
57 18 *ARBPW* (Richmond, 1835), p. 189; 19 *ARBPW* (Richmond, 1835), p. 479; and 21 *ARBPW* (Richmond, 1838), p. 267.

Did stockholders really believe these predictions? Overwhelming evidence suggests that they did not. If investors really expected large dividends, why did merchants and financiers from Richmond (in the case of Albemarle) or Philadelphia (in the case of Cumberland) invest so little in the enterprises? The expectation of large dividends should have brought investors from all over the county or region without regard to proximity to the improvement. Moreover, many of the local investors achieved considerable success as planters, farmers, and merchants. How could promotional literature fool these shrewd businessmen time after time? The correspondence of the investors themselves is remarkably silent about the prospect of large direct returns. The voluminous correspondence of John Cocke about the James River and Kanawha Company, analyzed in the last chapter, never once mentioned the expectation of large dividends. Cocke's letters represented a curious situation, at least to modern sensibilities: In *public* discourse, promoters predicted large dividends; in *private* correspondence, they claimed public benefits, patriotism, and friendship as their motives.

If stockholders probably discounted the exaggerated estimates of the corporations, they might well have understood predictions of large dividends as code that communicated the project's general viability. To openly admit that a corporation would pay zero dividends would hardly reassure investors, even those investing primarily to receive indirect benefits. Stockholders might have also expected that companies pay at least some dividends to offset their initial monetary losses – higher land values might have been their primary objective, but that did not rule out at least the possibility of direct profits. Investors had purchased a lottery ticket guaranteed to win a prize. If corporations somehow found a way to make the extravagant profits they promised, stockholders could count their blessings and good fortune; if the corporations never paid a dividend, appreciating land values more than covered their losses. Hence claims of profitability might have encouraged local investment, even if investors realized that the chances of direct profits were exceedingly low.

Claims of extravagant direct profits also played well in the political arena. Governments in both Pennsylvania and Virginia invested heavily in developmental corporations. The Old Dominion developed a systematic policy of "mixed enterprise" in which it provided 40 percent of the capital stock if other investors took the first 60 percent. The Rivanna Navigation Company, for example, received $30,000 of its $80,000 capitalization from the state government, while the Staunton and James River Turnpike received $20,000 of its $50,000 capitalization.[58]

---

[58] 19 *ARBPW* (Richmond, 1835), p. 479; 12 *ARBPW* (Richmond, 1828), p. 217. The James River and Kanawha Company, as befitting the central improvement of the

Pennsylvania invested more haphazardly in developmental corporations, but the state government was still a significant source of capital. The state invested $70,000 in the Harrisburg, Carlisle, and Chambersburg Turnpike (47 percent of its capitalization) and $10,000 in the Hanover and Carlisle Turnpike (14 percent of its capitalization).[59] The Pennsylvania legislature, one presumes, displayed much less generosity for an improvement that redirected trade away from Philadelphia toward arch rival Baltimore.

With the state government acting as an important investor, organizers had to convince legislators that a project merited the expenditure of scarce resources. Admitting that a company would pay nothing in the way of dividends hardly constituted a politically compelling argument. This was especially true in Virginia, where the intense boosterism among competing localities made securing state funds highly competitive. When one corporation declared it would pay exceptionally high dividends, it became incumbent for others to predict the same. Even projects funded through logrolling schemes – a common practice in both states – predicted high dividends to lend additional legitimacy to their enterprises. Deficit financing of state investment contributed to the escalating rhetoric. To avoid raising taxes, legislators in both states borrowed money to pay for their investment, hoping that the combination of higher dividends and higher land values would allow quick repayment of the loans. Developmental corporations paid precious few dividends into state treasuries, but they nevertheless had to play the game and exaggerate the potential profitability of their projects. Both private and public investors, therefore, had similar expectations of the stock in developmental corporations: They had unlikely dreams of direct dividends, but more certain prospects for large indirect benefits that would translate into higher tax revenues.

The large scale of government investment raises an important counterfactual question: What would have happened to these improvements without government support? The question is difficult to answer with any degree of precision, but it is safe to say that the Albemarle projects would have suffered more than their Cumberland counterparts. Cumberland residents might well have financed their improvements without state investment. Recall that that the Carlisle and Hanover Turnpike received only $10,000 in government support, yet the improvement was still built. Residents of New York and

state, had a more complicated relationship with the state government, but it received aid valued at $3 million in 1835. State policy toward the canal is discussed in more detail in Chapter 5.
[59] 31 *House Journal*, 1820–1821 (Harrisburg, 1822), pp. 442–43; Unpublished Report of the Hanover and Carlisle Turnpike Company, John Bear Papers, Microfilm, PSA.

New England, in fact, built entire systems of turnpikes and toll bridges without state assistance.[60] In thinly settled Albemarle, on the other hand, a small population meant a smaller pool of investors, thereby increasing the importance of state investment. Despite a long Jeffersonian heritage suspicious of government activism, residents of the Old Dominion found that a small population left them with few alternatives to state investment.

The Broader Context

The difference between Virginia and Pennsylvania shows the importance of local context to internal improvements, but do not forget the underlying dynamics of all developmental corporations: low direct profitability, vigorous local boosterism, and high indirect returns. Many early transportation corporations throughout Pennsylvania and Virginia displayed the same characteristics. In 1825, for example, the State of Pennsylvania held just over $1.8 million in turnpike investments and received a miserably low total of $540 in dividends. Investments in local canal and navigation companies, according to Louis Hartz, "appear to have been even less remunerative than those in turnpikes."[61] The direct profitability of most early Virginia companies was not much better. According one government report, most of the stock of Virginia's navigation and turnpike companies had "no public value," implying that stock values had dropped so precipitously that no buyers could be found.[62] Nor were Virginia and Pennsylvania unique. Despite poor direct returns, developmental corporations mobilized local capital in states ranging from New York to California.[63]

Developmental corporations were popular throughout America because they successfully mediated economic self-interest with community norms. They did not require an ethos of "possessive individualism" in which entrepreneurs and businessmen violated community standards to pursue economic gain.[64] Such behavior, in fact, was antithetical to developmental corporations, which required investors to suffer short-term losses to achieve long-run community gains. Developmental corporations, in essence, converted community ties, kinship networks, and political connections into what social scientist

---

[60] Taylor, *Transportation Revolution*, p. 25.
[61] Hartz, *Economic Policy*, p. 92.
[62] 31 *ARBPW* (Richmond, 1847), pp. xxxiii–iv.
[63] See, for example, Klein, "Voluntary Provision"; Klein and Yin, "Use, Esteem, and Profit"; and Goodrich, "Public Spirit."
[64] MacPherson defined a "possessive market society" as one in which markets "shape or permeate all social relations." *Political Theory of Possessive Individualism*, p. 48.

James Coleman has called "social capital" to help finance commercial infrastructure.[65]

For all of their popularity, developmental corporations had a number of important limitations. The most troubling problem was a dependence upon a fixed pool of capital and investors in a particular town or county. The low direct profits of developmental corporations, after all, ruled out any investment from large commercial centers. Entirely dependent upon local financing, developmental corporations were much less effective financing large-scale projects such as railroads, which often required far more capital than a single locality could provide. State and local governments, of course, could invest millions of dollars in developmental projects that private capital markets shunned. Yet as we shall see, Virginians in particular paid a high price for relying on a fragmented legislature wedded to local interests.

---

[65] Coleman, *Foundations of Social Theory*, pp. 300–21.

3

Railroads and Local Development

The Cumberland Valley Railroad immediately changed the commercial world of John Lefever. When the railroad was under construction
in 1836, the Cumberland farmer recorded more than a dozen times
that he "hewed," "drew," or "hauled" wood for the railroad, a task that
he would periodically perform for many years. More importantly, the
railroad made it more convenient and less expensive for Lefever to
market his crops – instead of long wagon journeys to Baltimore and
Philadelphia, Lefever now made short trips to the railroad depot. In
January of 1840, for example, Lefever reported that he "[c]ame to
Newville Depot. Sold my rye to Swoyer at 45 cts." Over the next few
weeks, he would continue hauling rye to Swoyer's mill until he had
sold more than 250 bushels.[1] It would be an exaggeration to say that
the railroad revolutionized Lefever's life – Cumberland's farmers had
been selling surpluses to Philadelphia markets for many decades – but
now the railroad had brought national and international markets to
the doorsteps of Cumberland's farmers.

Railroads had a similar impact on Albemarle residents such as T. L.
Jones. A moderately prosperous yeoman farmer, Jones steadfastly
recorded the details of farm life during the tumult of the Civil War.[2]
Even in the war-ravaged Virginia economy, frequent travel was an
essential part of Jones's routine. Within a single year, Jones took dozens
of trips to villages such as Warren and Scottsville, and traveled to
larger towns such as Charlottesville, Richmond, and Lynchburg about
once a month. On many of these latter trips, Jones often took advantage of a railroad. Entries such as "I went to Charlottesville carried

---

1 "John Lefever Diary", edited and transcribed by Robert J. Smith, CCHS, pp. 101–02.
   Hereafter cited as "Lefever Diary."
2 Jones owned a small farm and three slaves, a level of wealth that perhaps gave him
   more in common with Cumberland's family farmers than Albemarle's planter class.
   Jones owned 715 acres of land that was divided into three holdings: a mill worth
   $1,222, 524 acres of waste land valued $524, and 191 acres of farmland worth
   $1,241. His total holdings, including the mill, came to $2,987. In 1860, Jones owned
   three slaves as well as $300 worth of securities. 1850 Albemarle County Real Property
   Tax List, microfilm, VSLA; 1860 Albemarle County Personal Property Tax List,
   VSLA.

wool to Machine. I came up on railroad & home at night" appear frequently.[3] Virginia's severely damaged rail system often interfered with
Jones's plans, but wartime inconveniences did not deter him. By the
1860s, taking the train had become a hard habit to break.[4]

The experiences of Lefever and Jones typify the railroad's impact
on Albemarle and Cumberland. The Cumberland Valley Railroad
(CVRR) and the Virginia Central had much different sources of
finance, but they shared an obvious similarity all too easily overlooked:
Both railroads significantly improved links between their respective
counties and major marketing centers. Residents in both counties
responded quickly to the new opportunities: They specialized in the
most profitable crops, they slashed the output of home manufacturing and purchased more ready-made goods, and they strove to
increase the productivity of their farms through the greater use of
agricultural implements. The combination of improved transportation and higher crop prices created remarkable prosperity. Good
fortune did not visit every household, but many small farmers and
artisans did quite well in these increasingly commercial societies.

On a broader level, however, the Virginia Central and the CVRR
foreshadowed a crucial regional divergence. The financial contours
of the Virginia Central closely resembled the county's other transportation corporations. Merchants, retailers, professionals, and planters
in the Charlottesville area provided almost all of the railroad's private
capital, while the state government purchased the remaining shares.
The CVRR represented a sharp break from this developmental model.
Most of the CVRR's capital came from Philadelphia financiers, not
local investors. The influence of the Philadelphia investors grew as the
corporation matured. In 1858, the company moved its headquarters
to Philadelphia, symbolizing the completed transition from developmental corporation to urban enterprise.[5] As later chapters will argue,
the urban investors that dominated the CVRR and the rest of Pennsylvania's railroads would build trunk lines and integrated systems well
beyond the ability of Virginia's developmental corporations.

"Great Spirit, Zeal, And Activity":
The Virginia Central Comes to Albemarle

First known as the Louisa Railroad, the Virginia Central began its corporate life as a spur of the Richmond, Fredericksburg, and Potomac

[3] Journal of T. L. Jones in Kenneth Stampp, ed., *Records of Ante-bellum Plantations from
the Revolution Through the Civil War*, Series J, Part 9, microfilm (Bethesda, MD), p. 37.
Hereafter cited as "Jones Journal."
[4] On July 27, 1863, for example, he recorded that "I went to R. Road to go to Charlottesville but no train[.] I went to Bro. Bates and staid all night." "Jones Journal," p. 41.
[5] "Minute Book of the Board of Managers of the CVRR," Vol. II, MG-286, Box 70, PSA,
p. 350. Hereafter cited as "Minute Book."

Railroad (RF & P).[6] Built in 1836, the RF& P linked Richmond and Washington. The Louisa was built from Hanover Junction (25 miles north of Richmond) to Gordonsville, located in the Piedmont county of Louisa. The RF& P provided the Louisa with rolling stock and carried freight over its own tracks from Junction to Richmond. In all other respects, however, the Louisa Railroad operated as an independent company that issued its own stock, elected its own board, and paid its own dividends. When the Louisa proposed building its own tracks to Richmond in 1849 – and hence became a potential competitor of its parent company – the RF& P initiated a lengthy lawsuit that eventually failed. In 1850, the Louisa's directors renamed their railroad the Virginia Central to reflect its ambitious drive to become the state's primary transportation improvement. The legal battle, however, indicated the haphazard nature of the state's rail network. That the Virginia Central, the self-proclaimed grand trunk line of the Old Dominion, began its corporate life as a small spur line hardly boded well for the state's efforts to reach western markets.[7]

The Virginia Central's extension into Albemarle reflected the vigorous competition among the county's towns. Railroad schemes in Albemarle sprouted like mushrooms. Scottsville worked especially hard to win a railroad from the James River to Staunton (following the route of the turnpike), thereby securing the lucrative Shenandoah Valley trade once and for all. The town's boosters eventually prodded the state legislature into sponsoring a survey that strongly supported a Scottsville to Staunton railroad.[8] The surveyors noted that such a railroad would increase the business of the James River and Kanawha Canal, an important consideration because of the state's large commitment to that project. Scottsville interests, however, could not fund the road. The notoriously optimistic state engineers estimated that the road, forced to cross the rugged Blue Ridge, would cost nearly $825,000. Even if the state financed 60 percent of the project and residents from Staunton contributed another 20 percent, Scottsville residents would still have to provide $165,000, a very large sum for a small town that had difficulty raising $30,000 for the Staunton and James River Turnpike.

Charlottesville entertained its own share of fanciful railroad schemes, including a visionary enterprise that would have connected the town with New Orleans.[9] Its residents knew, however, that luring the Virginia Central westward was its best chance to get a railroad

---

[6] The company carried the name Louisa Railroad until 1850. I use the name appropriate for the year in question.
[7] Coleman, "Edmund Fountaine," p. 243.
[8] 20 *ARBPW* (Richmond, 1837), pp. 24–33.
[9] ACLP, 13 January 1836.

connection. In the late 1830s, the Louisa extended its line to Gordonsville, a stone's throw away from the northeastern corner of Albemarle and only 21 miles from Charlottesville. Once in Charlottesville, the road could then cross the Blue Ridge to Staunton. Claudius Crozet, the state engineer, declared in 1840 that "of the propriety of extending the Louisa road (The Virginia Central) to Charlottesville, there cannot be the least doubt."[10] Eager businessmen and planters in Charlottesville and Staunton agreed. An 1839 legislative petition mentioned that the Virginia Central was "preparing for commencement" toward Charlottesville and that the railroad had "a subscription that insures its completion."[11]

The bitter town rivalries of central Virginia, however, undermined these confident predictions. Instead of reaching the Valley via Charlottesville and Staunton, the Louisa proposed heading toward Harrisonburg, located in Rockingham county 50 miles northwest of Gordonsville. For almost a decade a furious debate raged between proponents of the "northern route" (Harrisonburg) and supporters of the "southern route" (Charlottesville and Staunton). The northern route clearly had the upper hand. The initial 1836 charter of the Virginia Central that authorized the company to cross the Blue Ridge "near the town of Harrisonburg," made no mention of either Staunton or Charlottesville.[12] As late as 1845 the Louisa's directors enthusiastically endorsed a resolution entitled "the extension of said road from Gordonsville to Harrisonburg, with a view to its ultimate extension to the Ohio River." The directors noted with great excitement the increased revenue resulting from the "vast and fertile valley in the neighborhood [of Harrisonburg], and the country for one hundred miles beyond, abounding in agricultural and mineral productions."[13]

Almost miraculously, Charlottesville prevailed. How the company decided upon Charlottesville became a subject of great public debate. The Board of Public Works, the state agency that oversaw the state government's railroad investments, was so shocked at the company's decision, it refused to allocate any funds until further investigation. In the lengthy newspaper debates that followed, Edmund Fountaine, the railroad's president, argued that surveyors considered the routes more or less equal. The enthusiastic residents of Charlottesville and Staunton, who eagerly purchased shares of the proposed railroad, pushed the scales in favor of the southern route. Indeed, Fountaine had warned Harrisonburg supporters that "the probable facility of

[10] 24 *ARBPW* (Richmond, 1841), p. 202.
[11] ACLP, 2 February 1839.
[12] As quoted in the 32 *ARBPW* (Richmond, 1847), p. 8.
[13] 30 *ARBPW* (Richmond, 1845), p. 67–69, quote on p 68.

getting the necessary stock must exert its due weight. I learn that there is great spirit, zeal and activity in Albemarle."[14] It seems that the crafty Fountaine had cleverly pitted one route against another to secure as much capital as possible. Shady dealings took place, especially in the eyes of outraged Harrisonburg residents, but nothing illegal. The courts eventually ruled in the company's favor, forcing the reluctant Board of Public Works to release the authorized state investment. Charlottesville, thanks to its "great spirit, zeal, and activity," would have its railroad.

The Virginia Central needed the enthusiasm of Albemarle residents, for almost all of its private capital would come from local investors. Of the 215 names linked from the 1847 list of stockholders to the 1850 census, 84 percent lived in either Albemarle or Augusta county.[15] (Since the Virginia Central quickly extended the railroad to Augusta once it finished the Albemarle section, Augusta residents could expect significant indirect benefits.) Even within Albemarle, investment was extremely localized. Almost 90 percent of the Albemarle investors linked to the county's property tax records owned property within 5 miles of the road, with half of them living in or near Charlottesville. The merchants and planters living in the rich plantation district near Scottsville hardly put a dollar in the Virginia Central. Their lack of investment made sense. Why help finance a railroad that would divert trade away from their town?

The local residents who invested in the Virginia Central represented the growing diversity of the Albemarle economy. The influence of Albemarle's wealthiest planters had hardly disappeared. Men such as Thomas Jefferson Randolph, Alexander Rives, and William C. Rives were among the county's largest slaveholders and the company's largest shareholders. The large number of merchants, professionals, and artisans who invested in the enterprise, however, distinguished the railroad from the county's earlier developmental corporations (Table 3.1). Whereas wealthy slaveholders had contributed 50 or even 80 percent of the capital for Albemarle's early corporations, they provided only 24 percent of the railroad's capital. The greater diversity of investors demonstrated that "nothing succeeds like success" when it came to economic development. The earlier improvement of the Rivanna and James Rivers led Charlottesville to grow more populous and more wealthy, thereby creating a new set of potential investors to help fund more ambitious projects. The same interactive dynamic, as will be demonstrated in later chapters, worked on a far larger scale in Pennsylvania.

[14] *The Richmond Enquirer*, 5 November 1847, p. 2.
[15] Please see the appendix for an overview of precise methods used to link stockholders to census records.

Table 3.1. *The Diversity of Albermarle Investors in the Virginia Central*

Occupation	Number of Investors in Sample	Shares of Stock Owned (percent of sample)	Average Real Estate Holdings	Average Slave Holdings
Large Planters	23	70 (24)	$24,874	26
Middling Planters	43	79 (27)	$7,125	9
Small Planters	17	29 (10)	$4,553	3
Professionals	18	54 (18)	$3,459	5
Merchants & Retailers	17	49 (16)	$4,533	3
Artisans	7	16 (5)	$3,000	4
Total	125	297	$9,316	10

Notes and Sources: Sample consists of 1847 stockholders whose names appear once or twice in 1850 Census index. The table includes only residents of Albemarle County; please see appendix for more precise methods of calculation. Large planters are defined as farmers owning more than 15 slaves; middling planters are defined as owning 6 to 15 slaves; and small planters owned 5 or less. Occupations and real estate holdings calculated from manuscript returns of 1850 census; number of slaves came from 1850 Albemarle Personal Property Tax List, microfilm, VSLA.

The diversity of investors reflected the Virginia Central's developmental roots. Although the aggregate amount of local investment was much larger than previous developmental corporations, most individual stockholders purchased only a share or two. The median investor, in fact, held only $100 worth of stock, a figure lower than most of the earlier corporations.[16] Perhaps investors feared poor direct returns, and therefore sought to spread the risk over a large number of shareholders. That way the railroad would get built – providing great benefits for the community – but no single individual would be saddled with a large block of unprofitable stock. The instincts behind the diversification of risk proved sound. From 1837 to 1859, the company's annual dividends averaged 2.6 percent. If one excludes the bonds that the company sometimes paid in lieu of cash, the average annual dividend was less than 2 percent per year.[17] No wonder the vast majority of investors lived near the line; they could best benefit from the road's favorable impact on local development.

What accounted for the Virginia Central's poor direct returns? This complex issue is best tackled in Chapter 5, when the railroad's lack of dividends can be put into the context of the poor financial

---

[16] Calculated from list of investors in the Albemarle extension of the Virginia Central, dated November 22, 1850 in the ABPW, Box 224, VSLA.
[17] Calculated from various annual reports filed in the *ARBPW*.

performance of Virginia's railroad network. For now, however, note that Albemarle's relatively low population density – 33 persons per square mile in 1840, versus 56 for Cumberland – meant fewer passengers and less traffic per mile of track.[18] The population density figures may well underestimate the Virginia Central's relative disadvantage in attracting passengers and traffic. Many travelers in southern Albemarle, for example, continued to use the James River and Kanawha Canal rather than make the long wagon journey to Charlottesville. The local nature of Albemarle's transportation network, in other words, carved up a small market into even smaller slices, further reducing profitability for each individual company.

The poor direct profitability of the Virginia Central led the company to depend on government support. Its far larger capital requirements, in fact, magnified the importance of state investment. Responding to the pressure for more state investment, the Virginia legislature voted to purchase 60 percent of the Virginia Central's capital stock. The state investment was conditional; only after the Virginia Central's directors had secured $100,000 in private investment for the Albemarle extension did the state government invest $150,000 in the railroad. The conditional nature of state investment undoubtedly eased the burden of raising local capital but it also had a pronounced drawback. Every time the company wanted to extend its line westward, it had to lobby the state legislature for new funds. As we shall see, rival improvements would make securing state funds difficult and uncertain.

The Virginia Central and Prosperity in the Piedmont

Reliance on state funds notwithstanding, the Virginia Central helped create a mini-boom when it reached Charlottesville in 1850. According to Richard Edwards, editor of *The Statistical Gazetteer of Virginia*, the population of the "flourishing town" had risen to 2,600 in 1853, an increase of 38 percent since 1849.[19] The town's growing population led to higher property values. In 1840, Charlottesville was divided into 81 lots valued an average of $1,480 apiece. By 1850, when the railroad had reached the town, the average value of these 81 lots had risen to $1,982.[20] Between 1840 and 1850 the town had also annexed an additional 50 lots, suggesting a brisk demand for Charlottesville real estate.

---

[18] Please see Table 2.1 for the complete breakdown from 1830–1860.
[19] Edwards, ed., *Statistical Gazetteer*, p. 205.
[20] Calculated from 1840 and 1850 Albemarle County Property Tax Lists, microfilm, VSLA.

A perusal of the Charlottesville newspapers shows how merchants and retailers put the new lots to use. Newspapers in the 1830s and 1840s contained advertisements for a small number of stores carrying a variety of goods. By 1860, the same newspapers advertised a broad range of specialty shops that included two dentist offices, several "Barbers and Hair-Dressers," two gun stores, a jewelry store, a marble workshop, a confectionery store, a gallery offering both paintings and photographs, and the Albemarle Insurance Company.[21] Charlottesville storekeeper Henry F. Dade hinted at the prosperity of Charlottesville's retailers when he wrote his father in 1856 that "We are very busy at this time assessing and marking new goods which are coming in very fast. We have not much time for marking in the day but have to do most of it at knight [sic]. I marked last knight to twelve a clock and I feel very, very sleepy and dull from the effects of it today."[22]

Prosperous Charlottesville presented a striking contrast to struggling Scottsville. When Charlottesville secured the Virginia Central, Scottsville attempted to enhance its connection with Augusta County with a plank road. By covering the Staunton and James River Turnpike with a wooden surfacing, Scottsville interests hoped for a smoother and more dependable road that would funnel more commerce into their town. Predictably, the wooden surface quickly decayed, and when the Virginia Central neared Staunton in 1854, traffic abandoned the toll road altogether.[23] Feisty Scottsville residents did not give up; they saw their salvation in the Orange and Alexandria railroad. Chartered in 1849, the Orange and Alexandria cut across the state in a southwestern diagonal, hoping to bring the trade of central and southern Virginia northward to Alexandria. Scottsville residents vigorously lobbied to have the railroad connect with their town.[24] Once again Charlottesville outflanked its James River competitor: the Orange and Alexandria connected with the Virginia Central at Gordonsville and shared the VCRR's tracks to Charlottesville before heading south to Lynchburg.[25] Without railroad access, Scottsville declined precipitously,

[21] These advertisements were found in the *Charlottesville Advocate*, 16 March 1860, pp. 1–4.
[22] Henry F. Dade to "father," September 21, 1856, Dade Family Papers, UVA.
[23] Young, "Brief History," p. 11. Scottsville was not alone in looking for economic salvation from plank roads. See Majewski, Baer, and Klein, "Responding to Relative Decline."
[24] For an example of Scottsville's efforts, see "Extension of the Orange and Alexandria Railroad from Gordonsville via Scottsville and Lynchburg," [by "Albemarle"], *Richmond Enquirer*, 19 January 1853, p. 2.
[25] The Orange and Alexandria actually shared 21 miles of the Virginia Central line that ran from Gordonsville to Charlottesville. The Orange and Alexandria then had a separate division extending from Charlottesville to Lynchburg. Unfortunately, I have not been able to locate any stockholder lists of the railroad, and because the connection between Charlottesville and Lynchburg was completed in 1860, it is also difficult to judge its impact on the Albemarle economy.

its free population falling from 460 in 1850 to 246 in 1860.[26] Scottsville's fate served as a grim reminder that the stakes of local competition were high indeed.

Charlottesville residents were not the only winners. The railroad also brought significant advantages to central Albemarle's planters and farmers through improved access to Richmond's markets. The business correspondence of planters such as William T. Brown gives concrete examples of the railroad's greater speed and reliability. In September of 1849, just before the railroad reached Charlottesville, Brown's Richmond agent complained "we have found it impossible to ship your goods, as Water being so low, that Boats can neither come down or go up – the prospect at this time is gloomy for rain."[27] A few years later, the same agent casually remarked that he had sent a barrel of brown sugar and two sacks of salt that Brown could pick up the next day at the Charlottesville railroad depot.[28] The railroad eliminated worries of low water or other adverse weather conditions that might interfere with canal operation.

The railroad, working in concert with higher crop prices, undoubtedly contributed to rising land values in the 1850s. Tax assessments show that Albemarle land values increased 34 percent between 1850 and 1856.[29] The higher land values partly stemmed from the railroad's faster and more reliable transportation, but steeply rising prices for tobacco and grain also helped raise real estate values. Tobacco prices, which hovered around 4 cents per pound in the mid-40s, increased to 8 cents per pound in 1850 and zoomed to 12 in 1857. Although they fell somewhat after the Panic of 1857, tobacco prices nevertheless remained high for the rest of the decade.[30] Wheat followed the same pattern, if in less dramatic fashion.[31]

With high prices and improved transportation, Albemarle's farm economy flourished. Ominous assessments of the county's future, so prominent in Jefferson's day, gave way to a new wave of optimism. Frank Ruffin, an Albemarle resident and the editor of the *Southern Planter*, beamed with pride at Albemarle's improved plantations and farms. In reviewing the model plantation of William Garth, Ruffin exclaimed that "Clover is luxuriant, wheat not yet dropped its bloom and the young corn thrifty as can be desired. It is worth a ride of 20

[26] Figures taken from Hess, "Four Decades of Social Change" (Ph. D. diss.), p. 102.

[27] Deane and Brown to William T. Brown, September 17, 1849, Brown Family Papers, UVA.

[28] Deane & Brown to William T. Brown, January 9, 1852, Brown Family Papers, UVA.

[29] "Virginia Statistics," *Southern Planter* 27 (August 1857), pp. 486–87.

[30] Robert, *Tobacco Kingdom*, p. 134. Robert reports the weighted average price in Richmond for the year ending September 30.

[31] Rising from $1.28 per bushel in 1850 to $2.44 in 1855, wheat settled at $1.50 per bushel in 1860. *Historical Statistics*, p. 209.

miles to see Mr. Wm. Garth's wheat fields at Midway farm."[32] Now that planters such as Garth had easy access to Virginia's urban markets, Ruffin predicted, they would soon diversify into fruits and vegetables.[33]

Here Ruffin was wrong. Specialization, rather than diversification, became the dominant trend. Small farmers, defined as those owning less than 160 acres of land, tripled tobacco production while cutting their wheat output in half (Table 3.2). Albemarle's small farmers did not completely abandon corn and wheat, but their warm embrace of tobacco showed a keen awareness of new opportunities.[34] Medium-sized farmers applied the same strategy, growing 20 percent less wheat while expanding tobacco output 260 percent. The largest Albemarle plantations increased both tobacco and wheat production, but even they produced somewhat less corn and wool.[35] For all groups, the value of home manufacturing plummeted; farm families presumably took advantage of the consumer goods readily available in Charlottesville. Albemarle's farmers and planters, trying to find new methods to raise overall productivity, also invested more in agricultural implements. The tremendous surge in tobacco cultivation – a crop which needed little in the way of sophisticated tools – made the growth of implements all the more remarkable.

The success of individuals who resided in Albemarle during the 1850s readily demonstrates the county's widespread prosperity. Linking a sample from the 1850 census to the 1860 census, I recorded the names, ages, occupations, and property holdings of 144 individuals who remained in Albemarle over the decade. The results show that the vast majority of these long-term Albemarle residents did remarkably well (Table 3.3). Small property owners enjoyed a substantial 985 percent increase in the value of their property holdings. Medium and large property owners also did well, often seeing the value of their holdings double in value. These results should be taken with considerable caution. Much of the gains among the small property owners resulted from inheritance rather than economic mobility. A son of a wealthy planter, owning little in 1850, might appear in the 1860

---

[32] "Correspondence of the Planter," *Southern Planter* 10 (July 1850), p. 211.

[33] "Correspondence of the Planter," *Southern Planter* 10 (August 1850), p. 252.

[34] The growth of tobacco production among small farmers is similar to what Lacy K. Ford has found for cotton in the South Carolina backcountry. See Ford, *Origins of Southern Radicalism*, pp. 244–63.

[35] Noe, *Southwest Virginia's Railroad*, pp. 32–43, notes the same trends of rising wheat and tobacco output even in mountainous regions of southwest Virginia. Part of the reason that large planters could increase both wheat and tobacco output was that their labor regimes meshed well: Wheat required heavy labor precisely when tobacco did not, and vice versa. In terms of land, however, the crops were competitive: A planter could not grow grain and tobacco on the same acre in the same year. A large planter could therefore devote some land to tobacco and some land to wheat, thus maximizing his use of slave labor. See Irwin, "Exploring the Affinity," pp. 295–322.

Table 3.2. *The Impact of Rising Crop Prices and the Virginia Central Railroad on Albemarle Agriculture*

	Improved Acres	Cash Value of Farms	Implements (in dollars)	Bushels of Wheat	Bushels of Corn	Pounds of Tobacco	Pounds of Wool	Home Manufacturing (in dollars)
Small Farmers								
1850 Mean (N=80)	79.49	1,429.84	52.25	69.80	316.13	592.75	32.81	27.61
1860 Mean (N=91)	94.28	2,758.00	93.61	37.06	327.67	2,373.67	16.76	12.13
Percentage Change	*18.61*	*92.89*	*79.16*	*-46.91*	*3.65*	*300.45*	*-48.94*	*-56.06*
Medium Farmers								
1850 Mean (N=60)	254.67	4,170.00	111.08	227.80	798.50	1,581.67	46.78	52.13
1860 Mean (N=60)	252.82	8,809.27	187.83	182.05	680.98	5,737.67	35.85	29.15
Percentage Change	*-0.73*	*111.25*	*69.09*	*-20.08*	*-14.72*	*262.76*	*-23.37*	*-44.09*
Large Farmers								
1850 Mean (N=28)	613.57	16,130.71	315.29	794.32	2,147.32	4,650.00	117.14	72.04
1860 Mean (N=39)	683.46	23,755.74	411.54	955.33	1,782.95	15,746.15	97.92	59.00
Percentage Change	*11.39*	*47.27*	*30.53*	*20.27*	*-16.97*	*238.63*	*-16.41*	*-18.10*
All Farmers								
1850 Mean (N=168)	231.07	4858.61	117.10	246.98	793.60	1622.14	51.86	43.77
1860 Mean (N=190)	266.19	9011.90	189.13	272.57	740.13	6201.01	39.57	27.21
Percentage Change	*15.20*	*85.48*	*61.51*	*10.36*	*-6.74*	*282.27*	*-23.70*	*-37.85*
All Farmers (Per Acre)								
1850 Per Acre	21.03	0.51	1.07	3.44	7.02	0.22	0.19	
1860 Per Acre	33.88	0.71	1.02	2.78	23.31	0.15	0.10	
Percentage Change	*61.08*	*40.26*	*-4.16*	*-19.01*	*231.97*	*-33.74*	*-46.03*	

Notes and Sources: Compiled from a sample of surnames beginning with "B" and "W" taken from 1850 and 1860 agricultural censuses. Please see appendix for details of calculations. Small farmers are defined as owning less than 169 acres, medium farmers are defined as owning between 170 and 399 acres, and large farmers are defined as those owning 400 acres or more.

Table 3.3. *Prosperity in the Piedmont:*
Changes in the Value of Property Holdings, 1850–1860

	Small Property Owners in 1850	Medium Property Owners in 1850	Large Property Owners in 1850
Number in Group	79	39	26
Average Value of Property in 1850	$196	$2,950	$13,162
Average Value of Property in 1860	$2,126	$6,423	$22,693
Average Increase in the Value of Property, 1850–1860	$1,930 (985%)	$3,473 (118%)	$9,531 (72%)

Notes and Sources: "B" and "W" sample compiled from manuscripts of the 1850 and 1860 Albemarle censuses. Please see text and appendix for description of collection of data and calculations. "Small" property owners are defined as those holding $1,500 or less of real estate, "medium" owners as those holding more than $1,500 but less than $5,000, and "large" owners as those holding more than $5,000 of real estate.

census as the master of a large plantation. A selection bias exists as well. Successful farmers and planters had good reason to stay in Albemarle, and hence were more likely to be linked; those struggling to meet their expectations may have left the county.[36] These biases are important, but the results nevertheless help explain the widespread community support for the railroad. The boosters who had promoted local investment in anticipation of rising land values and increased trade could smugly smile as the county's land rapidly appreciated. The long-term residents who benefited from the railroad provided highly visible evidence that the enterprise had indeed improved the lot of most citizens.

The prosperity of Albemarle did not necessarily undermine community values often associated with southern localities. Kinship networks were a case in point. In 1850, 43 percent of sampled Albemarle households lived within 25 dwellings of another household with the

[36] Indeed, Albemarle's population rose only a fraction during the 1850s, suggesting that many sons and daughters of Albemarle's farm families continued to stream out of the county. An optimist might point out that out-migration probably would have been significantly higher without the substantial development of the 1850s. And even if the county as a whole did not gain much in population, those areas closest to the railroad did.

same surname. Such kinship grouping became slightly more pronounced in 1860, when 47 percent of Albemarle households lived within 25 census dwellings of another household with the same surname. Statistics, of course, do not necessarily speak to the qualitative aspects of kin networks.[37] Evidence from store ledgers and account books, for example, suggests a trend that many historians have found elsewhere: a shift from trade based on barter and long-term debt to one built upon cash transactions. Yet if trade in general had become more commercialized, there was still room for more personal trading networks. Even during an economic crisis such as the Civil War, scattered evidence suggests that such networks still survived. In 1863, T. L. Jones recorded that "I went to Warren. [P]aid Dr. T. D. Shelton in full for Ten years practice in my family $120."[38] While we do not know what prompted Jones to finally pay Dr. Shelton, the fact that the payment covered a decade of service suggests that neighbors could afford to allow debts to remain unpaid for many years. Reciprocal exchanges also continued. "R. M. Childress borrowed 1 Barrell [sic] of flour to be returned when I want it," recorded Jones in March of 1863.[39] Jones conducted many cash transactions as well, but the point remains that commercial transactions and local exchanges could co-exist within Albemarle.

The real losers of Albemarle's commercial expansion were the county's slaves. A detailed account of the transformation of Albemarle slavery would require a full-scale social history well beyond this book, but fragmentary evidence suggests that market development often led ambitious masters to squeeze out the last ounce of toil and labor of their slaves. In wheat production, for example, planters using the most rational management techniques drove their slaves in large gangs. One economic historian has noted that gang labor on wheat plantations was so "arduous, intense, and unpleasant" that no free laborers would undertake it, despite the higher productivity it entailed.[40] For improving planters looking to raise productivity and reduce costs, it was all too easy to upgrade farm operations while ignoring the welfare of their slaves. The example of Thomas Jefferson Randolph, one of Albemarle's most well-known agricultural reformers, suggests how little slaves could benefit from the success of their master. A committee reviewing Randolph's plantation congratulated him "for the great improvement he has wrought in his lands." Yet the reviewers could not help note the poor condition of the plantation's

---

[37] Calculated from a sample of "Bs" and "Ws" from the manuscript, returns of the 1850 census. Please see appendix regarding sampling procedures.
[38] "Jones Journal," p. 37.
[39] "Jones Journal," p. 32.
[40] Irwin, "Exploring the Affinity," pp. 301–2.

slave cabins. "They appeared to be small and rather rude in the style of construction, and withal rather detracting from the general air of neatness and good management which characterized the farm."[41]

For all of the exploitation that Albemarle's slaves endured, at least some had good reason to wish their masters continued economic success. Unsuccessful planters might move westward or sell their slaves to traders. Slaves heading west would most likely endure an even more brutal work regime separated from family and friends. One particularly disturbing case highlights the conundrum in which slaves might find themselves. John Buckingham wrote to a Scottsville slave trader, James Brady, that he desired to sell a house servant named Harriet. Buckingham's decision to sell Harriet was not an easy one. "To the Strong and constant appeals of my wife not to let Harriet go yet, I am obliged to yield," wrote Buckingham.[42] Financial distress, however, left Buckingham with no alternative – all his other slaves were in families that he refused to separate. Buckingham's letter suggests that Harriet had no immediate family, but she may well have had ties to friends and kin that her sale might sever forever. Would Harriet have been better off under a ruthlessly efficient manager whose financial success kept families together and friendships intact? The question highlights the cruel alternatives confronting Virginia's slaves. It was bad to be a slave on an efficient and profitable plantation, but the long-term consequences of working on an unprofitable one could be even worse.

Developmental Corporations "on the Stocks": Philadelphia Capital and the CVRR

In free labor Cumberland County, the town rivalries that motivated so much of Albemarle's developmental efforts were virtually absent. Geography dictated that any Cumberland railroad would follow the contours of the Valley, beginning in Harrisburg and extending southwest through Carlisle and then Chambersburg in adjacent Franklin County. The gentle landscape of the central Valley, coupled with the absence of a competing river or canal, made the railroad an appealing prospect. Carlisle newspapers published detailed and optimistic articles about the iron horse as soon as the technology appeared feasible. In 1827 the *American Volunteer* printed a lengthy front-page article on the world's first successful steam-powered railroad, the Stockton to Darlington line in England. In the same issue, the *Volunteer* reported

---

[41] "Hole and Corner Club of Albemarle," *Southern Planter* 4 (May 1844), pp. 109–10. For examples of rational and scientific planters with less than caring attitudes towards their slaves, see Faust, *James Henry Hammond*, pp. 69–104 and Dusinberre, *Them Dark Days*, pp. 285–301.

[42] John W. Buckingham to James Brady, July 20, 1853, Brady Papers, UVA.

that stock in the nearby Baltimore and Ohio was selling well. "The contemplated Rail Road from Baltimore to the Ohio River has excited the attention of the public in every direction, and those who come within its range are *all alive* upon the subject."[43] Carlisle papers continued to report the latest triumphs of the iron horse, predicting in 1830, for example, that steam engines "would in all probability soon enable persons to travel upon RailWays, at the rate of a mile per minute."[44]

The enthusiasm for railroads soon took more concrete manifestations. In January of 1831, "[a] large meeting of the citizens of this county" resolved to appoint a committee "to memorialize the Legislature on the subject." The committee chose a single person from each township to ascertain the number of forges, furnaces, distilleries, tanneries, mills, and stores, as well as "[a]ny other information that may have a bearing on the question of the importance of a railroad through the valley." The reports, in turn, were turned over to a "Committee of Correspondence," which eventually published a pamphlet to promote the enterprise. The town meeting also decided to submit a petition to gently remind legislators that the recently approved Pennsylvania canal system had largely bypassed the Cumberland Valley. While they made clear that Cumberland residents would take "liberal subscriptions of stock," the petitioners argued that the railroad deserved state investment.[45] At this point, the railroad had the hallmark of a developmental corporation: enthusiastic local backing eager for state aid.

The legislature refused to invest in the road, but the petitioners succeeded in getting a charter passed in March 1831. It granted the company the right to build a double-track road from Carlisle to the Susquehanna River near Harrisburg. The charter also authorized a capital stock of $200,000, which was divided into 4,000 shares worth $50 apiece. To become an operating corporation, however, investors had to purchase at least 1,500 shares ($75,000 of the capital stock). The company had to organize itself within three years or else the charter would expire.[46]

The proposed venture flopped before building a single mile of track. Despite all of the enthusiasm for the project, the company could not find enough capital to meet the charter's requirements. As the *Volunteer* sarcastically remarked, "The Cumberland Valley Rail Road, from present appearances, will be a long time on the *stocks*." Investors stayed away from the project because the lack of a direct rail

[43] *American Volunteer*, 5 April 1827, p. 3.
[44] *American Volunteer*, 2 December 1830, p. 1.
[45] "Rail-road Meeting," *American Volunteer*, 27 January 1831, p. 3.
[46] Westhaeffer, *History of the Cumberland Valley Railroad*, pp. 5–6.

connection between Harrisburg and Philadelphia reduced the profitability of the short line from Carlisle to Harrisburg. The promise of a
local improvement was not enough to encourage investors to sink
their money into a new and risky technology. The *Volunteer* pointedly
observed how even the promise of indirect benefits failed to attract
the capital required to finance the railroad:

> From the anxiety that was manifested to get a *law* passed for incorporating
> a company to construct it, we thought there would have been *no difficulty*
> in disposing of sufficient stock to procure *a charter*; but, we understand, that
> our *merchants* and *farmers*, who would, unquestionably, receive the *greatest*
> *benefit* from it, are the most tardy in taking shares.[47]

The supporters of the railroad did not give up. In 1835, the legislature, perhaps responding to pressure from both the Cumberland
Valley and Philadelphia capitalists, modified the charter so that a
more ambitious 55-mile road from Harrisburg to Chambersburg
could be undertaken. In contrast to the attempt made four years
earlier, a railroad from Harrisburg to Lancaster was already under
construction, offering the promise of an all-rail connection to Philadelphia. Railroads in general had shown real-world glimpses of their
potential, lessening the risk of the proposed venture. Significantly,
supporters made appeals to Philadelphia *"capitalists* and *speculators"*
who would find the CVRR stock "a very profitable investment."[48] In a
departure from the practices of earlier corporations, an office was
opened in Philadelphia to help sell shares when the company was
organized in May of 1835.

The stockholder lists for the CVRR show that Philadelphia *"capital-*
ists and *speculators"* did indeed perceive the company as a profitable
venture. A total of 400 private investors purchased $531,750 worth of
stock in the enterprise, which meant the typical investment was
markedly higher than the Virginia Central's Albemarle extension
(Table 3.4). Indeed, 77 investors in the Cumberland Valley Railroad
owned at least $1,000 in stock. Linking the names of investors with tax
lists, local histories, and city directories reveals that a relatively small
group of Philadelphians accounted for almost half of the privately
subscribed capital. If the $200,000 invested by the Bank of the United
States is included, the importance of Philadelphia capital becomes
even more significant.

One can reasonably argue that the presence of outside capital did
not necessarily diminish the CVRR's developmental nature. Indirect

---

[47] *American Volunteer*, 26 May 1831, p. 3.
[48] "Cumberland Valley Rail Road," *American Volunteer*, 21 May 1835, p. 3. The editorial
urged Philadelphians to help "connect the Cumberland Valley with the Lancaster
and Harrisburg Railroad."

Table 3.4. *Contrasting Patterns of Investment:*
The Cumberland Valley Railroad versus the Virginia Central

Enterprise (capital stock)	Number of Investors	Average Investment	Median Investment	Percentage of Shares Held by Top 10%
Cumberland Valley	400	$1,050	$200	72
Cumberland Valley (excluding BUS holdings)	399	$550	$200	47
Virginia Central	501	$200	$100	31

Notes and Sources: All state investment was excluded. The Virginia Central figures include only the stock issued in 1847 to finance the Albemarle extension. The stockholder list for the Virginia Central was found in the ABPW; the stockholder list for the CVRR was found in MG 286, Box 93, PSA.

benefits of a larger magnitude may well have motivated the Philadelphia investors. In the struggle between Philadelphia and Baltimore for Cumberland's trade, the CVRR would be an important blow. The railroad's freight cars would bring the valley's grain, hay, and livestock to Philadelphia, much to the delight of the city's merchants. The appeals made to Philadelphia investors, while mentioning the certain profits that the company would produce, frequently dwelled upon the lucrative trade that the railroad would secure. The *United States Gazette,* for example, remarked that farmers and manufacturers in Cumberland and Franklin counties "are obliged to transport their agricultural products, iron and other manufactures almost entirely to Baltimore." The *Gazette* concluded that "the plan appears to us to offer some considerable advantages to our city, by drawing hither a portion of trade which has heretofore been given to Baltimore."[49] Here we see a crucial difference between Albemarle and Cumberland. While small town rivalry within Albemarle helped generate support for the Virginia Central, rivalry among large cities outside of Cumberland motivated financing for the CVRR. Even after the CVRR was chartered and financed, Baltimore interests did not give up. They chartered several different companies to build a railroad that ran parallel to the Susquehanna River, thus hoping to deflect Philadelphia's Cumberland trade southward. These companies were eventually merged into the Northern Central Railroad. When the Northern Central reached Cumberland in 1851, its local impact appears to have been minimal.

[49] "Cumberland Valley Railroad," reprint from the *United States Gazette* appearing in the *American Volunteer,* 21 May 1835, p. 2.

With a sizable head start and more direct connections, the CVRR would dominate the trade of the Cumberland Valley, much to the delight of Philadelphia merchants and manufacturers.[50]

The importance of the Baltimore rivalry notwithstanding, the size of the Philadelphia investments indicates direct dividends were just as important as indirect benefits. The economic logic of the free-rider problem comes into play once again. A Philadelphia merchant or manufacturer who purchased CVRR stock for its indirect benefits would find competitors who did not invest enjoying the same indirect benefits. There was no guarantee, after all, that the individuals who made the investments would be the same ones who benefited from the growing trade. With this logic in mind, merchants and manufacturers investing large sums probably expected dividend payments and stock appreciation. When it became apparent that the railroad was not immediately going to pay large dividends, a few urban capitalists attempted to renege on their promises to purchase stock, which led the company to successfully sue them in 1839.[51]

The biggest infusion of urban capital – the $200,000 worth of shares held by the Bank of the United States – had more complex motivations. Once Andrew Jackson had blocked the federal re-chartering of the Bank of the United States, Nicholas Biddle turned to Pennsylvania for a new charter. After lengthy debate, the legislature approved the new charter, but required the bank to invest in certain transportation enterprises, including the CVRR. The railroad received $100,000 from Biddle's bank, and another $100,000 one year later. Biddle's investment not only reflected his need to procure votes in the Pennsylvania legislature, but also his connections with several of the company's local supporters. Prominent among Biddle's local contacts was Charles B. Penrose, a Carlisle lawyer closely allied with the Biddle family through business partnerships and family ties.

Biddle's investment, though, almost spelled disaster for the railroad. When the bank failed, its assignees converted the stock into debt, an option apparently stipulated in the Bank's original stock purchase. The CVRR's horrified directors realized that the sudden appearance of a large debit on the railroad's accounting books might cause various creditors and contractors to lose confidence and call in their loans, which by March of 1844 amounted to "about sixty thousand dollars due in great and small sums." To avoid disaster, the Board sent several representatives to Philadelphia to "exercise an influence"

---

[50] Watts, *Mainline Railroads*, pp. 45–46 and Van Dolsen, "Transportation," pp. 29–30. While the CVRR enjoyed tremendous prosperity in the 1850's, the Northern Central had difficulty repaying its large debts, suggesting that Philadelphia had become the preferred destination for Cumberland's commerce.

[51] "Minute Book," pp. 2–3.

on those buying the debt.[52] They need not have worried. Thomas A. Biddle purchased the entire debt, which was converted into bonds that paid six percent interest.

The influence of the Biddles and other Philadelphia capitalists grew over time. When the need for new tracks forced the company to seek more capital in 1849, the company issued about $700,000 of preferred stock that replaced the company's debt and gave it enough additional capital to make the necessary improvements. As the name implies, preferred stock gave its owners the right to receive dividends before other stockholders. In the case of the CVRR, the holders of the preferred stock would receive an 8 percent return before owners of the common stock received any dividends. By 1851, 42 investors held the entire issue of the preferred stock, owning an average of $16,607 apiece. The real degree of centralization was much greater, as nine representatives of the Biddle family collectively owned $191,500 in the preferred stock.[53] Any similarities of the CVRR to earlier developmental corporations was now lost in a flood of Philadelphia capital.

Philadelphia capitalists, however, waited many years before receiving a profit. In its first decade the railroad edged perilously close to bankruptcy. To even finish the project, the company issued its own scrip (known as "shin plasters") to pay contractors and other debts. The scrip and other debts consumed most of the railroad's revenue, leaving nothing for dividends. The company attributed this poor performance to disappointing revenues stemming from the depressed economy of the late 1830s and early 1840s, as well as high repair costs stemming from the railroad's flimsy first track. The dividend picture, however, improved dramatically during the 1850s. Not only did the railroad's revenue steadily rise – gross receipts rose from $108,000 in 1849 to more than $180,000 in 1859 – but a new iron track and bridges kept repair costs in check.[54] The company's preferred stock became a financial boon to its holders. In sharp contrast to the stocks of turnpikes and other developmental corporations, the preferred stock of the CVRR sold above par in 1860.[55]

Urban investors sought to insure that the CVRR would run as efficiently as possible. In November of 1850, H. J. Biddle urged George Cadwalader to attend a meeting concerning "a system of management of the business of our C. Valley Company. I think it is exceedingly

---

[52] "Minute Book," p. 110.
[53] Balance Sheet and List of Subscribers, Cumberland Valley Railroad, MG 286, Box 93, PSA.
[54] The growth of the company's revenues is outlined in the various annual reports found in the Cadwalader Collection, George Cadwalader Section, Miscellaneous–C, HSP.
[55] Schotter, *Growth and Development*, p. 50.

important for all our interests that you be present and give us the
benefit of your judgment in the decision we shall make."[56] Biddle
informed Cadwalader that Frederick Watts supported Daniel Tyler
for the road's superintendent. Biddle considered Tyler an excellent
engineer, but thought that he was "a poor accountant and any road
under his management would be worked in such a way as to *prevent* the
directors *knowing anything about it.*" Strict accounting was vital, Biddle
argued, so that "[t]he Board can compare every department with the
best managed roads in the United States and ascertain the causes of
any excess of our expenses and how to remedy it. We can act know-
ingly in all modifications of tolls & fares & see whether the desired
effect is or is not produced."[57]

Local investment in the railroad was still important, but even its
character had changed considerably from the patterns of turnpikes
and tollbridges. Most of the railroad's local capital originated from a
relatively small group of professionals, merchants, and manufacturers. Members of the Cumberland bar invested particularly large
amounts in the enterprise – 10 Carlisle attorneys collectively purchased 229 shares, or almost 20 percent of Cumberland's entire con-
tribution. Kinship and profession linked these lawyers into a tight-knit
group that acted as a conduit for Philadelphia capital and influence.
Frederick Watts, the largest Cumberland investor in the CVRR
($5,000), had initially practiced with Andrew Carothers, another
investor in the CVRR. Watts had also been a reporter of Pennsylvania
Supreme Court decisions with Charles B. Penrose, whose firm Penrose and Biddle invested $2,250 in the railroad. Edward M. Biddle,
who served as treasurer of the CVRR for nearly 50 years, married
Juliana Watts, the sister of Frederick.[58] These Carlisle lawyers provided
local leadership for the company, managing it in alliance with the
Philadelphia capitalists who controlled its stock.

Another important contrast to earlier corporations was the relative unimportance of state investment. The only direct support the
Cumberland Valley Railroad received from the state legislature was a
$100,000 investment made in 1836. The state government's invest-
ment represented only 16 percent of the railroad's initial capitalization, a small amount compared to the Virginia legislature's lavish
spending on the Virginia Central. More importantly, no further aid
was forthcoming after this initial investment. After unsuccessfully
putting the CVRR stock up for auction in 1843, the state government

---

[56] H.J. Biddle to George Cadwalader, November 15, 1850, Cadwalader Collection,
George Cadwalader Section, Miscellaneous–C, HSP.
[57] Ibid.
[58] Biographies of the major figures in the Cumberland Valley Railroad are found in
Nevin, *Men of Mark*, pp. 307–9, 323–24.

gave 85 percent of its holdings back to the company, with the implicit understanding that capital for future improvements must come from private sources.[59]

Developmental concerns, of course, were not completely absent from the CVRR. A case in point was the heated struggles over the location of the railroad's stations. Here was the same type of rivalry found in Albemarle, but in Cumberland, competition pitted one city block against the next. To influence the railroad's board of managers, merchants in Harrisburg, Carlisle and other towns offered free land and cash payments to lure the road to a particular street or particular block. Rivals a block or two away would make similar offers, leading to bidding wars and flaring tempers. In 1836, for example, the Chief Engineer reported that merchants in Harrisburg "took an active interest in the expected decision of the Company and even offered liberal inducements to determine upon a particular place from crossing the [Susquehanna] river and entering Harrisburg." Even water towers became objects of contention. The citizens of one Cumberland town gave the company two free lots and purchased $600 worth of stock in exchange for a water tower and stopping place.[60] Local residents banked on these towers and stations to further spur local development. As we shall see in the next section, they were not disappointed.

The CVRR and Cumberland's Continued Prosperity

If urban capitalists and local lawyers provided most of the capital for the CVRR, many of Cumberland's farm families benefited from its construction. Running across the length of the county, the CVRR put even the remotest farms in the county within 12 miles of a railroad station. After a short wagon trip to a railroad depot, farmers could have their grains, livestock, cider, butter, and other products arrive in Philadelphia the next day. Documenting the railroad's precise impact is difficult because detailed data about farm operations was first collected for the 1850 census, more than a decade after the railroad was built. It is thus impossible to construct a detailed "before" and "after" comparison to chart the railroad's impact.

The 1850 and 1860 censuses indirectly suggest, though, that the railroad strengthened the regime of small but diversified family farms. One sure sign of agricultural prosperity were land values that rose 62 percent in the 1850s.[61] Diversified production for urban markets

---

[59] Hartz documents that the state only managed to auction off 300 of the 2,000 shares of CVRR stock it owned. *Economic Policy*, pp. 323–28.

[60] "Minute Book," pp. 139, 143.

[61] Calculated by dividing the "cash value of farms" in the 1850 and 1860 censuses by the number of improved acres.

remained the order of the day. The production of almost every major cash crop increased sharply during the decade, with wheat production increasing 40 percent, corn production 140 percent, hay production 36 percent, and butter production 12 percent. Wool output fell, but it dropped only 7 percent. One reason that yields rose so dramatically was that Cumberland farmers cultivated more land. With high grain prices beckoning in the ever-growing markets of Philadelphia and Baltimore, Cumberland farmers increased the county's total number of improved acres by 11 percent. The value of agricultural implements rose at an even higher rate (45 percent), suggesting that growing demand led Cumberland farmers to increase productivity.[62]

Part of the reason that the railroad increased diversification was that it expanded the range of goods that Cumberland's farm families could produce for Philadelphia markets. No better example exists than the relationship between butter production and the commercial activity of rural women. Butter production had long been part of the gendered division of labor that was so essential for the survival of the family farm. Farm wives and daughters, in fact, had begun marketing butter in Philadelphia in the late eighteenth century. With the railroad reducing the cost of selling butter in Philadelphia markets, butter became an even more important part of Cumberland's farm economy. In the 1850s, the typical Cumberland farm produced slightly more than 400 pounds of butter, representing nearly $279 in gross revenue.[63] As historian Joan Jenson has noted, the sale of even a few hundred pounds "was often enough to buy most of the commodities the family needed for the household."[64]

The production and marketing of butter, as well as other farm commodities, allowed Cumberland's farm families to purchase more consumer goods outside of the home. Home manufacturing dropped sharply, declining from 80 cents per person in 1840 to 16 cents in 1850. Instead of producing home manufacturers, Cumberland farm families purchased the large quantity of goods that the CVRR carried every year. By 1849, more than 1,368 tons of "dry goods" traveled westward along the road to shops in Cumberland and Franklin counties; in 1855, the figure exceeded 2,000 tons.[65] Cumberland consumers living in the smallest towns had convenient access to a wide

---

[62] *Seventh Census* (1850), p. 194; *Agriculture in the United States* (1860 census), p. 122.

[63] In 1850, the average was 426 pounds; in 1860 it was 415 pounds. The small drop came about primarily because of declining farm size between 1850 and 1860. Calculated from DeBow, *Statistical View* (1850 census statistics), p. 298, and *Agriculture* (1860 Agricultural Census), p. 124.

[64] Jenson, *Loosening the Bonds*, p. 83. For Philadelphia prices for butter, see Atack and Bateman, *To Their Own Soil*, p. 235.

[65] These figures taken from annual reports in the Cadwalader Collection, George Cadwalader Section, Miscellaneous–C, HSP.

variety of goods. In 1859, residents of the market town of Newville, for example, could browse the "QUEENSWARE AND GROCERIES of all kinds" at Wm. L. M'Cullough's store, take a look at the "Marble-top Dressing Bureaus, Sofas, Sofa-Tables and Wash-Stands, Tete-a-tetes" and other furniture at the New Cabinet Ware-Rooms, and then stroll down to W. R. Linn's to examine the "IMPROVED MELODEONS" and other musical instruments.[66]

If the trainloads of consumer goods benefited Cumberland's merchants and their rural customers, the same items might mean unemployment and dislocation for Carlisle's artisans. At about the same time that the railroad's boosters began organizing the railroad, Carlisle's artisans began a protest movement that called into question the benefits of closer connections to Philadelphia. The artisans feared that the continued importation of cheap manufactured goods would reduce their political and economic independence. In 1835, a meeting of "Mechanics and Workingmen" formed a society to oppose "the importation of any articles to this place from the cities or elsewhere, that can be manufactured by our own mechanics, and . . . we will use every means in our power to *prevent* such importation." As part of their strategy, the association promised "to support those and those only who support us." It is not clear how many other residents supported the boycott, but the mechanics expressed determination "to resist oppression, and protect the interests of the working class of society."[67] Economic development, instead of uniting Cumberland society, now threatened to divide it along class lines.

Despite the railroad's threat to the interests of the anti-import organization, its meetings never directly attacked the CVRR. Indeed, a smattering of evidence suggests that the organization might have even supported the enterprise. One of the officers of the anti-import organization – a wealthy tanner – owned stock in the company.[68] As we will see in the next chapter, the *American Volunteer*, the Democratic newspaper that published the proclamations of the anti-import society, strongly supported the railroad. How could Carlisle's artisans oppose the importation of Philadelphia goods, but then fail to attack an enterprise that promised to strengthen ties with the Quaker City?

A comparison of the town's 1838 occupational structure (when the road was just completed) with that of the 1850 census helps answer

---

[66] These are selections from advertisements carried in the Newville *Valley Star* reprinted in "Newville in 1859," pp. 51, 55.

[67] These various quotes come from the proceedings of the initial meeting, published in the *American Volunteer*, 12 February 1835, p. 3.

[68] The tanner was Andrew Blair, who was appointed to the committee charged with writing the constitution of the anti-import organization. *American Volunteer*, 12 February 1835, p. 3. Blair owned $3,500 in Carlisle real estate, putting him in the upper echelon of the town's wealth distribution.

this question (Table 3.5). As one might expect, the number of merchants and retailers increased significantly because the CVRR made Carlisle an even more attractive marketing and retailing center. More surprisingly, the number of skilled and semi-skilled laborers increased significantly. The rhetoric of the anti-import organization aside, what was good for merchants was also good for most artisans. The need for new buildings meant more jobs for bricklayers, carpenters, and other skilled construction workers. The same rural customers that purchased new consumer goods from retailers and merchants also needed blacksmiths to shod their horses, carpenters to repair their barns, and tanners to make more leather goods. Even the infusion of Philadelphia textiles meant more jobs for certain trades: The number of tailors in the city increased from 9 in 1838 to 23 in 1850. A few skilled occupations that competed more directly with Philadelphia manufacturers – especially watchmakers and wagonmakers – suffered losses. But some small-sized manufacturers found niche markets that flourished even in the face of Philadelphia competition. The number of furniture makers, for example increased from 9 to 19. In general, market development opened more opportunities than it closed.

More jobs, of course, did not necessarily make artisans better off. Historians have documented that in many major cities, commercial expansion increased the number of artisans, but the new "opportunities" also meant that work was increasingly performed in nonmechanized factories instead of craft shops. Journeymen became less like junior partners and more like wage laborers as inequality between entrepreneurial masters and their employees became more pronounced.[69] The evidence from Carlisle, however, indicates that most shops remained small. In 1860, the average Cumberland manufacturing establishment employed only four workers, a size unlikely to encourage a harsh and impersonal work environment.[70] Nor did the standard of living of Carlisle's artisans fall. On the contrary, more artisans owned real property in 1850 than in 1838 (Table 3.5).[71] The average value of the holdings also increased significantly. At least some artisans, one surmises, accumulated enough savings from Carlisle's prosperity to buy their own homes and shops.

The flourishing Carlisle economy produced more opportunities, but it produced more inequality as well. In 1808, the wealthiest 10 percent of Carlisle's residents owned 47 percent of the real property.

[69] See, for example, Wilentz, *Chants Democratic*, pp. 107–42, and Laurie, *Artisans into Workers*, pp. 45–73.
[70] *Manufacturers* (1860 Census), p. 68.
[71] For a similar analysis of how artisans fared in the antebellum period, see Stott, "Artisans and Capitalist Development," pp. 257–71 and Sokoloff and Villaflor, "Market for Manufacturing Workers," pp. 29–62.

Table 3.5. *The Impact of the CVRR on Carlisle Occupational Patterns, 1838–1850*

Occupation Group	Number in 1838	Number in 1850	Number Owning Real Property, 1838	Number Owning Real Property, 1850	Average Real Property, 1838 ($)	Average Real Property, 1850 ($)
Merchants and Retailers	53	68	22 (43%)	34 (50%)	585	1,860
Professionals	93	65	33 (35%)	29 (45%)	655	2,812
Laborers	57	76	10 (18%)	14 (18%)	62	292
Artisans and Semiskilled	191	259	62 (32%)	118 (46%)	353	803

Notes and Sources: Derived from 1838 tax list and 1850 population census for Carlisle. Please see appendix for precise methods of calculation.

In 1838 that figure stood at 67 percent, and by 1850 it had risen to 74 percent. Inequality rose because however many ordinary artisans benefited from the CVRR, those controlling the mercantile and retail sectors in Carlisle benefited even more. In 1838, the typical merchant or retailer owned real estate worth 66 percent more than the holdings of the typical skilled or semiskilled worker. In 1850, the figure was 131 percent.[72] If the distribution of bonds, stocks, and other forms of wealth could be calculated, the gap would have been even larger. Given this evidence, the fears of the anti-import organization take on new meaning. In a more commercialized economy, artisans fell further behind other social groups even if, in absolute terms, they were better off.[73]

Economic Prosperity, Political Controversy

Rising inequality within Carlisle suggests that the political impact of railroads may have been quite different than their economic consequences. We know that men such John Lefever and T. L. Jones frequently made great use of local railroads, but how did such farmers and other small producers perceive the corporations that built and managed the improvements? In the minds of some residents, the very popularity of railroads made them potentially dangerous entities. Would not the company's economic power create the temptation for corporate officers to acquire additional privileges from the state government? How could Americans protect the republic from the possible corruption that large-scale corporations might engender? Conflicting answers to these questions meant that economic prosperity, no matter how widely shared, would not end political controversy. The improvements that transformed the countryside of Albemarle and Cumberland, as we shall see in the next chapter, would also leave their mark on local politics.

---

[72] Calculated from Table 3.5.
[73] Easterlin makes the point that a sense of well-being is derived not from one's absolute standard of living but from one's relative position in society. See Easterlin, "Raising the Incomes of All."

4

The Local Politics
of Market Development

In the 1790s, Pennsylvania farmers warned of a new and insidious threat to American liberty: the turnpike corporation. In the 1793–1794 legislative session, prominent Jeffersonian Republicans submitted petitions that complained of "wealthy incorporated companies taking possession of public and private property." The petitioners made clear that they were not social levelers; they praised inequality for encouraging beneficial exchanges that were "the basis for public prosperity." Granting special privileges to turnpike corporations, however, introduced a form of political inequality that "must destroy the liberties of our country." The petitioners feared that eminent domain privileges would put property rights on a slippery slope that would eventually lead to their demise. "If the government has the right to take one acre of property of the farmer," the petitioners starkly concluded, "it has the same right to deprive him of his whole farm."[1]

Signed by more than 200 people, the petition attests to the powerful influence of republicanism in American politics. Although a notoriously complex set of ideas, republicanism can be defined as a political language expressly concerned with the precarious balance between liberty and power. How could Americans avoid the unhappy fate of Rome and other republics that had eventually fallen into despotism? Civic-minded virtue, defined as the ability to put the public good above self-interest, was the answer for many republican thinkers. The problem was that "corruption," the overly ambitious pursuit of economic gain and political power, constantly threatened to undermine virtue. Republican thinkers especially feared the centralization of power because it created great temptations for abuse. Any grant of power, no matter how small or trivial, could be the harbinger of a vast conspiracy that might lead to despotism.[2] To politicians such as Thomas Jefferson and Andrew Jackson, public debt,

---

[1] The petitions are found in RG-7, Box 1, PSA.
[2] The literature on republicanism is vast. Some of the most important works include Bailyn, *Ideological Origins*; Wood, *Creation of the American Republic*; Wood, *Radicalism of the American Revolution*; Watson, *Liberty and Power*; and Rodgers, "Republicanism: The Career of a Concept."

national banks, and business corporations were designed to "prepare the way for a change, from the present republican form of government, to that of monarchy, of which the English constitution is to be the model."[3]

Republicanism led many Americans to view the corporation with considerable suspicion. Was not the corporation a special grant of power, designed to enrich a few at the expense of the many? The Pennsylvania petitioners claimed that eminent domain privileges "enabled an incorporated Company, engaged in a *subordinate Occupation*, to make 25 *per Cent per Annum* on their Capital Stock."[4] Such an assertion would have surprised the many investors who owned unprofitable turnpike stock, but it nevertheless expressed widespread sentiments that the combination of commercial enterprise and centralized power threatened American liberty. The reference to "*subordinate Occupation*" also hints at a broad conflict between farmers and artisans – who embodied republican ideals of the virtuous and independent small-producer – with the corrupting influence of merchants and financiers.[5] As historian Pauline Maier has noted, such republican attacks on the corporation reverberated in American politics throughout the first half of the nineteenth century.[6]

The goal of this chapter is to understand how republican fears of corporate power influenced both public perceptions and public policy in Albemarle and Cumberland. One can hardly imagine a more discordant set of attitudes than the brash optimism of local boosters and the foreboding pessimism of anticorporate republicanism. How did residents square their vigorous boosterism and strong community support of developmental corporations with republican fears that the same corporations would lead Americans down a dark road of corruption and tyranny? The question gets at the heart of political conflict and local development in Albemarle and Cumberland.

Three distinct episodes allow us to analyze the tensions between local boosterism and republican rhetoric. In Albemarle, a protracted struggle between the proprietors of a large commercial milling site at Shadwell Mills and the Rivanna Navigation Company highlighted fears that transportation companies could endanger property rights.

---

[3] Thomas Jefferson to George Washington, May 23, 1792 in Peterson, ed., *Jefferson: Writings*, pp. 994–95.
[4] RG-7, Box 1, PSA.
[5] A number of labor historians have emphasized the importance of small-producer republicanism, including Wilentz, *Chants Democratic* and Laurie, *Artisans into Workers*. See also Merrill and Wilentz's analysis of William Manning's distinction between the "Few" and the "Many" in *Key of Liberty*, pp. 59–70.
[6] Maier, "Revolutionary Origins," p. 68. Maier's excellent essay is perhaps the best summary of anticorporate opposition in the early republic. See also see Klein and Majewski, "Economy, Community, and Law," and Hartz, *Economic Policy*, pp. 69–79.

The dispute began in 1818, when Thomas Jefferson sued an early version of the company for damaging his milling complex. Throughout the first half of the nineteenth century, the corporate entities charged with improving the river clashed with the millowners. In both the court of law and the court of popular opinion, the corporation was a big loser. Judges and juries held that a company could not damage property without paying for it, even if that company produced important public benefits. By the company's own reckoning, many of the county's residents opposed its aggressive stance against the millowners. The episode shows that however eagerly Albemarle's residents supported the developmental goals of the navigation company, they could quickly turn against it if it overstepped its bounds.

Banks generated even more suspicion and distrust. Possessing immense control over capital and credit, banks represented a volatile mixture of government privilege and economic power that led to continual controversy in Jacksonian America. Popular hostility directed against banks was not entirely absent in Albemarle, but the intense boosterism that pervaded county politics undermined the political impact of these misgivings. The fierce struggle for trade between Charlottesville and Scottsville led each town to petition for their own bank. The economic benefits that a bank would bring to each locality – and the probability that the state legislature would only allow one such institution in the county – led to protracted political infighting that solidified probanking sentiments. Even as many of the county's residents supported Jackson's Bank War in national politics, they frequently reaffirmed the importance of banking to the local economy.

Cumberland residents, on the other hand, directly confronted the Bank of the United States when it became the major investor in the Cumberland Valley Railroad. The county's Democrats, in particular, feared that Nicholas Biddle and his allies within Carlisle's legal elite would dispense railroad jobs and patronage to corrupt local politics. These fears came to a head in 1837, when Charles B. Penrose, a Carlisle lawyer and director of the CVRR, sought reelection for his state senate seat. The tense campaign that followed reflected acute anxiety over the changing social origins of the corporation. That Philadelphia capitalists controlled the county's most important economic institution worried many of Cumberland's farmers and artisans. Yet for all of the anticorporate sentiment expressed in the bitter political campaign, Cumberland residents rarely implicated economic progress itself as a villain. They feared that the CVRR's economic and political power might imperil free elections, but they also realized that the railroad created new jobs and increased land values. Democratic critics of the Cumberland Valley Railroad therefore treaded carefully, clearly distinguishing their attacks on the railroad's political connections from its important economic advantages.

The Penrose reelection campaign suggests how Cumberland's Democrats sought to synthesize the best of boosterism and republicanism: They wanted to reap the advantages of commercial expansion while preventing its potential corruption of politics. Such pragmatic attitudes help to explain the coexistence of republicanism and boosterism. Residents took republican fears about the corrupting power of corporations quite seriously. Republican fears, however, motivated a set of specific reforms rather than a generalized movement aimed at stopping market expansion altogether. Juries and judges curtailed eminent domain privileges without questioning the benefits of improved transportation; politicians condemned the Bank of the United States on the national level while vigorously lobbying for a local bank; and Cumberland Democrats denounced the leader of a railroad corporation while supporting the railroad itself. The specificity of the issues transformed republicanism from a coherent, anti-commercial ideology into a more elastic vocabulary that selectively accommodated a commercial economy.

The Shadwell Mills Case: Public Good versus Private Property

The most controversial issue involving transportation companies was the right of eminent domain. No matter how eagerly landowners supported better transportation, they continually fretted over the ability of a company legally to take or damage their land. Canal and navigation companies, that often flooded hundreds of acres of land in fertile river valleys, could be particularly dangerous to landowners. How did the legal system handle such cases? Some historians have argued that legislators and judges often granted canal and river improvement corporations the right to take land cheaply and easily. "[E]limination or reduction in damages," writes Morton Horwitz, "created a new source of forced investment, as landowners whose property values were impaired without compensation in effect were compelled to underwrite a portion of economic development."[7]

In Albemarle County, the Rivanna Navigation Company and the James River and Kanawha Company did indeed generate a large number of eminent domain cases. But if any group received a legal subsidy, it was the landowners. The James River and Kanawha Company, for example, paid 11 Albemarle landowners (who collectively had 167 acres condemned) an average of $109 per acre. The real

---

[7] For example of the legal subsidies view, see Horwitz's enormously influential *Transformation of American Law*, pp. 63–108, quote p. 70. See also Kulick, "Dams, Fish, and Farmers," pp. 25–50.

estate holdings of the same 11 landowners had been valued for tax purposes at an average of $26 per acre, suggesting that the canal company paid more than *4* times the "official" value of the land. The same pattern held for town lots that the company flooded. The corporation paid owners an average of $173 per lot; tax valuations showed that most lots were unimproved, worth no more than $60 on average.[8] Tax assessors, of course, usually valued land and lots below market value.[9] Nevertheless, most property owners seemed to have found these settlements agreeable – only one planter appealed a decision, and he was granted a $600 increase in his award.

The economic standing of the property owners suggests why the James River and Kanawha Company paid dearly for the land it damaged. Landowners near fertile river valleys tended to be planters of considerable wealth and influence. In the James River cases, the landowners involved in condemnation proceedings owned an average $18,500 worth of real estate and 21 slaves, putting them at the very top of Albemarle's economic hierarchy.[10] As corporations quickly learned, these planters could make their wishes known in local courthouses, local elections, or even in company meetings. Anecdotal evidence suggests that companies listened carefully when wealthy planters complained. In 1847, John Hartwell Cocke wrote the board of the James River and Kanawha Company to complain that the leaky canal banks not only damaged his crops, but resulted in "sickliness" during the summer. The ditches the corporation had built for drainage were "soon filled by slides from the embankment & rendered useless." Cocke recommended lining portions of the canal banks with clay in order to prevent the leakage. Although this solution would require "considerable labour," it was the only alternative left given that "[t]emporary expedients of various kinds have been tried and failed."[11] Cocke mentioned that he had already met with an agent of the company who had agreed with the planter's views. The agent's quick agreement with Cocke is understandable. Cocke was not only a

---

[8] Damage awards were listed in the annual reports of the James River and Kanawha Company. See 21 *ARBPW* (Richmond, 1837), p. 236, and 23 *ARBPW* (Richmond, 1839), pp. 272–75. Tax valuations taken from 1840 Albemarle County Real Property Tax Lists, microfilm, VSLA.

[9] The tax valuations are the average per acre for an entire tract of land, thereby including acres not adjacent to the river. Since the land near the river tended to be the highest valued, it is natural that the average for the entire tract should be lower.

[10] See Majewski, "Commerce and Community," pp. 264–69 for a more detailed analysis of the James River and Kanawha Company and eminent domain disputes. For a similar take on eminent domain proceedings in the Middle Atlantic states, see Freyer, *Producers Versus Capitalists*, pp. 137–95. Freyer stresses the importance of "constitutionalism" in limiting the eminent domain power of corporations, which is consistent with public attitudes toward the Rivanna Navigation Company.

[11] Draft of a letter from John Hartwell Cocke to the Board of Directors of the James River and Kanawha Company (1840), Cocke Papers, Box 123, UVA.

major investor, but a former member of the board and one of the most
vocal proponents of the enterprise. The company could ill afford to
lose the support of such men.

The legal and political issues, however, became more complicated
when the right to water itself was contested. Rivers, after all, not only
provided convenient transportation, but also power for merchant
mills, tanneries, and other rural manufacturers. Which users should
have the primary right to the river's water? The question became
especially important in Albemarle County because the Rivanna River's
narrow confines created a zero-sum situation in which a company
improving navigation would inevitably run afoul of local millers. The
resulting cases became heated controversies that made their way
into legislative petitions, newspaper editorials, and public addresses.
Although the specific legal issues were quite complicated, the debates
almost always addressed the fundamental question of how much
power developmental corporations should possess when performing
their important public mission.

No other than Thomas Jefferson began the long legal battle. In
order to repay his heavy debts, Jefferson built a substantial manufacturing complex known as Shadwell Mills that was completed in
1806.[12] The "old" Rivanna Navigation Company – that improved navigation only between Charlottesville and Milton – wanted to raise Jefferson's dam, widen his channel, and build a lock near his mill. Jefferson, ever the public-spirited gentleman, graciously offered to modify
his dam while giving the corporation his "assurance of every aid and
accommodation which my lands adjacent can afford."[13] But even the
accommodating Jefferson found the encroachments of the company
intolerable – raising the mill dam made it more vulnerable to damage,
the wider channel eroded the adjacent bank, and the lock sometimes
shut down the mill for weeks. In 1818, he finally sued the corporation
for damages.[14] The dispute remained an issue of controversy when the
"new" Rivanna Navigation Company took over the works of the older
corporation in 1827. The man who took great pride improving navigation had, ironically enough, erected a major legal obstacle to its
accomplishment.

Another local millowner added an additional legal headache. In
1814, the state legislature granted William Wood the right to collect
tolls if he promised to maintain dams, locks, and canals at key points

[12] Wertenbaker, "The Rivanna," p. 4, and Merrill, *Jefferson's Nephews*, p. 60.
[13] Thomas Jefferson to Peter Minor, March 3, 1811, VHS. See also Wertenbaker, "The
Rivanna," pp. 4–5.
[14] The details of the Jefferson case were discussed in a lengthy newspaper exchange
between the new owners of Shadwell Mills and the Rivanna Navigation Company. *Virginia Advocate*, 9 July 1830, p. 2.

from Milton to the James River. The "old" Rivanna Company had the right to improve navigation only from Charlottesville to Milton, leaving most of the river unimproved. As owner of several strategic mills along the Rivanna, Wood seemed to have the means to keep the river passable. To prevent Wood from exploiting his potential monopoly, the legislature regulated toll rates and profit levels. The right for one man to collect tolls, even if regulated, still raised troubling questions. What happened if Wood failed to improve navigation along the River, yet still collected tolls? Who would insure that Wood gave an accurate account of his expenses to regulators? How would Wood be compensated for his outlays if the arrangement proved completely unprofitable?

To complicate matters further, the partnership of John Timberlake, Jr., John Magruder, and James Magruder purchased both Shadwell Mills and Wood's rights to improve the river. As befitting shrewd businessmen, Timberlake and the Magruders acquired these properties from the debt-ridden estates of Jefferson and Wood.[15] Timberlake and the Magruders could well afford to snatch up such bargains, for they were among the wealthiest businessmen of central Virginia. The partnership of John Timberlake and John Magruder owned the Union Mills complex, a sprawling collection of enterprises located on the Rivanna in Fluvanna County. The Union Mills holdings included a merchant mill, saw mill, cotton factory, company store, and blacksmith shop. Employing more than 100 people, it was one of the largest manufacturing concerns in central Virginia. Suffice to say, the financial resources of Timberlake and the Magruders made them formidable legal opponents.

The deep pockets of Timberlake and the Magruders were soon put to the test. Charlottesville interests began a long campaign to end the millowners' monopoly over navigation of the Rivanna. An 1823 petition signed by nearly 250 Albemarle residents complained that the millowner's locks were made of "slight and perishable materials" that were "Dangerous, and often impassable." The petitioners also charged that the millowners apathetically witnessed "produce and merchandise of the most valuable and perishable kinds, rolled out in the mud, exposed to every injury, from weather, theft, & pillage, to be reshipped in other boats." For Albemarle residents who depended upon the River for cheap transportation – especially those living near

---

[15] Precise details on the purchases have been difficult to find, but the legal papers of Timberlake and the Magruders clearly indicate that the millowners purchased Shadwell Mills from Jefferson's estate. See "Notes of the Plaintiffs," (undated), Ended Chancery Case 429, Albemarle County Court Records, VSLA. As for the purchase of Wood's right to improve navigation, an 1823 petition claimed that Wood was "bankrupt and Dead," having "transferred at a loss his right & interest in the tolls." ACLP, 15 December 1823.

Charlottesville – the result of this alleged mismanagement was disastrous. Farmers had produce "left unproductive and wasting in our
barns" while local merchants "have been driven from market."[16]

Timberlake and the Magruders did not give up their right to collect
tolls without a fight. They strenuously denied the charges of neglect,
claiming that freight rates had dropped considerably under their
stewardship. To bolster their case, the millowners presented the legislature depositions from boatmen and local residents, forcing the
opponents of Timberlake and the Magruders to take depositions of
their own. The resulting testimony – which came to almost 100 pages
in length – testified to both the conflict's high stakes and each side's
considerable financial resources.[17] The testimony also showed the
complex nature of the conflict. Witnesses disagreed over when locks
were repaired, how long it took to navigate the river, the exact height
of dams, and the degree to which debris blocked channels. The
detailed, technical nature of the arguments created a legal morass
that was bound to befuddle even the most knowledgeable jurists
and legislators.

The millowners lost the first round when the legislature reorga-
nized the new Rivanna Navigation Company in 1827, which super-
seded the original legislative grant made to William Wood in 1814.
As with many local issues, the precise political mechanics of the millowners' defeat remain mysterious. It seems reasonable to assume,
however, that many legislators felt that the river's navigation was too
important for a few men to control.[18] In this regard, the initial 1814
arrangement with Wood had been highly atypical. It was predicated
upon individual initiative and direct profit, not community action and
indirect benefits. By securing the participation of scores of local merchants, retailers, and planters, a corporation could mobilize more
community support and more capital. A corporation could also
receive substantial state investment ($30,000 in the case of the
Rivanna Navigation Company) that would be politically indefensible
to give to three wealthy businessmen.

Yet even in defeat, the millowners gained much from the new
corporation's charter. The charter acknowledged that the millowners
had a valid claim to the river's water. The legislature authorized disinterested commissioners to settle the millowners' compensation claims
for the loss of their right to take tolls. The commissioners would also

---

[16] ACLP, 15 December 1823.
[17] The depositions are filed with the ACLP, 15 December 1823.
[18] An 1826 petition from the Albemarle Agricultural Society reminded the legislature
   that thousands of residents depended upon "the provision of safe, cheap, and practi-
   cable channels of transportation," yet the Rivanna was "entirely useless" because of
   the millowners. ACLP, 20 December 1826.

determine if the company's activities affected the operation of
Shadwell Mills, and fix suitable compensation.[19] Here the legislature
upheld the point that no corporation, however public its purpose,
could violate preexisting property rights without compensation. Even
the members of the Albemarle Agricultural Society, strong supporters
of the new corporation, agreed that the millowners should receive "a
ratable compensation for the injury that they may sustain."[20]

The legislative settlement led to a fragile peace, but relationships
between the Navigation Company and the millowners remained
tense. The millowners claimed that they had spent more than $4,000
for improvements before the navigation company had been chartered. They argued that the company, which had inherited the
improvements, should pay for them in full. The corporation maintained that the millowners had collected the $4,000 (with interest)
through the collection of tolls, so that any additional compensation
would be unfair. The independent commissioners ruled in favor of
the corporation, finding that it owed Timberlake and the Magruders
only $464. The incensed millowners took the decision to court, but
eventually lost. The company triumphantly heralded the case as "favorable to the rights of the community upon all litigated questions."[21]

The millowners, though, soon struck back. Timberlake and the
Magruders argued that irrespective of compensation for past improvements, the company's actions interfered with the operations of Shadwell Mills. Timberlake and the Magruders filed a number of separate
complaints against the company, but their main point of contention
was a dam that the company had erected downstream from the milling
complex. This dam created a "reflux of water" that diminished the fall
of water from the Shadwell dam and impaired the operation of the
mills. The millowners asked for an injunction against the company's
operations, compensation for the damage that the dam had already
done to Shadwell Mills, and a court order forcing the company to
reduce the dam's height.[22]

The corporation's legal response centered on the public's right to
improved navigation. Improved navigation, the directors argued, was
a community benefit that transcended the individual concerns of
the millowners. The directors drew an analogy between river navigation and public roads – just as the county government had the right
to take land for public highways, the navigation company had the
right to take land for public navigation. The directors never tired of

---

[19] *Laws of Virginia*, 1826–1827 Session (Richmond, 1827), c. 65.
[20] ACLP, 20 December 1826.
[21] "Report of the President and Directors ... for 1831," ABPW, Box 210.
[22] "Notes of the Plaintiffs," (undated), filed in Ended Chancery Case 429, Albemarle
   County Court Records, VSLA.

proclaiming that navigation along the river was "an inalienable &
indefeasible right of the public, which would never accrue to any individual in opposition to the Public."[23] In a series of legal briefs and
court documents written in the early 1830s, the corporation represented itself as "agents of the public in the execution of a work of
utmost importance," an enterprise "upon which the prosperity of a
large community intimately depended," and a project "anxiously and
impatiently demanded by the wants and claims of the community
interested in the important work."[24]

The company portrayed Timberlake and the Magruders as engross-
ing monopolists. The company planned to lease some of the excess
water created by its dam near Shadwell to "respected gentlemen"
engaged in the milling business. These rival millowners, the directors
declared, were the real targets of the litigation, for Timberlake and
the Magruders sought to derail any potential competitors in a business that "they have too long exclusively monopolized."[25] The millowners, the corporation warned, sought "to hold a whole community
in a state of perpetual vassalage." Timberlake and the Magruders,
"self-created lords of the domain," wanted the public to pay "a mon-
strous exaction" for the right of free navigation.[26] "[P]rivate interest
and private profits," the directors of the company declared in an 1830
newspaper editorial, were the "bitter pill by which the public is to be
drugged out of its rights."[27]

The director's language was filled with the vivid metaphors of
republicanism. Most obvious was the sense of conspiracy and impend-
ing corruption. The millowners were not merely legal opponents, but
selfish aristocrats plotting to preserve an invidious monopoly. The
case was not a dispute over complicated issues, but a clear-cut battle
between the public good and corrupt monopolists. Such republican
language was common enough in the Jacksonian era – the directors
might well have been describing the Second Bank of the United States
instead of a local milling concern. The real irony was that the corporation had cleverly usurped the metaphors of corruption and aristocracy, so frequently used to discredit corporate power, to justify its own
ends. The company's status as a developmental corporation allowed
the directors to make this rhetorical turnaround. Paid little in the way

---

[23] "Report of the President and Directors ... for 1830," ABPW, Box 210, VSLA.
[24] "Reply to the Bill of Complaint," (undated), filed with Ended Chancery Case 429,
Albemarle County Court Papers, VSLA, p. 1; "A Memorial in Behalf of the President
and Directors of the Rivanna Navigation Company," (undated), filed in the papers of
Ended Chancery Case 429, Albemarle County Court Records, VSLA, p. 2. Hereafter
cited as "Memorial."
[25] "Memorial," p. 3.
[26] "Memorial," p. 5.
[27] Virginia Advocate, 11 June 1830, p. 2.

of dividends, the company's investors had made considerable financial sacrifices for the entire community, a stark contrast to the apparently self-interested motives of Timberlake and the Magruders.

The key mistake of the company was assuming that its public interest somehow made private property irrelevant. The millowners never questioned the public's right to unimpeded navigation along the Rivanna. But did that right mean that private parties were somehow undeserving of compensation? The millowners turned the corporation's public road analogy on its head, arguing that while it was true that a county could take land for public highways, the landowners received compensation for their losses. As the rightful owners of the mills, Timberlake and the Magruders thought that they had "a clear, absolute and indefeasible vested right to all the fall acquired by the dam and canal." Such a right entitled them "to redress equally with every other property owner whose property may be unlawfully injured or trespassed upon."[28] The argument that the company could ignore private property rights boiled down to "a principle too arbitrary and despotic in its character ... to be tolerated in any government of equal laws."[29]

The requirement for compensation was especially strong for the Rivanna Navigation Company because the corporation was not a true representative of the public good. Timberlake and the Magruders pointed out that if the corporation provided a public benefit, then some members of the public benefited more than others. The millowners asserted that the corporation could have simply deepened the channel of the river instead of building a dam. The corporation had chosen to build a dam, the millowners charged, so that they could sell water to rival millowners. The legal briefs of Timberlake and the Magruders declared that the company's plan was an "illegal and unrighteous contract." A director of the company was actually a partner in the rival milling establishment, while the other partners were "near relatives, by affinity at least, of some of the said Directors."[30] Such cozy relationships undermined confidence that a corporation, even a developmental one, could be trusted to put aside self-interested motives to pursue its public mission.

The evidence is fragmentary, but the millowners seemed to have won the battle of public opinion. In 1831, the company reported "extraordinary hostility" from juries deciding other eminent domain

[28] "Notes of the Plaintiffs," (undated), Ended Chancery Case 429, Albemarle County Court Records, VSLA. Hereafter cited as "Plaintiff's Notes."
[29] Bill of Complaint by John Timberlake, Jr., John Magruder, and John B. Magruder, October 3, 1831, Ended Chancery Case 429, Albemarle County Court Records, VSLA, p. 5. Hereafter cited as "Bill of Complaint."
[30] "Bill of Complaint," pp. 2–3.

cases involving the corporation. Indeed, these juries had awarded "the most exorbitant estimate which the most extravagant calculator could possibly have made." The directors blamed the widespread hostility on the proprietors of the Shadwell Mills, for "they [the directors] have not been able to escape from the latent influence of their vile genius."[31] The corporation's frank assessment of its public image was an ironic admission for a project supposedly representing the wishes of the community. Local juries apparently believed that even the cause of improved transportation failed to justify the uncompensated taking of private property.

So, too, did Virginia's courts. For more than two decades, the corporation and the millowners heatedly disputed damage claims. Scores of depositions were taken as the courtroom battles intermittently flared.[32] The case file does not contain any court decrees, but the rough outline of the case's progress can be followed from company reports. In 1838 the company reported that the courts had thrown out two injunctions of the millowners, but also warned that Timberlake and the Magruders had taken fresh depositions. "We have every confidence in the justice of our cause," the corporation's directors declared, "but this will avail nothing against so indefatigable an opponent without great attention on our part."[33] The great attention of the company was of little avail. In 1843, court-appointed commissioners found that the corporation's works had done considerable damage to the mills. The corporation paid Timberlake (now sole owner) more that $3,100 with the hope that "this unpleasant controversy is forever at rest."[34]

The corporation's hopes were once again disappointed. In 1845 the navigation company reported that Timberlake had filed yet another injunction seeking to reduce the height of the dam. The exasperated directors made clear that the suits "are cause of much trouble to the directors, and not a little expense to the company."[35] The lawyer for the company, the prominent Whig politician V. W. Southall, asked the court "[a]re the defendants and the public to be eternally harassed with its renewal?"[36] The answer was not clear. The last court record mentions another injunction filed in 1852, but the court's

---

[31] "Report of the Board of Directors ... to the Board of Public Works, 1832," ABPW, Box 210, VSLA, pp. 2–3.
[32] The case file contain more than 60 depositions.
[33] "Report of the Rivanna Navigation Company for 1838," 23 *ARBPW* (Richmond, 1839), p. 407.
[34] "Annual Report of the Rivanna Navigation Company, 1843–44," 29 *ARBPW* (Richmond, 1844), p. 287.
[35] "Report of the Rivanna Navigation Company for 1844–45," 30 *ARBPW* (Richmond, 1845), p. 39.
[36] "Notes of the Defendants," (May 19, 1847), Ended Chancery Case 429, Albemarle County Court Records, VSLA.

decision was not recorded in company records or found in the case files. Nevertheless, the case became a major distraction from the company's primary purpose, irrespective of the damages it paid. To a large extent, the company's directors had only themselves to blame. Their aggressive stance toward the millowners reflected a bedrock faith in the importance of the public good they provided. But Virginia's courts – and most of Albemarle's citizens – believed that even important community improvements had to respect established property rights.

Boosterism and Republicanism in the Albemarle "Bank War"

For all of its legal fireworks, the Shadwell Mills dispute paled in comparison to the heated conflict over the location of Albemarle's bank. Residents in the central and northern portions of the county lobbied for a bank in Charlottesville; residents in the southern portion of the county wanted the bank in Scottsville. Boosters in the two towns collectively filed more than two dozen legislative petitions between 1831 and 1839, with some having more than one thousand signatures. The rivalry for the bank was especially remarkable given the backdrop of national politics. While Andrew Jackson, Albemarle's overwhelming choice for president, attacked the Bank of the United States on the national level, local residents fought tooth and nail to secure one of their own.

The Albemarle banking controversy had its roots in the Virginia state legislature, which strictly limited the number of banks it chartered. As of 1830, the legislature had chartered only four banks that established branches around the state.[37] Even the opening of a branch, however, required legislative permission. The legislature's miserly policy regarding bank charters and branch permissions reflected widespread suspicion that banks were agents of political corruption. Antibanking sentiment had deep roots in eighteenth-century Virginia republicanism. Thomas Jefferson, for example, wanted to "interdict forever, to both the State and national governments, the power of establishing any paper bank."[38] Many politically influential planters and merchants had more self-serving reasons to limit bank charters: The absence of competitors made the stock of the previously existing banks all the more valuable.[39]

---

[37] Schweikart, *Banking in the American South*, pp. 122–23; Shade, *Democratizing the Old Dominion*, pp.40–41; and Wallis, Sylla, and Legler, "Interaction of Taxation and Regulation," pp.138–39.
[38] Quoted in Swanson, "Bank Notes," p. 50.
[39] Wallis, Sylla, and Legler add an important point. Since the state had large investments in banks, the state could maximize its dividend revenue through restricted

Residents of Albemarle, who lived 50 miles from the nearest branch, felt the brunt of the state's restrictive chartering policy. In numerous petitions to the legislature, Albemarle residents outlined the inconveniences they suffered. Most obvious was the shortage of specie and notes, especially those of small denominations. "In Charlottesville," an 1834 petition complained, "it is always impracticable to get a note changed, unless you make a purchase, and then it is difficult."[40] Others noted the "*risk, inconvenience,* and *positive loss* in the transportation of money from Richmond."[41] In towns such as Charlottesville and Scottsville, the flour trade alone sometimes required that $5,000 change hands in a single day. Without a local bank, merchants had to "either keep large sums of money idle, or be subject to the expense and risk of frequent trips to Richmond, in order to meet the demand for Cash."[42]

The intense efforts of Charlottesville and Scottsville reflected the more general rivalry for trade between the two counties. A bank would attract more commerce to the winner, resulting in significant population growth and rising property values. As an 1834 Charlottesville petition noted, almost everybody in the town stood to benefit from a bank. "Besides the great increase of trade and manufactures which must be very beneficial to all merchants and mechanics, the bank will call many strangers from a distance, who, of course, must feed themselves and horses, to the immediate benefit of the inn-keeper, and ultimate profit of the farmer."[43] The losing side of the bank battle, on the other hand, would have to travel more than 20 miles of uncertain public roads for banking services.[44] Thomas R. Bailey, working to gather petitions in Charlottesville, wrote to an unnamed recipient in 1834 that "I am affraid [sic] if they get one in Scotsville [sic] it will hurt this place very much."[45]

The battle for the local bank also involved an overlapping party conflict between the two sections of the county. As the Second Party System crystallized in Albemarle during the 1830s, residents in the

---

chartering. They conclude that "the nature of the state's fiscal interest in banking retarded banking development in Virginia for most of the antebellum decades." See "Interaction of Taxation and Regulation," p. 139.

[40] ACLP, 8 December 1834.
[41] ACLP, 29 December 1836.
[42] ACLP, 19 December 1831.
[43] ACLP, 8 December 1834.
[44] As one Charlottesville petition noted, communications were so poor as to make frequent communication almost impossible. "Even ordinary *mail* facilities for that purpose are wanting ... being now afforded by the slow and awkward contrivance of a *weekly horse mail.*" ACLP, 14 February 1839.
[45] Thos. R. Bailey to "Dear Sir," December 29, 1836, filed with Albemarle County Legislative Petitions.

northern and central portions of the county tended to support the Whigs. The Democrats, on the other hand, dominated the southern portion of the county. Part of the geographic split reflected differing religious affiliations: Scotch-Irish Presbyterians dominated northern and central Albemarle, while most residents of southern Albemarle belonged to Baptist and Methodist churches.[46] The banking petitions never mentioned the political and religious splits within the county, but these divisions undoubtedly contributed to the intensity of the commercial rivalry. Albemarle county had its own version of the bank war that, like the national dispute, involved the complicated interaction of religion, ethnicity, geography, and economics.

Unlike the national battle between Jackson and Biddle, the participants in Albemarle's bank war agreed on the fundamental legitimacy of banking. The importance of banking to local development all but assured widespread community support. Even those suspicious of banks had to think twice about rejecting an institution that could secure their town the trade of the surrounding countryside. The strong relationship between local boosterism and probanking sentiment was apparent in an 1836 letter from a Charlottesville town meeting to Col. Samuel Carr, the area's state senator. The letter noted that at first very few people would sign the petition to locate a bank in Charlottesville, apparently out of fear that it would become a controversial party issue. The House of Delegates, however, had recently voted to increase the state's banking capital. The legislature's decision transformed the bank controversy into an issue of distribution – which locality would secure the new bank? After "a strong disposition was manifested in various quarters to locate a Bank in this county," the bank question soon became an issue "of considerable interest here." According to the letter, "almost every person applied to has signed the petition, [and] some have come forward voluntarily & offered both to sign & to get signatures." The petition that accompanied the letter contained more than 1,000 signatures.[47] Seven months later, Thomas R. Bailey reported that "I have been geting [sic] signaturs [sic] for a bank in this place, [and] I can say that there is not more than five or six persons that has refused to sine [sic] the petition for a bank in Charlottesville."[48]

With local support for a bank running high, the petitioners rejected Jeffersonian strictures on the evils of banking. Recognizing that "many

---

[46] Shade, *Democratizing the Old Dominion*, pp. 134–37.
[47] Letter from a Town Meeting of Charlottesville to Col. Samuel Carr, March 1, 1836, included with the Albemarle County Legislative Petitions.
[48] Letter from Thomas R. Bailey to "Dear Sir," December 29, 1836, included with the Albemarle County Legislative Petitions.

members of the Legislature of Virginia are opposed in principle to all Banks," the petitioners proceeded to lecture legislators on the benefits of banking.[49] A Charlottesville petition noted that some opposed banks for "affording too great facilities for going into debt." The petitioners answered that all commercial institutions had the same effect. Even stores and taverns offered "every imprudent man an opportunity of ruining himself, as fast as possible." "[N]o individual," the petitioners continued, "should be prevented from using his means and enterprise for the benefit of himself and the community, because of want of prudence or judgment he may be injured."[50] Such forthright defenses of banking and speculation, however, were rare. Petitioners usually eschewed economic didacticism for a more pragmatic approach, arguing that if banks were here to stay, then it made sense to have one in Albemarle. As an 1833 petition mentioned, "the Banking System seems too firmly fixed to afford any prospect of its abandonment."[51]

The national debates over banking helped petitioners strengthen their case. An 1834 petition noted that with the eminent demise of "that giant monopoly of monopolies, the Bank of the United States," more capital would have to come from Virginia's own banks. The only alternative would be having banks of other states furnish more capital for Virginians, a solution that the petitioners regarded as "the very greatest of evils."[52] Here the petitioners cleverly used fear of outside powers – the Bank of the United States, banks of other states – to justify a more liberal chartering policy on the part of the state legislature. To control their own commercial "independence" – another key republican concept – Virginians would need more banks.

But even if Albemarle residents succeeded in securing a bank, where would it be located, Charlottesville or Scottsville? Answering this question required Albemarle residents to craft their petitions in a republican rhetoric that cloaked their commercial ambition within traditional claims of benefiting the public good. The petitions were filled with reasons why a bank in Charlottesville or a bank in Scottsville would benefit the state as a whole: It would deflect trade away from Baltimore to Richmond; it would help strengthen the trade of western and eastern Virginia; and it would increase the business of various state works. Petitioners knew that a forthright appeal based on their own self-interest would surely fail. One Charlottesville petition went so far as to claim that if "it shall seem best for the public interest, and that the greatest good of the greatest number be served by the location of

[49] ACLP, 8 December 1832.
[50] ACLP, 8 December 1834.
[51] ACLP, 3 December 1833.
[52] ACLP, 8 December 1834.

the branch bank at *Scottsville*," then the legislature should establish it in that town.[53]

Republican claims for the public good, however necessary to write an acceptable petition, could never survive the rough and tumble of legislative politics. In a political environment of intense local competition, mild forms of self-interested corruption were likely to occur. In an 1832 letter to Thomas Jefferson Randolph, Peyton Harrison urged the Albemarle Democrat to continue his efforts to secure a Scottsville bank. Harrison warned that "If this last effort is not made I feel assured that there will be some dissatisfaction among your constituents, and you will have no votes to use."[54] Harrison's letter seems to have been part of a systematic lobbying campaign. A few months earlier the Scottsville merchant John Hartman had sent a list of petition signatures to Randolph, asking him to show them to the senator from neighboring Augusta county. "Our citizens expect every exertion of our representatives as it is a matter of very great interest to the county & the country around – however it is known that this will be done," Hartman wrote. "Mr. Harrison expects to hear from you as soon as you ascertain the probable destiny of the bill."[55] Neither Harrison nor Hartman was disinterested in the eventual outcome. According to tax lists, both men owned Scottsville real estate and mercantile concerns that would have profited from a bank.

The lobbying of Harrison and Hartman suggests that republican fears that banks would corrupt politics created a self-fulfilling prophecy: Efforts to limit banking charters created intense competition, which then led to the wheeling and dealing so distasteful to republican ideals. As demands for banks multiplied throughout Virginia, competition for banks and branch banks became increasingly fierce. Throughout the 1830s, the legislature slowly altered its restrictive policy, chartering one bank in 1834, one in 1837, and one in 1839, as well as authorizing a number of new branches. Although the legislature did not charter any new banks in the 1840s, it passed a free-banking law in 1851. As long as specified requirements were met, any group could form a bank without receiving special permission from the state legislature. In response to the free-banking law, the number of banks and their branches increased from 36 in 1850 to 70 in 1860, while banking capital rose from $9.6 million to $17.3 million.[56] By 1860, Virginians had more banks and banking capital per capita than

[53] ACLP, 11 February 1839.
[54] Peyton Harrison to Thomas Jefferson Randolph, February 25, 1832, Randolph Collection, UVA.
[55] John Hartman to Thomas Jefferson Randolph, January 7, 1837, Randolph Collection, UVA.
[56] Calculated from Wallis, Sylla, and Legler, "Interaction of Taxation and Regulation," p. 131.

more industrialized states such as Pennsylvania and Maryland. To fight political corruption and insure fairness, Virginians no longer limited bank charters, but made them more available.[57]

As for Albemarle's bank war, Charlottesville won the day long before the free-banking law was passed. In the 1837–1838 session, the legislature finally authorized the Farmers Bank of Virginia to locate a branch in Albemarle, with its exact location left to the bank's stockholders. Residents of both towns expressed unhappiness over the decision. According to one petition, the location of the bank had too much "*public* character" to be left to stockholders who "would scarcely have time to act with deliberation and care."[58] After reconsidering the issue in 1839, the legislature finally decided in favor of Charlottesville. The exact political maneuverings that led to Charlottesville's victory are unknown, but both of Albemarle's representatives to the House of Delegates, Thomas W. Gilmer and Valentine W. Southall, were Whigs with substantial investments in Charlottesville real estate.[59] The peculiar combination of self-interest and public spirit had once again allowed Charlottesville to secure a crucial commercial institution.

"Miserable Dependents of Bank Power"?
The CVRR and Cumberland Politics

"Let it be established, and the freedom of elections is gone," thundered Charles B. Penrose on the floor of the Pennsylvania state senate, "and we sir, instead of being representatives of the free people, must hold our seats as the miserable dependents of Bank power." Penrose's fiery 1834 oration demonstrated the ferocity of the Jacksonian onslaught against the Bank of the United States. The Cumberland lawyer and state senator attacked the Bank as a corrupter of democracy, a threat to republican institutions. He praised Jackson's heroic veto for exposing "the startling truth that we had fallen into vassalage to a power which ... would have crushed the political institutions of our country." He railed against "sordid avarice, inordinate luxury and unbounded wealth" that subtly destroyed the vigilance and backbone of good republicans. As for the prosperity that the bank supposedly

---

[57] Shade argues that a majority of Democrats "attacked the morality of banks, paper money, and soulless corporations." A number of "soft" Democrats, however, voted with the Whigs for the free banking law of 1851 that "permitted the general incorporation of banks of issue under state authority without the taint of special privilege that characterized earlier laws." *Democratizing the Old Dominion*, p. 187. See also Lamoreaux, *Insider Lending*, pp. 31–51 for attempts in New England to liberalize the region's bank chartering process.

[58] ACLP, 4 Feburary 1839.

[59] In 1840, Gilmer owned two lots collectively worth $4,000; Southall owned two lots collectively valued at $5,000. 1840 Albemarle County Real Property Tax Lists, microfilm, VSLA.

promoted, Penrose steadfastly vowed that he would rather taste the "black broth of Sparta" than submit to the Bank's despotism.[60]

A few years later Penrose was drinking a hearty serving of Sparta's black broth. Despite his seemingly implacable opposition to the Bank, Penrose became one of the first Democrats to support its 1836 state charter. Not only did Penrose vote for the bill, but he actively worked with Biddle's highly paid lobbyists to secure its passage. One of Biddle's lieutenants reported that "Mr. Penrose is now all confidence and in conjunction with Dr. Burden and Mr. Stevens is now engaged in arraigning [sic] every thing [sic] for to morrow [sic]."[61] Thanks largely to Penrose and four other "turncoat" senators, the Bank's new charter passed the Democratic-controlled senate. Penrose's actions gave prophetic irony to the prediction in his 1834 speech that bank lobbyists would corrupt "representatives of the free people" into becoming "miserable dependents of Bank power."[62]

The Cumberland Valley Railroad loomed as a central motivation behind Penrose's sudden conversion. As one of the initial directors of the CVRR, Penrose had substantial economic and personal ties to the road. The state charter of the Bank of the United States stipulated that Biddle invest $100,000 in the road, an amount he would later increase to $200,000. The bank's investment not only benefited Penrose personally, but it also aided his friends, family, and colleagues who composed Carlisle's legal elite. To clinch Penrose's support for the bill, Biddle even purchased a Harrisburg antibank newspaper that was sure to rake the Senator over the hot coals of Pennsylvania politics.[63]

Unfortunately for Penrose, Biddle's deep pockets could not silence opposition within Cumberland County. Penrose's vote for the Bank immediately generated angry cries of corruption from the antibank faction of Cumberland's Democratic Party. The protests were certainly not new. Many Cumberland Democrats had long distrusted Penrose's privileged economic background and his close connections with prominent Whigs. Born and raised in Philadelphia, Penrose studied law before moving to Carlisle. He soon became a prominent lawyer, in part because of his connections to the Biddle family. He married Valeria Fullerton Biddle, and entered into partnership with William M. Biddle, whose father was a first cousin of Nicholas.[64] These connections to Philadelphia financiers, as well as his own wealth, did not sit well with many Democrats. The *American Volunteer*, which served

---

[60] *Speech of Charles B. Penrose*, [delivered March 18 & 19, 1834], pp. 5, 15.
[61] Charles S. Baker to Nicholas Biddle, February 5, 1836, in McGrane, ed., *Correspondence of Nicholas Biddle*, p. 264.
[62] *Speech of Charles B. Penrose*, p. 28.
[63] Snyder, *Jacksonian Heritage*, p. 78.
[64] Wiley, *Biographical and Portrait Cyclopedia*, pp. 100–1.

as the mouthpiece of antibank Democrats, accused Penrose in 1833 of being "an office hunter," "a FEDERAL LAWYER," "an aristocrat at heart," and "a vacillating politician without any fixed principles."[65]

The charges of political vacillation would later prove true, but the *Volunteer's* heated attack also reflected a growing rift within Pennsylvania's Democratic Party. After dominating the state for eight years, Pennsylvania Democrats split between supporters of incumbent governor George Wolfe and challenger Henry A. Muhlenberg. The Democratic rift – based more on political patronage and personal rivalries than ideological principles – gave the election to Joseph Ritner, who ran as the joint candidate of the Antimasons and the Whigs.[66] Penrose was tied to the disgruntled Muhlenberg faction, which joined the Whigs and Antimasons to dominate the legislative session of 1835–1836. While the Muhlenberg faction continued to claim the mantel of Old Democracy, leaders such as Penrose had decidedly Whiggish leanings. Penrose would later make an outright conversion and became treasury solicitor for William Henry Harrison in 1841.

The bickering among Democrats gave Nicholas Biddle a golden opportunity to reorganize the Bank of the United States as a state institution, the Bank of the United States of Pennsylvania. With Ritner as governor and a Whig and Antimasonic majority in the House, Biddle needed five votes from antibank Democrats in the state senate for a new charter. Biddle's task was difficult, but the Philadelphia banker and his legislative assistants masterminded an effective strategy. Biddle realized that offering large investments in transportation corporations would put the Democrats in the political dilemma of voting against internal improvements. As legislator William B. Reed knew, funding for local projects was an almost irresistible inducement:

> Every one at all acquainted with matters and things here, particularly of late years since the Canal policy has been pursued, knows that the temptation of a turnpike, or a few miles of canal and rail road as a beginning on a favorite route is nearly irresistible, and I am strongly inclined to think that now a few of the many members who have toiled year after year for branches, and who look to this session as their last chance, could vote against legislation that would give them their extensions and entrench upon nothing but party prejudices and antipathies.[67]

Reed's assessment proved unerringly accurate. Other Democratic senators besides Penrose found the charter's $675,000 in appropriations to various railroads and turnpikes difficult to spurn. One Democratic

[65] *American Volunteer*, 3 October 1833, p. 3.
[66] Snyder, *Jacksonian Heritage*, pp. 50–67.
[67] William B. Reed to Nicholas Biddle, December 12, 1835 in McGraine, ed., *Correspondence of Nicholas Biddle*, pp. 258–59.

senator confided to a friend that "I must confess that I do not like the bill but ... I must go for the bill or loose [sic] my appropriations."[68]

Changing political realities also prompted Penrose to make a more optimistic assessment of the Bank. Earlier in the 1836 session, the Whigs and the Antimasons had managed to reapportion the Senate districts so that Penrose's old district, the solidly Democratic counties of Cumberland and Perry, would consist of Cumberland, Adams, and Franklin Counties. Franklin and Adams had strong Antimasonic and Whig sympathies that would offset Cumberland's traditionally strong Democratic vote. The reapportionment generated charges of corruption from chagrined Democrats, for it was a clear victory for the Whig and Antimasonic coalition.[69] It forced politicians such as Penrose to change political constituencies in order to win reelection in 1837, thereby precipitating a shift away from the Democrats.

For the antibank Democrats, of course, one form of corruption (legislative gerrymandering) was no excuse for a second form of corruption (passage of the new bank charter). Pennsylvania Democrats immediately called for an investigation of possible bribery regarding the charter. A legislative hearing found no evidence of overt bribery, but the taint of corruption never left the bill. As for Cumberland's Democrats, they took Penrose's probank vote as a serious abrogation of representative government. They saw the "bribery bill," as the bank's charter came to be known, as a clear example of how corporations could undermine republican institutions. Penrose's support of the bank generated public meetings and calls for his resignation. "Those who gave him the trust he has so shamefully and wantonly *abused*," declared the *American Volunteer*, "now demand it of him in a voice not to be misunderstood or disregarded."[70] Penrose's notoriety made him the pivotal figure in Cumberland politics in the 1837 elections. For enraged Democrats out for revenge, all other local races became inconsequential to the defeat of their turncoat senator.

The Panic of 1837, which struck just months before the elections, added another controversial tie between the banking system and the CVRR. The failure of several New York and Philadelphia banks led to the suspension of specie payments, prompting a great shortage of circulating medium throughout the country. The town council of Carlisle, following the lead of cities throughout the state, issued notes

[68] Quoted in Snyder, *Jacksonian Heritage*, p. 78. Biddle also included a cash bonus of $4.5 million to the state government, a sum large enough to allow the legislature to repeal Pennsylvania's state property tax. This gave reluctant legislators another politically popular reason to pass the charter.

[69] After the 1837 election, the editors of the *American Volunteer* noted that Penrose would have lost by a considerable margin if the district alignments had not changed. *American Volunteer*, 19 October 1837, p. 3.

[70] *American Volunteer*, 3 March 1836, p. 3.

of small denominations known as "shin plasters." The shin plasters operated as a medium of exchange during the crisis. The town council had no legal authority to take such action, but argued that "a still more imperious obligation rests upon us, to provide for the wants of those who have no other means to provide for themselves."[71] Significantly, Penrose's business associates dominated the town council. Council president Frederick Watts would become president of the CVRR, and four of the seven councilmen held stock in the railroad.

Economic circumstances forced the railroad to issue shin plasters of its own. On May 22, 1837, the Chief Engineer grimly reported that work had been "seriously retarded in consequence of want of funds."[72] With the railroad not yet complete, its funds exhausted, and no other sources of credit available during the Panic, the managers decided to issue shin plasters to pay contractors and suppliers. According to the company's minutes, the railroad issued almost $30,000 worth of shin plasters by July of 1837, promising to redeem the notes (with interest) as soon as possible. In the meantime, the company and its allies hoped that the shin plasters, which were issued in denominations as small as 25 cents, would circulate as cash. The *Carlisle Republican*, a strong supporter of Penrose and the railroad, announced that the railroad's notes "will be taken by us in payment of Groceries and Subscription."[73]

Support from the *Republican* notwithstanding, the railroad's issue of its own money seriously undermined public confidence in the enterprise. The road's contractors and their employees had to accept notes of questionable value for work already done. Given that the railroad had not yet opened, there was a real possibility that the notes would not be repaid. Even the railroad's engineer realized in May of 1837 that "[t]he Contractors are nearly all men of small capital, & however favorably disposed toward our company, they are, under the existing state of things, unable to maintain the confidence of workmen beyond a limited extent."[74] To buttress flagging public confidence, the Board of Managers (which included Penrose) pledged their personal fortunes as security for the shin plasters.[75] The personal endorsement of Carlisle's wealthiest men, widely announced in local papers, seemed to have restored confidence. The completion of the road allowed the company to begin redeeming the shin plasters from operating revenues, and within a few years most had been retired.

Before the railroad's notes had been repaid, however, the shin

---

[71] *American Volunteer*, 29 May 1837, p. 2.
[72] "Minute Book of the Board of Managers," Vol. I, MG-286, Box 69, PSA, pp. 161–62. Hereafter cited as "CVRR Minute Book."
[73] *Carlisle Republican*, 22 June 1837, p. 3.
[74] "CVRR Minute Book," p. 162.
[75] "CVRR Minute Book," pp. 169-70.

plaster issue provided antibank Democrats with explosive political ammunition. In August of 1837 a Democratic party meeting roundly condemned shin plasters as the work of "monied aristocrats and Bank monopolists." The resolutions endorsed at the meeting claimed that shin plasters smacked of political corruption. Neither the borough of Carlisle nor the Cumberland Valley Railroad possessed banking privileges, making "the issue of illegal paper money . . . [a]n open defiance of the laws of the commonwealth."[76] Perhaps more important than the legalities of the shin plasters was the frightening ability of banks and other corporations to manipulate the money supply. The resolutions echoed the fears of "Republican," who had written three years earlier that the power of banks was their ability to "make money plenty or scarce" and thus "make or break fortunes."[77] The note issue controversy added to the specter of outside capitalists controlling the local economy. The railroad not only owned the area's most important transportation artery, but it could also induce inflation or deflation at a whim through the issue of its own currency.

In the boisterous campaign in the fall of 1837, the Cumberland Valley Railroad was a potent symbol for Democrats worried about the connections between corporate power, economic centralization, and political corruption. The Democrats derisively labeled the pro-Penrose forces as the "shin plaster party" and the "railroad party," which suggests their eagerness to tap into popular hostility surrounding the CVRR. The Democrats clearly had little trouble tying Penrose to the CVRR's wealthy supporters. A year before the election – when Penrose had cast his ballot on behalf of the Bank of the United States – Penrose's supporters sponsored a large public dinner on behalf of the Senator. Almost all of the railroad's most important local investors attended the event. Thirty-six stockholders – representing a total investment of $19,600 in the enterprise – could be linked to the list of guests appearing at the dinner.[78] The pro-Penrose shareholders included Frederick Watts, the road's largest local investor, and seven other local investors who owned at least $1,000 worth of stock. All of these large investors were Cumberland lawyers, merchants, or manufacturers. No wonder that the American Volunteer claimed that most of Penrose's supporters were "BANK LAWYERS from Carlisle and Chambersburg, BUSH WHACKERS, RAIL-ROAD MANAGERS, CONTRACTORS, &c."[79]

The Democratic message was clear: Penrose and the CVRR would

[76] *American Volunteer*, 17 August 1837, p. 2.
[77] *American Volunteer*, 26 June 1834, p. 4.
[78] For the list of subscribers to the Penrose dinner, see "Republican Barracks Dinner," *Carlisle Republican*, 4 August 1836, p. 3.
[79] *American Volunteer*, 5 October 1837, p. 3.

corrupt politics in much the same way that Nicholas Biddle and the BUS had corrupted the 1835–1836 legislative session. The anti-Penrose forces openly raised the issue of "whether the Road itself is to be made tributary to the political designs of Mr. Penrose and one or two others?"[80] The *Volunteer* went so far as to claim that "Mr. Penrose has promised office on the Rail Road to about FIFTY persons in this Borough ... This will account for the zeal manifested by many for his election."[81] This specific charge was never substantiated, but there was still good reason to believe that Penrose would use the railroad to his own advantage. Newspaper accounts from both sides make clear that railroad meetings and celebrations before the 1837 election had pro-Penrose overtones. In many of these events Penrose himself would speak, bolstering the image that the CVRR was a tool for his reelection.

A striking feature of the debate over the Cumberland Valley Railroad, however, was the Democrats' acceptance of the railroad's economic promise. Like their political opponents, the Democrats celebrated the commercial advantages of the road. Less than two months before the election, the *Volunteer* noted the opening of the railroad's first division between Harrisburg and Carlisle, praising "the perseverance and industry of those entrusted with its management."[82] When the entire length of the railroad opened three months later (a month after the election), the *Volunteer* published a poem to honor the event. The poem's last stanza captures its decidedly boosterish spirit:

> Success to our State, she's the keystone complete,
>   All her mighty improvements we hail good —
> And above all the rest is the last and the best,
>   Success to the Cumberland Rail Road.[83]

Not surprisingly, Penrose used the railroad as his own campaign issue. His campaign biography exalted the Cumberland Valley Railroad as a tribute to his ability to promote "the prosperity of this section of the country."[84] Penrose was undoubtedly trying to capitalize on the close association between internal improvements and public service that developmental corporations had fostered. The shin plaster episode, ironically, gave him the means to do so. Whereas anti-bank Democrats saw the shin plasters as an example of corporate privilege, the Penrose supporters saw the managers' personal endorsement of the notes as a courageous and public-spirited act. In one of

[80] *American Volunteer*, 6 July 1837, p. 3.
[81] *American Volunteer*, 5 October 1837, p. 3.
[82] "Cumberland Valley Railroad," *American Volunteer*, 24 August 1837, p. 3.
[83] *American Volunteer*, 23 November 1837, p. 3.
[84] "Charles B. Penrose," *Carlisle Republican*, 5 October 1837, p. 3.

the railroad's first annual reports (published in Carlisle), the CVRR's chief engineer praised the managers for their "bold and liberal course" in having pledged "their individual fortunes in behalf of the improvement, & thus secured for the Company the funds and credit which enabled us to prosecute the work to a point so near completion."[85]

When Penrose took credit for the railroad, the Democrats fumed that "*Charley's* bump of modesty . . . is as BIG as a 'locomotive.'"[86] The difficult political quandary of the Democrats was typified by Colonel Charles McClure, Cumberland's delegate to the U. S. House of Representatives and an ardent Jacksonian.[87] Attending the celebration marking the opening of the road's first division, McClure was called upon to deliver a toast. Despite previous Democratic attacks on railroad meetings, McClure could only salute the road as "a connecting link of much public importance" and praise the managers for "the promptness with which the work has been undertaken and executed."[88] McClure's praise for the railroad, while more reserved than the other toasts, attests to the fact that the CVRR received support from all of Cumberland's political factions. Cumberland Democrats had to walk a fine line of praising the railroad while condemning the capitalists and lawyers responsible for its completion.

Democrats walked this fine line well, but not well enough to win. Penrose lost Cumberland County, but had sufficient majorities in Adams and Franklin Counties to win the closely contested race. Penrose managed to narrowly win Carlisle, but the Democrats did extremely well in the rural districts.[89] One should keep in mind that the family farmers in these areas – the political backbone of the Democrats – would be among the biggest beneficiaries of the CVRR. No wonder that even staunch Democrats drew a clear distinction between the railroad's pernicious ties with outside capitalists and its salutary effects on local development.

Markets and Politics in Jacksonian America

The attitude of Cumberland Democrats toward the CVRR is yet another piece of evidence suggesting the presence of a widespread consensus in favor of commercial expansion. A general consensus

[85] "CVRR Minute Book," p. 191.
[86] *American Volunteer*, 24 August 1837, p. 3.
[87] One toast to McClure at a Democratic party meeting praised his "devotion to the interests of the democratic party." *American Volunteer*, 6 July 1837, p. 3.
[88] "Cumberland Valley Railroad," *Carlisle Republican*, 31 August 1837, p. 3.
[89] The election results were published in the *American Volunteer*, 19 October 1837, p. 3. The race pitted four candidates – two Democrats, two Whigs/Antimasons – for two seats in the state senate. Penrose lost Cumberland county by 419 votes to the highest ranking Democrat, but managed to win the total vote by a margin of 261.

about the viability of market development, however, did not imply an absence of conflict about its particulars. The ensuing debates, couched in terms of republican rhetoric, showed that many residents in Cumberland and Albemarle genuinely feared that the corporation could easily become a vehicle for abuse. Juries in Albemarle prevented the Rivanna Navigation Company from minimizing compensation in eminent domain disputes; many Virginians, including Thomas Jefferson himself, feared the power that banks exerted over the economy; and Cumberland Democrats feared that Charles B. Penrose would abuse the CVRR for political gain. All of these disputes involved the intersection of economic and political power. Like many other Americans in the early nineteenth century, residents in Albemarle and Cumberland feared "the corruption of mixing public and private spheres."[90]

For those suspicious of the corporation, republicanism's vivid descriptions of corruption and tyranny provided the perfect language for attacking abuses of corporate power. Those using a republican vocabulary, however, selectively criticized specific misdeeds. In neither Albemarle nor Cumberland did politicians, petitioners, or editorialists offer a general condemnation of economic change. Attention instead focused on particular issues: eminent domain, shin plasters, legislative bribery. The very specificity of political debate limited the scope of the republican critique of the corporation. Key republican concepts such as virtue, corruption, and the public good were freely available to all, including the corporations themselves. The association between developmental corporations and public service, in fact, often put companies in an excellent position to claim that they represented the "true" public good. If such claims were not always persuasive – witness the trials and tribulations of the Rivanna Navigation Company – they still spoke to the elastic nature of the republican vocabulary.

Perhaps a more precise way of summarizing the political debates was that for all the misgivings about the corporation, nobody seriously questioned the desirability of commercial progress. A new bank or a new railroad, boosters firmly believed, would help all residents regardless of their circumstances. Here was a sharp contrast to many eighteenth-century versions of republicanism, which associated commercialization with the erosion of virtue and the spread of self-destructive individualism. Residents in Albemarle and Cumberland, to be sure, knew that the instrument of progress – the corporation – opened up new possibilities for political corruption. They optimistically believed, however, that selective reform and unceasing vigilance would offer the best of both worlds: the commercial expansion that they so eagerly sought without the political corruption they so desperately feared.

---

[90] Hartog, *Public Property*, p. 146.

5

Urban Capital and the Superiority of Pennsylvania's Transportation Network

Some time in the 1850s John Hartwell Cocke, the James River planter who had worked so hard to improve Virginia's transportation network, sat down to scribble a few "Notes on Starting a Great Commercial City." Cocke sought to demonstrate that a "point of land forming the northern bank of [the] James River at its entrance into Hampton Roads" could become the site of a grand metropolis that would dominate the trade of America's Atlantic coast. He predicted that with a little courage and enterprise "[a] city will spring up at the mouth of [the] James River – which for rapidity of growth & accumulation of wealth will ecliyspe [sic] the famed History of St. Louis and Chicago." Even by the rather generous standards of nineteenth-century American boosterism, Cocke's effort to show how Virginians could build a port that would quickly surpass New York and Philadelphia bordered on the ridiculous. The location for his great commercial city, he freely admitted, was nothing more than "a barren promontory without a house." All of the city's infrastructure would have to be built from scratch, along with several rail and canal connections that would link it to the Ohio Valley. Nor did Cocke have a clear idea of how Virginians could finance such a venture other than to assert vaguely that "we are likely to engage foreign capital."[1] No wonder that Cocke's notes remained safely tucked away in his papers, never to see widespread circulation.

For all of the plan's obvious holes and unanswered questions, Cocke had stumbled upon the central problem thwarting antebellum Virginia's drive for commercial independence and economic diversification. Sounding something like a modern economic geographer, the Virginia planter argued that thriving cities generated wealth and opportunity for a vast hinterland. Build a great commercial city, he declared, and "what N.Y. has done for her adjacent county will spring into existence here in like effects from like causes especially as we have a more genial clime & better Soil." Cocke's emphasis on a metropolitan

---

[1] John Hartwell Cocke, "Notes on Starting a Commercial City," Cocke Papers, Box 142, UVA, p. 7. Hereafter cited as "Notes."

"central place" had a political element as well. The Virginia planter had correctly surmised that the Old Dominion's urban landscape – a collection of small cities vigorously competing for commerce and trade – had undermined Virginia's program of state investment. First-hand experience with legislative battles over location and funding of internal improvements prompted Cocke to write that foreign investors should finance his great commercial city because they were "free from all local bias in the all important question of the site." Once the city was started, Cocke maintained that it would eliminate the local rivalry and centralize Virginia's population and transportation network, thereby helping the Old Dominion achieve commercial supremacy over her northern rivals. "[T]he whole policy of Virginia has been hitherto adverse to concentrating her population in Cities, but there are new Changes – a crisis in her history – [that] makes building up a great commercial city an indispensable requisite to her future prosperity as well as that of the southern section of the Union."[2]

Cocke's analysis identified a complex relationship between urbanization, government policy, and commercial infrastructure in antebellum America. Somewhat surprisingly, historians and social scientists have been slow to investigate these relationships. Determined to undermine the myth that Americans have always promoted laissez-faire capitalism, historians, economists, and political scientists have documented how states, counties, and municipalities spent many millions of dollars to build turnpikes, improve rivers, dig canals, and construct railroads before the Civil War.[3] The ideological motivation underlying most of this scholarship was obvious. As legal scholar Morton Horwitz has noted, the net effect of these studies was to provide the New Deal with "its own historical pedigree."[4] Despite its obvious success in documenting widespread government investment, the literature's single-minded focus on attitudes and ideology has left relatively unexplored the question of how basic economic factors – slavery, urbanization, industrialization – influenced state economic policy. Since most scholars have assumed that state policies were part of a "constructive liberalism" that pragmatically solved problems that private enterprise could not, they have sometimes overlooked how social and demographic characteristics influenced the success of state policies.[5]

[2] Cocke, "Notes," p. 7.
[3] Classic works in the "Commonwealth Tradition" include Handlin and Handlin, *Commonwealth*, and Hartz, *Economic Policy and Democratic Thought*. For a general overview of this literature, see Scheiber, "Government and the Economy," pp. 135–51.
[4] Horwitz, *Transformation of American Law*, p. xiii.
[5] The phrase "constructive liberalism" is taken from Heath's study of economic policy in antebellum Georgia, *Constructive Liberalism*.

The comparison between Pennsylvania and Virginia reveals that John Hartwell Cocke was near the mark when he argued small cities and local interests had short-circuited Virginia's commercial policy. In Pennsylvania, the political and economic power of Philadelphia and Pittsburgh led to the completion of the Mainline Canal between the two cities. Although the Mainline was a pronounced failure, it at least expanded the hinterlands of Philadelphia and Pittsburgh, helping these cities acquire the population and trade to build a trunk railroad line without state aid. In Virginia, however, competing localities consistently diluted state funding, preventing the completion of the James River and Kanawha Canal and several later railroad projects. The political infighting among the small, evenly-matched Virginia cities delayed legislative funding for key routes, led to wasteful duplication of effort, and promoted the use of inefficient technologies. As the Civil War approached, Virginians found themselves stuck on an economic treadmill: The failure to complete important projects slowed the growth of Virginia's cities, exacerbating the lack of a central place, and further diluting state investment. The irony of Cocke's call for a "Great Commercial City" was rich. Far from providing a blueprint for the Old Dominion's commercial rejuvenation, Cocke had uncovered the dynamic relationship between urban growth and transportation networks that would ultimately foil Virginia's hopes for economic diversification and commercial independence.

The failure of Virginia's transportation network, it should be emphasized, was not the result of lagging interest in economic modernization. The statewide evidence suggests canals and railroads provoked the same enthusiasm throughout Virginia as they had in Albemarle County. Beginning with a network that amounted to less than 500 miles, Virginians almost quadrupled their railroad network in the 1850s, adding just under 1,300 miles. Pennsylvania – a state with a far larger population and huge reserves of iron and coal – added only 1,600 miles during the decade, putting the Old Dominion well ahead of the Keystone state in terms of mileage per person.[6]

Yet despite these impressive accomplishments, many Virginians considered their railroad network a failure when compared to northern counterparts. Most conspicuous was the lack of a central trunk road to the West that could add system and structure to the Old Dominion's rail network. Charles Bruce, a state senator, fumed that the Old Dominion's motley collection of local lines "have built up no town, and hardly a single village" because it lacked connections to the

---

[6] These figures calculated from Baer, *Canals and Railroads*, table "Cumulative Railroad Mileage 1826–62." In 1860, Pennsylvanians had built slightly less than one mile of track per thousand residents; Virginians had built 1.43 miles of track per thousand residents.

West. Tidewater planter and politician Joseph Segar noted that New
York alone had built three great trunk railroads while "sectional jeal-
ousies, and local feuds, wrangling among ourselves about this road
and that" had prevented Virginians from building a single trunk line.[7]
M. F. Maury noted with similar disdain that Virginia did not have "a
single railway or canal in operation" that connected the coast to the
western interior. The consequence of Virginia's incomplete transportation network, Maury wrote, was nothing less than the loss of "the
business of an empire."[8] Bruce, Segar, and Maury would have agreed
with historian Ulrich B. Phillips's stern pronouncement that "the
building of railroads [in the South] led to little else but the extension
and the intensifying of the plantation system and the increase of the
staple output."[9] Phillips's assessment was exaggerated, yet his larger
point was essentially correct. Local railroads, no matter how boisterous and enthusiastic their supporters, did not have the same impact as
trunk lines emanating from major urban centers.

Urban Interests and the Pennsylvania Canal System

In the early nineteenth century, many Philadelphia residents felt the
same anxiety that Virginians would later experience. Long thought
of as the commercial capital of the nation, Philadelphia had already
lost its mercantile preeminence to New York City and was steadily
losing ground to nearby Baltimore. The completion of New York's
Erie Canal deepened the sense of decline. With a single bold stroke,
the Erie left New York's rivals flatfooted in the race for the growing
trade of the Midwest. Fearing permanent commercial stagnation, in
1825 Philadelphia's mercantile and manufacturing elite called for
their own improvement that would capture the western trade and
revive their city's falling fortunes.[10] After a year and a half of debate,
Philadelphia's civic leaders devised a state-run system of canals and
railroads that would connect the City of Brotherly Love with Pittsburgh
and the Ohio River. Pennsylvania's Mainline System would have the
dubious honor of being one of the costliest failures of the antebellum
period. Yet Pennsylvania's ability to respond quickly to the challenge
of the Erie Canal showed how large urban areas could concentrate the
state's financial resources on the completion of a central line.

The geographic barriers to completing an east – west canal were
daunting. Whereas the Erie Canal was built on the gently rolling

---

[7] Segar, "Speech of Joseph Segar," p. 22.
[8] "Virginia," *American Railroad Journal* 10 (18 November 1854), pp. 725–26.
[9] Phillips, *History of Transportation*, p. 20.
[10] Philadelphia's reaction to the Erie Canal is described in Rubin, *Canal or Railroad*, pp.
15–62. See also Rubin, "An Imitative Public Improvement," pp. 67–70.

landscape of the Mohawk Valley, a Pennsylvania canal would have to surmount the Allegheny Mountains with an elevation of more than 2,200 feet. The ominous mountain barrier, most Pennsylvanians realized, would make any improvement too costly and too risky for any private venture. Philadelphia politician John Sergeant spoke for many when he argued that private corporations "would make the parts of the line that were least expensive, and at the same time would be most productive of toll, while difficult parts would be left undone, and thus the main object would be frustrated."[11] Instead of counting on private enterprise or a state-subsidized corporation, supporters of the Mainline advocated a state-run public works program.

Convincing Pennsylvania voters and the state government to plan, build, and operate such a large public work would not be easy. While supporters of the Mainline could count on the support of Philadelphia and Pittsburgh, many of the state's most populous rural counties already had excellent connections with either Philadelphia or Baltimore. They had little desire to contribute their tax dollars to a project that principally benefited urban merchants and manufacturers. Overcoming "the great power of anti-mainline sentiment" would require considerable political skill.[12]

A small group of Philadelphia lawyers, politicians, and businessmen provided the influence and know-how to pass the needed legislation. In October of 1824, the well-known publicist Mathew Carey issued a broadside to announce the formation of the Pennsylvania Society for the Promotion of Internal Improvements in the Commonwealth. Forty-eight of Philadelphia's most important civic leaders, including the likes of Nicholas Biddle, Charles J. Ingersoll, and William Duane, paid an initiation fee of $100 to join the organization. The Society's official purpose was to "educate" the public through the dissemination of detailed, technical information, but the organization was also a well-oiled lobbying machine that acted with "the passion of a religious campaign."[13] The Society flooded newspapers with editorials, deluged the legislature with memorials and petitions, and organized a well-publicized internal improvements convention in Harrisburg.[14]

The success of the Pennsylvania Society was remarkable. The legislature made the first appropriation for the Mainline System in the spring of 1826, a mere 18 months after the Society was formed. Remarking on the importance of the Pennsylvania Society, historian Julius Rubin concludes that the Mainline movement was "led by a

---

[11] Quoted in Hartz, *Economic Policy*, p. 139.
[12] Rubin, *Canal or Railroad*, p. 50.
[13] Hartz, *Economic Policy*, p. 131.
[14] Rubin, *Canal or Railroad*, pp. 19–20; Rubin, "An Imitative Public Improvement," pp. 70–71; Hartz, *Economic Policy*, pp. 131–33.

centralized group of relatively wealthy men with unequaled access to the best technical data available, a group obviously able to give the movement direction and focus."[15]

The legislative victory, however, was far from complete. Despite the Pennsylvania Society's extensive campaign, opposition from the eastern rural counties with canals and turnpikes of their own remained difficult to overcome. Given that in 1825 the Philadelphia and Pittsburgh delegations constituted only 19 percent of Pennsylvania's legislature, Mainline supporters had to make alliances to overcome the project's political opposition.[16] Allies did not come cheaply. Rural areas in the more remote central and western portions of the state would support the Mainline, but only if the state built canals in their own locality. The most politically expedient solution was a log-rolling arrangement that provided for the simultaneous construction of both the Mainline and branch canals. Leaders of the Mainline movement knew the branch canals slowed construction of the east–west improvement and endangered the state's credit, but they had little choice in the matter. The policy of constructing branch lines, as Carey remarked in 1827, was "the only one that afforded a reasonable prospect of success ... Any other system would be as impolitic as unjust."[17]

The strategy of logrolling got the Mainline built, but it led to a huge increase in state spending on projects of dubious value. Before the start of the Mainline, the Pennsylvania state government had invested $2 million in transportation improvements through the purchase of shares in turnpike and bridge corporations. The "mixed enterprise" policy continued into the 1830s, but spending on the state-owned canals soon dwarfed expenditures on roads and bridges. The Commonwealth spent almost $39 million on canals (Table 5.1). Branch lines accounted for about 55 percent of that total. Many Pennsylvanians looked upon the branch canals as wasteful projects, but their popularity in rural districts made them politically sacred, especially if Philadelphia and Pittsburgh wanted a completed east–west canal. Pennsylvania's canal expenditures show both the political strengths and weaknesses of the state's urban interests: They managed to push for rapid funding of the Mainline, but had to make significant logrolling compromises to do so.

Legislative opposition forced the advocates of the Mainline to make several technological compromises as well. Since the Mainline was an "imitative" enterprise attempting to replicate the success of the Erie Canal, its advocates initially envisioned an all-water route. Given the difficulties of building a canal across the mountains, some

[15] Rubin, *Canal or Railroad*, p. 20.
[16] Klein, *Pennsylvania Politics*, pp. 412–13.
[17] Quoted in Rubin, "An Imitative Public Improvement," p. 99.

Table 5.1. *The Magnitude of State Investment
in Antebellum Pennsylvania and Virginia*

Type of Improvement	Total State Investment by 1860 (in millions of $)	Per Capita State Investment, 1860 (in $)
Pennsylvania		
Canals	38.7	13.3
Railroads	0.6	0.2
Turnpikes and Bridges	2.3	0.8
Total	41.6	14.4
Virginia		
Canals	13.5	11.6
Railroads	21	18
Turnpikes and Toll Bridges	5.4	4.6
Total	39.9	34.2

Notes and Sources: Pennsylvania's state investment is calculated from Hartz,
pp. 82–87; Poor, pp. 559–60; Goodrich, *Promotion*, pp. 65–68; and Ransom,
p. 375. Expenditures for Mainline railroads included under canals.
Virginia's state investment is calculated from *Annual Report of Rail-Road
Companies* (1860), p. 605; Goodrich, *Promotion*, pp. 94–96; and Goodrich,
"Virginia System of Mixed Enterprise," p. 368.

supporters of the Mainline urged that a railroad should be built
instead. In the ensuing debate, the rival railroad and canal supporters
reached a compromise in which three sections of the system would be
canal and two would be rail. The hybrid system pleased nobody,
reflecting once again the institutional weakness of state legislative
funding. Because the Mainline's supporters needed to overcome significant opposition in the legislature, they perceived the need to act
quickly while the political irons were hot. Any delays to better study
the relative merits of railroads and canals meant potential political disaster. According to one Philadelphian writing in 1825, "if at this
moment we permit our attention, or the public opinion, to be dis-
tracted to railroads, or any other supposed improvements, we shall fail
in both plans." [18]

Finished in 1834, the Mainline system was an economic flop. The
long chain of transshipment points made service slow, expensive, and

---

[18] Quoted in Rubin, *Canal or Railroad*, p. 50. Philadelphians also sought to complete the
east–west system before the Erie Canal had permanently captured the western trade.
This economic factor undoubtedly contributed to the hasty engineering decision to
combine canal and railroad technology.

undependable, prompting one Philadelphian to describe the Mainline as "an amphibious connection of land and water, consisting of
two railways separated by a canal, and of two canals separated by
a railway – happily elucidating the defects peculiar to both methods
of transit, with the advantages of neither."[19] Transportation costs
between Pittsburgh and Philadelphia remained prohibitively expensive for shippers of agricultural goods and other bulky commodities,
severely limiting the ability of the Mainline to compete with the Erie
Canal for western trade. At its high point in 1845, the through trade
on the Mainline amounted to just under 84,000 tons, a fraction of
what was shipped annually along the Erie. Even worse, the Mainline's
high cost made the state less willing to charter a rival railroad across
the mountains. A rival railroad, some Pennsylvanians surmised, would
cut into the already slim operating revenues of the canal, leaving the
state without means of paying its huge debt. Rather than provide an
answer to the Erie Canal, the Mainline would delay for years the construction of a truly competitive western connection.[20]

   Pennsylvania's canal system at least had a silver lining within its dark
clouds of failure. While the Mainline proved ineffective as a competitor for the Trans-Appalachian trade, it contributed to a more limited
expansion of Philadelphia's western hinterland, which in turn helped
fuel the city's industrial growth. Falling transportation costs between
Philadelphia and central Pennsylvania increased the ability of farm
families to sell more surpluses, thereby increasing incomes and
enlarging the market for manufactured goods.[21] The Mainline had a
similar impact on Pittsburgh. The canal dramatically lowered the
price of shipping iron from Pittsburgh to Philadelphia, eventually
becoming "a virtual life saver" for the Pittsburgh iron industry.[22] It also
increased the availability of resources for the city's iron manufacturers, allowing Pittsburgh manufacturers to import raw iron and coal
from the surrounding countryside.[23] The Mainline's boost to urban
manufacturers in Pittsburgh and Philadelphia did not necessarily
make the canal beneficial to the state as a whole. Economic historian
Roger Ransom's calculations on the system's external savings suggest
that the Mainline's reduction of transportation costs did not justify the
system's high price tag.[24] The Mainline, in essence, subsidized Philadelphia and Pittsburgh interests at the expense of the entire state.

---

[19] Quoted in Rubin, "An Imitative Public Improvement," p. 110.
[20] Rubin, *Canal or Railroad*, pp. 16–17.
[21] Lindstrom, *Economic Development*, pp. 1–18, 112–19.
[22] Reiser, *Pittsburgh's Commercial Development*, p. 106. See also Rubin, *Canal or Railroad*,
     p. 1.
[23] Rubin, *Canal or Railroad*, p. 16.
[24] See Ransom, "Canals and Development," pp. 365–89.

The Transition from State to Urban Investment in Pennsylvania

The financial failures of Pennsylvania's canals created a series of financial emergencies that pushed Pennsylvania perilously close to bankruptcy. The Mainline's revenues were never enough to repay the interest on the loans that financed the improvement.[25] The costly lateral canals that became part of the Mainline's political package further undermined the state's shaky financial situation, as these projects rarely covered their operating and repair expenses. Pennsylvania's spending policy depended upon a fresh infusion of loans and credit, which became increasingly difficult to find in the aftermath of the Panic of 1837. Faced with a rapidly mounting debt, in 1842 the state government suspended payments to the state's creditors while halting construction on works in progress.[26]

Although the state would not give up on its canal system for another 15 years, the financial woes of the Pennsylvania government led to a general retrenchment of state expenditures that left most new transportation projects to local governments and private investors. State investment resumed in 1846 and continued until 1858, with the legislature spending $6 million to finish some of the branch canals and repair the Mainline. Amounting to only $500,000 per year, these expenditures never approached the size of the large appropriations of the 1830s and early 1840s. The state also dramatically curtailed investment in turnpike, bridge, and railroad corporations, deciding to auction off its shares in these enterprises in 1843. State investment in Pennsylvania's railroad network was therefore relatively unimportant. As Table 5.1 shows, it never exceeded $700,000, a minuscule amount given that the capital stock of Pennsylvania's railroad network in 1860 was more than $82 million.[27]

In the absence of significant state investment, local governments – particularly those of Philadelphia and Pittsburgh – picked up the slack. Pennsylvania localities invested a total of $18 million in railroad companies, with the Philadelphia and Pittsburgh areas accounting for more than 85 percent of all local investment. The rest of local expenditures were spread out over a number of towns and counties attempting to build branch roads or local feeders.[28] That Philadelphia and Pittsburgh dominated municipal investment is not at all surprising. In 1850, Philadelphia and Allegheny Counties accounted for 25 percent

---

[25] Calculated from Poor, *History of the Railroads and Canals*, p. 559.
[26] Pennsylvania's financial woes are chronicled in Grinath, Wallis, and Sylla, "Debt, Default, and Revenue Structure," p. 8.
[27] Hartz, *Economic Policy*, p. 87; Poor, *History of the Railroads and Canals*, p. 423.
[28] Goodrich, *Government Promotion*, p. 71.

of Pennsylvania's total population and more than 75 percent of the state's manufacturing output. Each city, disappointed with the canal system's inability to capture western trade, had wealthy and influential residents eager to invest in railroads that would extend markets for their new mills, foundries, and factories. The population and wealth of Philadelphia and Pittsburgh also created large tax bases that allowed the two cities (at least in theory) to pay back municipal debts necessary to fund large railroad investments.[29] Philadelphia had the additional advantage of serving as the state's banking headquarters, giving the city government easier access to capital markets and financial expertise. By the late 1840s Philadelphia and Pittsburgh no longer needed the rest of the state to finance a central trunk line.

Historians have often thought of urban expenditures as just another form of government investment, but the advantages of municipal investment over state investment were pronounced.[30] Although Pennsylvania municipalities made their fair share of mistakes in railroad investments, at least local governments did not have to bargain with remote rural areas, thereby dispensing with the costly logrolling associated with the fractious state legislature. Even the choice of a project's exact route was easier, as more attention could be paid to economic factors rather than satisfying political allies in the state legislature.

The rapid and profitable expansion of the Pennsylvania Railroad reflected the advantages of urban investment. The PRR, chartered in 1846, received more than a third of all local investment when Philadelphia county purchased $5 million worth of shares and Allegheny county invested another $1 million. Completed in 1853 from Harrisburg to Pittsburgh, the Pennsylvania Railroad was the key link of an all-rail route from Philadelphia to the Ohio River. Without the decisive investments from Pittsburgh and Philadelphia, the PRR would probably not have begun construction in 1853, much less finished its mainline.[31]

Philadelphia's residents also provided large infusions of private capital that supplemented (and then transcended) investment from municipal governments. Before municipal governments invested in the Pennsylvania Railroad, thousands of urban investors provided the initial "seed" capital of nearly one million dollars in the summer of 1847. To raise this capital, the backers of the PRR stressed the large benefits of a trunk line that would accrue to all Philadelphians. These indirect benefits initially gave the PRR a vague resemblance to the earlier developmental corporations. The company's first annual report

---

[29] Philadelphia accounted for 15 percent of all assessed real and personal property in 1815; by 1845 that figure had risen to 28 percent. Lindstrom, *Economic Development*, p. 29.

[30] See, for example, Goodrich, *Government Promotion*, which often groups state investment and municipal investment as "government enterprise" without distinguishing the different characteristics of each.

[31] Ward, *J. Edgar Thompson*, p. 75.

told how the road's promoters managed to raise this capital through arm-twisting methods that would have been quite familiar to residents of Albemarle, Cumberland, and other rural localities: "The subscription of the stock was considered by many as a patriotic endeavor to retain and extend a trade which legitimately belonged to this city ... The books at that time were carried from house to house by the active friends of the road, who solicited even single shares."[32]

The importance of these indirect benefits, however, did not rule out the opportunity for direct returns. Of the first 1,000 investors in the railroad, 74 held at least 50 shares (representing an investment of at least $2,500). These investors collectively provided more than $350,000 in capital for the enterprise. The combination of direct and indirect returns that motivated such investment was noted in the company's second annual report: "Although a subscription to this work has been earnestly impressed upon the businessmen of the community, as a means of saving and extending their trade, it may, with equal propriety be presented to the capitalists as a sure and profitable investment."[33]

Basing their investment strategies on the same mix of direct profits and indirect benefits, urban capitalists extended their hold on the Pennsylvania railroad network. One way of measuring the increasing influence of urban capital in the Keystone state is by determining the location of the road's directors. The logic here is simple: If a majority of a railroad's directors lived in Philadelphia, then it would be a good bet that a significant portion of the railroad's financing came from the Quaker City. It would be hard to imagine local investors financing a railroad and then turning over control to urban outsiders. Companies in which the majority of directors resided in Philadelphia accounted for more than two-thirds of the state's railroad capital, with New York City a distant second (Table 5.2). While some of the investment in Philadelphia and New York City companies might very well have come from local sources, urban capitalists nevertheless controlled most of Pennsylvania's railroad network.

Urban capitalists encouraged the integration of Pennsylvania's railroad network. They began the long process of what Alfred D. Chandler has called "system-building" in which a single corporation controlled a vast network of roads and connections.[34] The PRR, under the aggressive leadership of J. Edgar Thompson, was particularly relentless in securing connections and unifying control. When

---

[32] *First Annual Report of the Directors of the Pennsylvania Rail-Road Company* (Philadelphia 1847), p 9.

[33] *Second Annual Report of the Directors of the Pennsylvania Rail-Road Company.* (Philadelphia 1848), pp. 10–11.

[34] Chandler, *The Visible Hand*, pp. 145–87. As Chandler makes clear, system-building was not completed until the early twentieth century.

Table 5.2. *The Importance of Philadelphia Capital:*
The Residence of Railroad Directors, 1859

Residence of Majority of Board Members	Number of Companies	Total Capitalization (millions of $)	Average Capitalization (millions of $)
Philadelphia	26	55.7	2.1
New York City	3	11.2	3.7
Pittsburgh	5	10.9	2.7
Local	12	4.7	.4

Notes and Sources: Capitalization refers to value of stock actually purchased. In a few cases, Poor did not list the residences of directors but included either the company headquarters or the residence of a railroad's president, which was used to classify the roads. Data taken from Poor, *History*, pp. 424–518.

chartered in 1846, the Pennsylvania Railroad was designed to connect Philadelphia to Pittsburgh, but two holdovers from the Mainline system – a railroad from Philadelphia to Columbia, and a system of inclined planes over the most difficult section of the Appalachians – remained in hands of the state government. Even before the railroad was finished, the company wanted to eliminate these state-owned segments, arguing that the costly interchange at the inclined plane impeded a cost-effective through route to the West. The company also distrusted political control of crucial links. The trade of the West, the company's 1850 annual report argued, would never be secured "while any link, however small, shall remain under the ever-varying management incident to the incessant changes of State and local politics."[35]

The railroad built its own link around the inefficient inclined planes, and eventually purchased the entire Mainline system from the state government in 1857. The sale, pegged at a price of $10 million, demonstrated the political influence of the railroad and its Philadelphia backers. One opponent of the sale declared that the bill authorizing the purchase "was engineered through by the paid borers of the Pennsylvania Railroad Company, who infested the legislative halls, to tell the representatives of the people that they demand the sale of the public works."[36] The claim was probably true, but the point remains that the political power of the Pennsylvania Railroad, no matter how insidious it appeared to anticorporate critics, resulted in a more efficient and reliable trunk line between Philadelphia and Pittsburgh.

---

[35] *Fourth Annual Report of the Directors of the Pennsylvania Rail-Road Company* (Philadelphia 1851), p. 11.
[36] Quoted in Hartz, *Economic Policy*, pp. 164–65.

The same political and financial clout helped standardize railroad gauges within the state.[37] A recurrent problem with railroad integration was differing track widths, which prevented the easy interchange of cars and often resulted in lengthy delays. In 1852 the Pennsylvania legislature mandated that all railroad gauges in the state conform to the standard of 4 feet 8 ½ inches. The law, as more than one commentator noted, was clearly designed to limit competition from New York's Erie Railroad, which had a five-foot gauge. If the Pennsylvania law demonstrated its unwillingness to integrate all northeastern railroads into a network, it nevertheless implicitly endorsed the declaration of the Philadelphia-based *North American* that Pennsylvania "should be ramified by railroads uniting in Philadelphia as the human body is coursed by arteries centering on the heart."[38] As the Civil War approached, complete railroad integration in the Northeast was still many years away, but at least the Pennsylvania Railroad had made considerable progress.

The benefits of the PRR for Philadelphia were pronounced. The Midwest was now within easy reach of Pennsylvania's manufacturers and merchants. In 1849, it took freight nine weeks to pass from Philadelphia to Chicago; in 1859, the same journey took only three days.[39] During the mid-1850s, the tonnage of manufactured goods moving between the two cities almost doubled.[40] Although New York City exerted increasing influence over the nation's international trade and domestic marketing network, Philadelphia's direct link to the Midwest, as we shall see in the next chapter, solidified the city's importance as a manufacturing center. The Pennsylvania Railroad aptly demonstrated the interactive nature of urban growth and transportation improvements: The initial concentration of population and wealth in Philadelphia was essential for the creation of the trunk railroad, which created larger markets to further increase urban population and wealth.

Despite the stunning success of the PRR, Pennsylvania voters rejected both state *and* municipal investment. In 1857, the legislature passed amendments to the state constitution barring all investment by state and municipal authorities. Popular support was overwhelming – the amendments passed by a landslide vote of 122,658 to 13,653.[41] Why the abrupt about-face? The industrial growth of Philadelphia

---

[37] The difficulty in standardizing gauges in America is discussed in Dunlavy, *Politics and Industrialization*, pp. 197–99. According to Taylor, "Between Philadelphia and Charleston there were at least eight changes in width of track." Taylor, *Transportation Revolution*, p. 82.
[38] "Pennsylvania," *American Railroad Journal* 8 (13 March 1852), p. 161.
[39] Chandler, *The Visible Hand*, p. 122.
[40] Pred, *Urban Growth*, p. 92.
[41] Hartz, *Economic Policy*, pp. 105–22.

made municipal investment unnecessary; by the late 1850s, private financial markets could handle most railroad projects without recourse to municipal investment. Moreover, many municipal-backed projects such as the Pittsburgh and Connellsville Railroad teetered on the edge of bankruptcy, forcing city and county governments to absorb considerable losses.[42] Property owners feared that they would shoulder the financial burden through higher property taxes if these financial failures proliferated. The last vestiges of government investment had disappeared.

The Failure of Virginia's James River and Kanawha Canal

Just as the Mainline Canal shaped most of Pennsylvania's canal policy, the James River and Kanawha Canal was the centerpiece of Virginia's early internal improvement efforts. Over the first half of the nineteenth century, the James River project accounted for most of the $13.5 million the state spent to improve its canals and rivers during the antebellum period. Although the project was organized as a "mixed-enterprise" corporation with both private and public investment, the vast majority of funding came from state and municipal governments. Virginia's canal expenditures never rivaled those of Pennsylvania, but the Old Dominion's investment was nevertheless significant, especially when considered in per-capita terms. The Virginia state government spent more than $9 for every resident on the James River and Kanawha Canal and $11.6 for all of the state's artificial waterways during the antebellum period (Table 5. 1). Virginians, it would seem, had few qualms about state investment even in the early stages of the transportation revolution.

Yet despite the considerable resources the Old Dominion put into its canals, the state never got much for its money. If the Mainline System was a disappointing failure, the various James River projects were utter disasters. While many Pennsylvanians complained of the Mainline's slow progress, it was lightning quick compared to the James River and Kanawha Company, which was still more than 120 miles away from the Ohio River as the Civil War approached. Nor did the financial performance of the completed sections of the canal match the low standards of the Pennsylvanian improvement. Throughout the 1850s, the company's net revenue fell about $500,000 short of its interest payments, prompting the Virginia state government to guarantee the company's loans.[43] In 1860, the state simply forgave

---

[42] Poor, *History of the Railroads and Canals*, pp. 490–91.
[43] Goodrich, *Government Promotion*, p. 95.

the loans, converting them into stock with a par value of more than $7 million and a market value of close to nothing.[44]

Geography had much to do with the failure of the James River and Kanawha Company. The formidable mountain barrier of the Appalachians almost guaranteed that an ambitious canal along the James and Kanawha Rivers would never effectively compete for western trade. Virginians supporting the James River and Kanawha Canal constantly referred to the tremendous success of the Erie Canal. "The great canal of New York has not only given a most powerful impetus to the commerce and agriculture of that state," a resolution from an 1828 internal improvement convention declared, "but has attracted to its metropolis a large portion of the commerce of the West."[45] Virginians who compared the prospects of the James River and Kanawha Company to the Erie Canal – like Pennsylvanians who trumpeted the Mainline system – ignored the basic geographic realities of building an economically feasible waterway more than 2,000 feet above sea level. The best Virginians could possibly have done was to build a hybrid canal–railroad system which would have met the same fate as the Mainline. Yet the Old Dominion did not manage to complete this task, raising the question of why Virginia's canal policy failed even more miserably than that of the Keystone State.

The answer to that question hinges on the inability of Virginia's state government to focus resources on the completion of key projects. The amount that the state government spent on the Canal was impressive in its final total, but funding came in fits and starts over long periods of time. In 1785, a company was chartered to build a canal around the falls at Richmond and make various improvements along a 224-mile stretch of the James itself. Capitalized at only $140,000, the company made few significant improvements, drawing the ire of farmers and planters who nevertheless had to pay tolls for using the river. Responding to political pressure, the legislature took over the improvements in 1820, paying the original proprietors a princely sum in the process.[46] Over the next decade and a half, the state spent $1.3 million to build canals over the most difficult sections of the James, made improvements on the Kanawha, and financed a turnpike connection to Covington.

For Virginians eager to unite eastern Virginia with the Ohio River, the long chain of river improvements and turnpikes was clearly inadequate, leading to calls for the formation of an entirely new company. After much debate and lobbying, in 1835 the state chartered the James River and Kanawha Company, capitalized at $5 million, including

---

[44] Goodrich, "The Virginia System," p. 368.
[45] *Virginia Advocate*, 19 July 1828, p. 1.
[46] Dunaway, *History of the James River and Kanawha Company*, pp. 26–43.

$3 million in government aid consisting of the state's old works (valued at $1 million) and an additional $2 million in new funds.[47] The contrast with Pennsylvania was sharp: As the Keystone State was finishing the Mainline system, Virginians had begun serious efforts to build an intersectional canal.

The limited capitalization of the James River and Kanawha Company was inadequate to build a canal to the Ohio. The work already completed by the state government, supposedly worth more than $1 million, had to be rebuilt, slowing progress and consuming precious capital. The company opened the first division of the canal from Richmond to Lynchburg in 1840, which resulted in a significant growth of the company's revenues. When combined with the task of rebuilding the state works, however, the completion of the Richmond to Lynchburg division exhausted the company's funds. Having already started on the second division of the canal extending from Lynchburg to Buchanan, the company pleaded for $6 million in new capital, with $3 million coming from the state government itself. The legislature refused, instead giving the company loan guarantees worth $1.5 million. The state government kept the project alive, but never gave enough funds to finish it.[48]

The James River and Kanawha Company received tepid legislative support because it lacked a big city to champion its cause. If Philadelphia and Pittsburgh did not have the political power to push completion of the Mainline without resorting to logrolling politics, Richmond and its allies had hardly enough influence to allocate funds under any circumstances. In 1830, the two most populous Virginia cities to directly benefit from the canal (Richmond and Lynchburg) accounted for about 4 percent of the Old Dominion's free population, while Philadelphia and Pittsburgh contained about 18 percent of the Keystone state's free population.[49] Nor could Richmond, home to less than 17,000 free residents in 1830, muster enough wealth and influence to form organizations such as the Philadelphia-based Pennsylvania Society for Internal Improvements.

The canal's promoters, of course, could appeal to residents along its line for economic and political support, but even here the James River and Kanawha Company was at a disadvantage. The number of residents living in counties along the James River project amounted to only 23 percent of the state's population, while the comparable figure

---

[47] The cities of Richmond and Lynchburg, the Bank of Virginia, and a number of private individuals invested the remaining $2 million into the company. Goodrich, *Government Promotion*, pp. 94–95.

[48] Dunaway, *History of the James River and Kanawha Company*, pp. 155–56.

[49] U. S. Bureau of the Census, *Abstract of the Returns of the Fifth Census* (Washington, D. C., 1832), pp. 14–19. These figures refer to the counties of each city.

for the Mainline was 41 percent.[50] Nor did all of the residents along the canal's path have an incentive to complete the western segment of the project. Eastern Virginia's planters and farmers wanted local transportation improvements that would increase their land values, but they had no economic reason to support an expensive intersectional canal. The differing economic motivations of commercial and landed wealth help explain why the Keystone State's merchants and manufacturers, eagerly seeking larger markets in the Midwest, pushed for the completion of intersectional lines, while the Old Dominion's eastern planters and farmers were content with local projects.

The urban rivalries that continually divided Virginians created a related problem for the James River and Kanawha Company. No fewer than five cities in the Tidewater and Piedmont regions (Alexandria, Lynchburg, Norfolk, Petersburg, and Richmond) vied to become the state's leading commercial center. Historian David R. Goldfield notes that Virginia cities perceived that "[i]ntrastate adversaries were potentially more dangerous than rivals beyond state borders. Pride as well as logic demanded that hegemony in the region or even in the nation could not be attained until leadership within Virginia was secure."[51] Just as competition between Charlottesville and Scottsville frequently delayed legislative approval of railroad routes and bank charters, the competition between Richmond, Norfolk, and other rival towns delayed funding for the James River and Kanawha Company.

Urban rivalries, of course, were hardly unique to Virginia, as commercial duels between Philadelphia, Baltimore, New York, and Boston motivated scores of important transportation projects. But while competition between northern cities often served to unify a state or a region against a distant competitor – Philadelphia and Pittsburgh, for example, could appeal to state patriotism to mobilize public sentiment against New York City or Baltimore – the rivalry among Virginia's small cities shredded any pretensions to harmonious cooperation. The lack of legislative unity impressed northern observers. In 1842 New York engineer Benjamin Wright, visiting Richmond as a consultant for the James River and Kanawha Company, told John Hartwell Cocke that "you have a timid body here – and so many conflicting interests that they do not harmonize very well." Wright hopefully concluded that "your people are coming to the conclusion that good policy requires the means of the State to be concentrated on this central line of improvement until it is carried thro."[52] Wright was a better

---

[50] Calculated from *Abstract of the Returns of the Fifth Census*, pp. 14–19.
[51] Goldfield, *Urban Growth*, p. 202.
[52] Benjamin Wright to John Hartwell Cocke, January 3, 1842, Cocke Papers, Box 103, UVA.

civil engineer than political prophet. Urban rivalries, as we will see, would throw the James River and Kanawha Company into heated competition with Virginia's railroad companies.

State Policy and Virginia's Haphazard Railroad Network

The financial performance of the James River and Kanawha Company was by no means unique. Many of Virginia's railroads had the same low rates of return. The generally dismal dividend performance of the Virginia Central documented in Chapter 3 was high compared to most Virginia railroads (Table 5.3). Ten of the Old Dominion's railroads never paid a single dividend, and as a whole, dividends for Virginia's railroads averaged far less than 1 percent. The source used to construct Table 5.3 – government records of dividends it received from its investment – might well have missed some payments. The number of unrecorded or missed payments, however, would have to be very large to raise the average annual rate of return to even 1 percent. One might be tempted to blame these poor profits on the short but sharp Depression of 1857, but Virginia's rural economy weathered the storm far better than the manufacturing economy of the Keystone State. Yet the 20 Pennsylvania railroads that Philadelphia and New York capitalists owned paid dividends averaging 4.25 percent between 1855 and 1859.[53] While hardly a windfall, Pennsylvania railroads at least showed the potential to make large direct profits that few railroads in the Old Dominion exhibited.

The primary reason behind the large differential in profitability stemmed from Virginia's lack of concentrated population and wealth. Here was the Achilles' heel of a rural economy composed primarily of farmers, planters, and slaves. The population density of the Keystone State in 1850 (almost 52 persons per square mile) was twice as great as Virginia's (22 persons per square mile). By 1860, this already large gap had widened considerably – 65 persons per square mile for Pennsylvania versus 25 for the Old Dominion.[54] Perhaps even more telling was the greater degree of centralization within Pennsylvania's economy. While Philadelphia and Allegheny Counties accounted for 21 percent of Pennsylvania's population in 1850, the 5 largest urban counties in the Old Dominion contained 9.4 percent of Virginia's total population.[55] Virginia railroads had to zigzag along the countryside in a forlorn search for passengers and traffic, while the commanding presence of Philadelphia and Pittsburgh created natural centers

[53] Calculated from the dividend information provided by Poor, *History of the Railroads and Canals*, pp. 414–518.
[54] *Historical Statistics*, pp. 33,36.
[55] Calculated from DeBow (ed.), *Statistical View*, pp. 298–99, 320–31.

Table 5.3. *The Poor Rate of Return of Virginia Railroads, 1856–1860*

Railroad Company (date chartered)	Total Capital Stock of the Company, 1860 (dollars)	Number of Dividends Issued, 1856–1860	Average Annual Dividend, 1856–1860
Richmond & Petersburg (1836)	836,100	10	5 %
Virginia Central (1836)	3,162,854	3	1.4 %
Richmond & Danville (1847)	1,981,197	2	.68 %
Alexandria, Loudon, & Hampshire (1853)	1,631,248	0	0
Fredericksburg & Gordonsville (1853)	220,665	0	0
Manassas Gap (1850)	3,188,313	0	0
Norfolk & Petersburg (1851)	1,700,974	0	0
Orange & Alexandria (1848)	2,039,603	0	0
Richmond, Fredericksburg, & Potomac(1834)	1,041,880	0	0
Richmond & York River (1853)	669,957	0	0
South Side (1846)	1,365,300	0	0
Virginia & Tennessee (1848)	3,452,810	0	0
Winchester & Potomac (1831)	300,000	0	0
Totals	$29,115,801	15	.11 %

Notes and Sources: Because the state government invested in these companies, all dividend payments made by the railroads should have been recorded. It is possible that a company simply did not pay the state government, or that the Second Auditor failed to record some payments. The records, however, appear to be complete. Similar dividend payments for turnpike and navigation companies, as well as money received from the collection of bonds, appear in the records of the Second Auditor. Several Virginia railroads – including the Petersburg Railroad Company, the Northwest Virginia Railroad Company, and the Seaboard and Roanoke Railroad Company – received no state investment. It is therefore impossible to estimate their rate of returns from this data. The aggregate capital stock of these companies amounted to $2.2 million, so it is unlikely that they would significantly improve the general profitability of the Virginia railroad network. All dividends are from Fund for Internal Improvement Journals, A–D. Archives of the Second Auditor, VSLA.

for trade that dramatically enhanced Pennsylvania's prospects for building a profitable trunk line.

Not only did Pennsylvania have a more concentrated population, but that population produced more wealth and hence the potential for greater railroad traffic and profitability. One way of measuring the advantage of Pennsylvania's railroads is calculating the "income per square mile" (per capita income multiplied by people per square mile) to take into account both higher population density and greater economic productivity.[56] "Income Per Square Mile" was $2,100 for the Old Dominion versus $11,765 for the Keystone State. To put it another way, railroads in the Keystone State could tap into a market for transportation five times richer than that of the Old Dominion. The Keystone State's rapidly industrializing economy produced more traffic to boost the potential profitability of railroads, which further enlarged the market for manufactured goods.

Instead of riding an upward spiral in which additional railroads boosted industrialization and future earnings, Virginia railroads faced a much less enviable cycle in which the expectation of low profits accentuated poor dividend performance. The financial troubles of Virginia's railroads made it difficult for even potentially profitable companies to raise capital. The shortage of capital in turn forced Virginia railroads to spend most of their revenues on the completion of their lines, thereby reducing or eliminating dividend payments. The Virginia Central was an excellent example of this conundrum. An 1858 resolution from the stockholders indignantly noted that the railroad had spent "$600,000 in net revenue of the company" to finish the westward expansion of the road. Declaring that this money "rightfully belonged to those stockholders who were incorporated to build the road," the company refused to allocate any additional revenues for further construction.[57] The Virginia Central's predicament represented a peculiar catch-22: The company's inability to raise capital forced it to use net revenues to fund construction, which made raising capital even more difficult.

With low population densities creating small direct dividends, Virginia's railroads depended upon the familiar combination of local capital and government financing. Local investors could hardly afford to pay for an entire railroad (remember that the residents of Albemarle, a particularly wealthy Virginia county, could barely raise $100,000 for the VCRR), which meant that the state and local governments had to make large investments to get projects built. In 1860, the state government had invested $17.1 million in the capital stock of Virginia's railroads, which accounted for 60 percent of the network's total capitalization. The state government was also willing to provide loans and guarantees, which by 1860 amounted to more than $3.5 million.[58] Most of this investment was paid through deficit financing.

The substantial state investment did little to increase the power of the state government to rationally "plan" the Virginia railroad network. As befitting a system of developmental corporations, local interests

[56] Per capita income taken from Fogel, *Without Consent or Contract*, p. 85.
[57] *Annual Reports on the Rail Road Companies* (Richmond, 1859), p. 135.
[58] *Annual Reports on the Rail Road Companies* (Richmond, 1860), p. 605.

still called the shots. Almost all of Virginia's railroad investment was funneled to individual companies through the Board of Public Works, the public agency that oversaw the state's investment program. On paper, the Board of Public Works was a powerful organization that not only distributed state investment to individual corporations, but also appointed state proxies and directors, and acted as a clearing house of engineering information. For most of its existence, however, the Board left companies to their own devices. The hands-off policy was due partly to necessity. The Board's administrative budget averaged less than $11,300 per year in the 1850s, leaving it without the manpower to oversee the hundreds of internal improvement companies that received state funds.[59] In appointing proxies and directors, the Board often followed the recommendations of the company in question, thereby increasing the power of local stockholders who often took a dim view of statewide considerations.[60]

Instead of concentrating investment into a few key lines, the legislature and the state spread investment over a number of competing projects. After a great deal of debate, the legislature usually passed an omnibus bill that authorized the Board of Public Works to buy 60 percent of the capital stock in selected roads. In order to satisfy localities that did not receive railroad funding, the legislature continued to make liberal expenditures on river improvements and turnpikes even when these enterprises competed with railroads. Between 1845 and 1860, the state invested just over $32 million in all transportation improvements. Observers were quick to point out that many of these transportation companies were "schemes of purely local character, some of them are wholly impracticable, and others such as by their construction would inflict injury upon interests already in existence, without furnishing any compensating advantage."[61]

Just as urban rivalry had prevented Virginians from concentrating investment on the James River and Kanawha Company, competition between the Old Dominion's small cities fragmented state railroad policy as well. Internal improvements led to incessant bickering in all states, but the political battles in Virginia were particularly noteworthy for their protracted strife and conflict. The battle for state appropriations led cities and their rural allies to forge legislative deals that often collapsed under charges of back stabbing and duplicity. Tensions ran so high that several Norfolk newspaper editors recommended that their city secede from Virginia when the legislature refused to allocate

[59] Calculated from Goodrich, "The Virginia System," p. 366.
[60] Goodrich, "The Virginia System," pp. 378–80. For particular examples of the Board's lack of power to resolve important controversies, see Majewski, "Commerce and Community," (Ph.D. diss.), pp. 115–16.
[61] *Richmond Enquirer*, 10 January 1854, p. 1.

funds for an important rail connection. One writer declared that "I go in for hitchin' teams with the Old North State, for it has long been my notion that Virginia cares little for Norfolk. Huzza for North Carolina and annexation!"[62]

The plight of the Virginia Central testifies to the political realities that prevented Virginians from centralizing investment into key improvements. The Virginia Central "system" was composed of three distinct railroads designed to connect Richmond to the Ohio River: the Virginia Central Railroad itself as well as the state-owned Blue Ridge Railroad and the state-owned Covington and Ohio. The state government paid for most of the system, including $1.6 million for the Blue Ridge Railroad, $2.6 million for the Covington and Ohio, and $2.2 million for the Virginia Central itself.[63] Yet the state's money was always painfully slow in coming. By 1860, the Virginia Central itself was out of funds and stranded many miles from its ultimate destination of Covington. Progress on the Covington and Ohio – the crucial state-owned link over the mountains to the Ohio River – was slower still. The road was not chartered until 1854, a year after the completion of the Pennsylvania Railroad's mainline. The legislature's allocation of only $1 million for construction was barely enough to finish the surveys and begin the grading. In 1856, the company's chief engineer, Charles Fisk, complained that a shortage of funds had forced the company to dismiss contractors and workmen that would take months to reassemble.[64] Between 1856 and 1860, the road received a total of $1.3 million, a woefully inadequate amount that slowed construction to a crawl. Although the legislature authorized $2.5 million in 1860, the onset of the Civil War suspended construction. The Virginia Central system became another of the half-completed projects that littered the Virginia landscape.[65]

Despite its claims as Virginia's primary trunk line, the Virginia Central never overcame Virginia's incessant commercial rivalries. Lynchburg residents feared that Richmond's direct connection with the West would completely bypass the James River and Kanawha Company, thereby eliminating a substantial portion of Lynchburg's tobacco trade. Rather than support completion of the Virginia Central system, Lynchburg residents pushed for continued construction of the canal and a railroad between Lynchburg and the Ohio River. In 1858, the Lynchburg *Daily Virginian* vigorously objected to a bill allocating

---

[62] Quoted in Goldfield, *Urban Growth*, p. 205.

[63] *Annual Reports on Rail Road Companies of the State of Virginia* (Richmond, 1860), p. 665.

[64] Charles B. Shaw, "Report of the Covington and Ohio Railroad," Document No. 20, *Journal of the Senate of the Commonwealth of Virginia* [for 1855–1856 session] (Richmond, 1856), pp. 5–8.

[65] *Annual Reports on Rail Road Companies of State of Virginia* (Richmond, 1861), p. xxiii.

$2 million to the Covington and Ohio Railroad. "This large sum to the Ohio road defeats all hope of securing any State assistance to the Canal," the chagrined editor declared. "The Canal must first receive the encouragement, and protection, and patronage of the Common-wealth before we plunge into the costly enterprise of a road from Covington to the Ohio."[66] Indeed, the canal's supporters were dreaming of a waterway not only to the Ohio, but a project that would eventually reach the Rocky Mountains.[67] Lynchburg and its allies never had the political power to have these grandiose plans enacted, but, as historian Robert F. Hunter has noted, "they did have the power to hamper competing projects in Virginia, which is essentially what they did."[68]

That the canal's supporters remained political players in the 1850s aptly highlights how Virginia's state investment program politicized even relatively easy economic decisions. With a remarkable lack of foresight, the supporters of the canal proclaimed the technological advantages of canals over railroads. "[T]here is not a railroad in the county," wrote the canal's chief engineer Walter Gynn in 1848, "whose road is engaged in the general business of traffic, that would not gladly get rid of the transportation of bulky articles."[69] Gynn's statement undoubtedly would have puzzled the directors of many Pennsylvania railroads, who profited handsomely from the carriage of anthracite coal and many other "bulky articles." The ultimate success of northern railroads such as the Pennsylvania Railroad persuaded many Virginians that railroads had a decided technological advantage in crossing mountain barriers.[70] Yet if the Virginia Central won the battle, it lost the war. Whereas the Pennsylvania Railroad purchased the Mainline system in 1858 to eliminate trunk-line duplication in the Keystone State, the Virginia legislature continued to finance two competing projects, which helped to insure that neither would be finished. The prospect of the state financing two competing and unfinished trunk lines led one exasperated correspondent to the *Southern Planter* to bitterly remark in 1856 that "Thus we see a canal made at enormous expense half way to the Ohio River, and a rail road as long made in the same direction, and then the makers stand in stupid amazement that the two halves have not reached the wealth of the great Mississippi Valley."[71]

---

[66] "The Governor's Message," *Lynchburg Daily Virginian*, 8 December 1859, p. 1.
[67] Meinig, *The Shaping of America*, p. 368. The pamphlet was written on behalf of Norfolk interests, who were aligned with Lynchburg in the hopes that the canal would bypass Richmond.
[68] Hunter, "The Turnpike Movement in Virginia, 1816–1860," (Ph.D. diss.), p. 282.
[69] *Report of the Chief Engineer to the President and Directors of James River and Kanawha Company* (n.p., 1848), p. 11.
[70] *Letters of Charles B. Shaw, Engineer, Comparing the Projected Railroad from Covington to the Ohio* (Richmond, 1851), p. 14.
[71] All Sides, "Agricultural Education," *Southern Planter* 16 (February 1856), p. 44.

Other rivals also fought to limit appropriations for the Virginia Central. The Virginia and Tennessee Railroad (which ran from Lynchburg to Bristol, Tennessee) attempted to extend a branch to the Ohio River, putting it in immediate conflict with the Virginia Central. After heated and protracted debate, the Virginia Central finally won out, in large part because the Virginia and Tennessee (V & T) had been built on a 5 foot gauge instead of the increasingly standard 4 feet 8 ½ inch gauge. The Virginia and Tennessee used the larger gauge because the company erroneously believed that a bigger track would give it a technological advantage over its rivals.[72] The plan backfired because, as the Virginia Central's partisans gleefully noted, "the roads in Kentucky and Ohio, the States with which we are aiming to connect, are all of the same width of the Central road, 4 feet 8 ½ inches."[73] The Virginia and Tennessee's large gauge also hurt its connections within Virginia. The V&T met the Orange and Alexandria Railroad in Lynchburg, thus forming a seemingly impressive line stretching from the Tennessee River Valley to Tidewater Virginia. The problem was that the Orange and Alexandria used a standard gauge, creating an expensive transshipment point that severely hampered the effectiveness of this potential trunk route. Virginia's commercial rivalries had once again discouraged integration and trunk lines.

Virginia railroad rivalries also discouraged direct connections within cities. Since Virginia railroad companies were designed to increase local commerce, merchants had no desire to see their city become another stop on the line. Allied with teamsters and other local interests, they worked hard to prevent railroads from directly transferring their freight to other railroads. Although Richmond became the hub of Virginia's internal improvement network – six railroads and the James River and Kanawha Canal entered the city – each railroad had its own separate depot so that freight had to be transferred using wagons. The lack of direct connections was disastrous from the standpoint of efficiently routing through freight. The local interests were so strong that even during the Civil War direct connections through Richmond and other Virginia cities could be used only for military purposes.[74] Once again the lack of a large commercial city such as Philadelphia – and the politically powerful mercantile, financial,

---

[72] Charles Garnett, the chief engineer of the Virginia and Tennessee, wrote an open letter to the President of the Virginia Central erroneously declaring that "a large majority of the [civil engineering] profession prefer a wider gauge than 4 feet 8 ½ inches. I believe that the best gauge to be five and a half feet, and in that opinion many practical men agree with me." *American Railroad Journal* 8 (17 January 1852), p. 86.

[73] *Letters of Charles B. Shaw ... on the Subject of a Connection between Richmond and the Valley of the Ohio* (n. p., 1851).

[74] Taylor and Neu, *American Railroad Network*, pp. 46–47.

and industrial elite that came with it – meant that local interests triumphed in the Old Dominion.

State Spending and Political Discrimination Against the West

The absence of a large city was not the only factor preventing Virginians from focusing resources on a single trunk line. The state's political institutions, which gave the eastern half of the state a disproportionate amount of political power, also played a significant role. Eastern Virginia asserted political dominance from the very beginning. Virginia's first constitution, passed in 1776, based political representation more on geography rather than population, conferring upon the Tidewater a disproportionate number of seats in both the House and Senate.[75] After long years of protest, reformers finally secured a new constitution in 1831. Basing representation on the 1820 federal census, the new constitution corrected the grossest inequalities of the 1776 document, but still discriminated against the fast-growing trans-Allegheny West. By 1850, the West had nearly 37 percent of Virginia's white population, but only 23 percent of the house seats and 22 percent of the senate seats. A new constitution passed in 1851 finally gave the West proportional representation in the House, but the region still suffered discrimination in the Senate.[76]

Despite the belated and partial acknowledgment of western equality, the lack of proportional representation undoubtedly weakened the region's bargaining power in the quest for state investment. Calculating cumulative state investment for each of Virginia's four distinctive regions shows that counties in the Piedmont, the Valley, and Tidewater captured most of the state investment (Table 5.4). Western Virginia, for example, had 39 percent of Virginia's free population, paid 23 percent of the state's taxes, yet received only 14 percent of the state's spending on canals and railroads.[77] Legislative petitions from the Wheeling area indicate the frustration felt by residents in the western part of the state. The Wheeling Board of Trade warned that the lack of state investment and good transportation "has had the effect of weakening in the minds of all our fellow-citizens of the section embraced, the reverence which they have heretofore felt for the government and institutions of Virginia."[78] Such warnings often went

[75] Freehling, *Drift Toward Dissolution*, pp. 270–71. By 1830, the Tidewater contained a quarter of Virginia's white population, yet held half of the senate seats. In contrast, the Trans-Allegheny region held less than 10 percent of the senate seats despite having 27 percent of Virginia's white population.

[76] Freehling, *Drift Toward Dissolution*, pp. 237, 239, 271, 286.

[77] The seventeen-percent figure includes funding for the Covington and Ohio Railroad, a decidedly bittersweet victory since it remained unfinished until after the Civil War.

[78] Quoted in Hunter, "Turnpike Movement," (Ph.D. diss.), p. 295.

Table 5.4. *The Uneven Regional Distribution of Virginia State Investment*

Region	Free Population	Annual Taxes Paid	State Investment (through 1859)	Per Capita Investment
Tidewater	253,777 (23%)	$768,495 (30%)	$7,683,375 (23%)	$30.27
Piedmont	243,065 (22%)	$782,093 (30%)	$15,155,139 (45%)	$62.35
Valley	178,817 (16%)	$434,892 (17%)	$6,101,300 (18%)	$34.12
West	429,839 (39%)	$598,501 (23%)	$4,523,875 (14%)	$10.52

Notes and Sources: The "Annual Taxes Paid" column is for the year 1858. "State Investment through 1859" is the cumulative amount of money each region received from the state government for canals and railroads. The regional distribution of state investment was calculated from *Annual Reports on the Rail-Road Companies* (1860), p. 606. The tax burden was calculated from "Biennial Report of the Auditor of Public Accounts," Doc. No. V., *House Documents* (1860), Table C.

unheeded, especially since some eastern planters feared that western-ers harbored abolitionist sentiments. John Randolph of Roanoke, the untiring champion of Tidewater interests, predicted legislation would be proposed "for the emancipation of every slave in Virginia" if the region's economic and political power expanded.[79]

The political discrimination against western Virginia, while certainly severe, was only part of the complicated story of how that region received less state funding. True enough, some eastern planters, following Randolph's example, opposed funding internal improvements in the western counties, where slaves made up less than 7 percent of the population. But by the 1850s, a large number of influential planters and politicians supported western improvements as a means of strengthening economic and political ties not only with western Virginians, but with free states such as Ohio as well. The growing anti-slavery movement in the North provided a powerful political argument for linking eastern Virginia with the Ohio River Valley. As early as 1838, state senator Joseph Segar declared that "The opening of one lone line of communication between the James River and the Ohio, will do more to check the progress of abolition in the free states of the west than all the appeals which eloquence can make, and all the arguments that ingenuity can urge." Almost 20 years later, Segar was making the same appeal as one of the Virginia Central's most influential supporters.[80] Another supporter of the Virginia Central asked in 1854 "[I]s it not the part of wisdom for Virginia to prepare for the

[79] Quoted in Freehling, *Drift Toward Dissolution*, p. 68.
[80] Quoted in Watson, "Slavery and Development," p. 60 and Segar, "Speech of Joseph Segar."

coming storm – to make it the interest of Western States to stand by her in any difficulties that may occur, and to increase her population and resources as much as possible?"[81] Even opponents of a direct rail link to Ohio – who feared the "interference in free states with slave property" – nevertheless supported building a railroad through western Virginia to Kentucky.[82] If slavery lessened the economic incentive of Virginia's slaveholders to build an intersectional railroad, it at least gave them a strong political reason to improve links with the west.

Political discrimination – at least as a lone explanation for the distribution of state investment – also fails to account for how the Tidewater region lagged significantly behind the Piedmont and Valley regions in securing state transportation funds. Although residents of the Tidewater paid 30 percent of the Commonwealth's taxes, they received only 23 percent of the state investment in canals and railroads. The culprit for the Tidewater was geography. Blessed with excellent access to either navigable rivers or the Chesapeake Bay, many Tidewater counties had little need for canals and railroads. Large planters in these areas, who paid relatively high taxes while receiving little state investment in return, understandably opposed spending on internal improvements. It was these planters who provided the kernel of truth to the myth that conservative slaveholders opposed state spending on internal improvements.

Regression analysis confirms a political dynamic in which the central portions of the state benefited the most from state investment, while the east and west fared poorly. The dummy variables for the regions show that the Piedmont and Valley Counties did well in securing state investment, the Tidewater less so, and the West (represented by the intercept) lagging far behind (Table 5.5). The dummy variables suggest the political dynamic in which planters and farmers of the Piedmont and Valley secured significant sums of state investment, while ignoring trunk line connections with the western region. When slavery is thrown into the mix, the regional dummies tend to change dramatically, but the overall picture remains the same. The "Percentage of the Population Enslaved" variable is large and statistically significant, representing the disproportionate power of slave-dominated counties in the Virginia legislature. After the effects of slavery are held constant, the Tidewater region lagged behind all others in securing state funds, while the regional dummies for the Piedmont, Valley, and West were statistically insignificant.

The developmental implications for western Virginia were profound. Without an eastern manufacturing and mercantile center to

---

[81] R. G. Morriss, "Speech," in *Proceedings ... At White Sulpher Springs*, p. 10.
[82] Shaw, "A Statement of the Reasons which controlled the Location of the Covington and Ohio Railroad," August 10, 1853, Charles B. Shaw Papers, UVA.

Table 5.5. *Regression Analysis of State Investment in Virginia*

Independent Variables	Regression One: Regional Dummies	Regression Two: Regions and Slavery
Dependent Variable: Cumulative State Investment in Virginia Counties through 1860.		
Intercept	9.97 (1.59)	2.76 (.44)
Tidewater Dummy	10.07 (1.36)	-47.90 (-2.64)
Piedmont Dummy	74.51 (6.93)	20.45 (.18)
Valley Dummy	32.64 (2.55)	13.04 (1.06)
Percentage of County Population Enslaved	—	1.51 (4.00)
Adjusted R-Square	.24	.32
F-Statistic	16.80	17.92

Notes and Sources: Please see Table 5.4. The intercept represents a county in the western region. T-statistics are in parentheses next to the regression coefficients.

pour funds into a trunk line, many residents of the Old Dominion's trans-Allegheny region lacked the ability to buy and sell in rapidly expanding commercial markets. Significantly, the one trunk line that would reach western Virginia was the urban-dominated Baltimore and Ohio Railroad, which reached Wheeling at about the same time that the Pennsylvania Railroad was completed. As the Civil War approached, most western Virginians were willing to cast their lot with the Union rather than the Confederacy. The Old Dominion's inability to build a trunk line helped turn western Virginia the region into West Virginia the state.

The Long-Run Impact of the "Missing" Big City

It bears repeating that the dismal results of Virginia's state investment policy did not result from anticommercial attitudes on the part of the state's farmers and planters. If anything, Virginia's state economic policy demonstrates the inadequacies of historiographical dichotomies such as "capitalist" versus "anticapitalist" that fail to adequately characterize the Old Dominion's eclectic blend of the traditional and the modern. As Carter Goodrich and other historians have suggested, Virginia's obvious concern for economic development and its reliance on deficit financing imbued the mixed enterprise system with elements of modern public policy.[83] Virginia's legislature, after all, spent more state money per capita on internal improvements than the

[83] Goodrich, "The Virginia System," pp. 289–311.

state government of "capitalist" Pennsylvania. On the other hand, the lack of planning and centralized direction meant the retarded development of trunk lines, thereby limiting opportunities for manufacturers and reinforcing the Old Dominion's agrarian orientation. One could call the efforts of planters to improve their links with outside markets the mark of modern entrepreneurs; one can also label their failure to build western connections as yet another manifestation of southern localism.

Rather than focusing scholarly energy on the "capitalist" versus "anticapitalist" interpretations of planter behavior, the comparison of Pennsylvania and Virginia railroads shows how urban capital greatly sharpened the regional differences between the two states. Large cities provided a steady supply of passengers and cargo that would make costly trunk lines profitable. Investors from large cities, flush with mercantile wealth, integrated trunk lines into coherent systems. In this sense the description "colonial" – if the term is taken to mean a system built by outsiders unconcerned with local development – is more apt for Pennsylvania than Virginia. It was "foreign" investors from Philadelphia, after all, that provided the bulk of the capital for the railroads that traversed the Pennsylvania countryside. Resident landowners steadfastly concerned with local development and an enthusiastic state government, on the other hand, financed Virginia's railroads. For a region concerned with dependency on northern capitalists and other outsiders, the state's railroad development offered delicious historical irony. It was precisely Virginia's reliance on its own resources – local capital and state investment – that led the state to develop its awkward railroad network.

Virginia's experience was typical of the older southern states. Scholars have documented the extensive state investment programs of Georgia, South Carolina, and North Carolina.[84] Despite large government investment programs, these states never managed to build a true trunk line to the Ohio or Mississippi Rivers.[85] It was no coincidence that Virginia, Georgia, North Carolina, and South Carolina did not have a city with a population larger than 50,000 people. The failure of these slave economies to generate a large city would have tremendous consequences for the region's transportation system and economic development. With a population spread out over a wide area, these states depended upon state investment to build railroads, opening the Pandora's box of legislative infighting. Planters and farmers in these areas would continue to grow cotton, tobacco, and rice profitably, but the absence of a great commercial city meant that

[84] Ford, *Origins of Southern Radicalism*, pp. 219-31; Heath, *Constructive Liberalism*, pp. 286-89; and Trelease, *North Carolina Railroad*, pp. 111-14.
[85] Phillips, *History of Transportation*, p. 220.

dreams of commercial greatness and economic independence would have to wait many decades. So what prevented the growth of a large commercial city in these slave states in the antebellum period? Using the comparison of Virginia and Pennsylvania as a guide, the next chapter attempts to answer that question.

6

Why Antebellum Virginians Never Developed a Big City: Comparative Urban Development in Philadelphia and Eastern Virginia

Many Virginians in the antebellum period would have readily agreed with Jane Jacobs, the twentieth-century sociologist who declared that great cities are "the wealth of nations."[1] Lacking a large city of their own, they realized through hard experience that metropolises were engines of development that made innovation and improvisation part of everyday economic life. George Tucker, a political economist at the University of Virginia, wrote in 1859 that cities "are more favorable to the cultivation of science and the arts of every kind. If they also more favor human depravity and misery, they afford readier means of punishing the one, and of alleviating the other."[2] State Senator Charles Bruce wrote in 1858 that "I care not how gentlemen cry out against towns and cities, as being sores upon the body politic, for they are, nevertheless, unfailing indices of the wealth and prosperity of the country."[3] Even George Fitzhugh, the most famous of Virginia's proslavery writers, argued that an independent South "must manufacture for itself, build cities, erect schools and colleges, and carry on all the pursuits and provide for all the common wants of civilized man."[4] No matter how reactionary their politics, most Virginians could not part with the idea of cities and the progress that they represented.

This chapter tries to explain why antebellum Virginia never came close to developing a city of the size and wealth of Philadelphia. Such a comparison, involving 200 years of crop choices, income levels, population densities, political institutions, economic attitudes, and geographic variables, necessitates a broad, synthetic approach. To make the task somewhat more manageable, important developments in the West, including the rivalry between Wheeling and Pittsburgh, are excluded. The focus on Philadelphia and Virginia's eastern cities, narrow as it is, allows us to get at the more general problem raised at the end

[1] Jacobs, *Cities and the Wealth of Nations.*
[2] Tucker, *Political Economy*, p. 63.
[3] Bruce, *Speech of Charles Bruce*, p. 7.
[4] Fitzhugh, *Sociology for the South*, p. 16.

of the last chapter: Why did states along the southern Atlantic (the Carolinas and Georgia, as well as the Old Dominion) never develop a true "central place" that could anchor an integrated transportation system and accelerate industrial growth? In 1860, Charleston and Richmond, the two largest cities in the South Atlantic region, had respective populations of 41,000 and 38,000, a far cry from the 565,000 people living in Philadlephia.

What emerges from the comparison of urban growth in the Philadelphia region and eastern Virginia is a complex narrative that can be divided into three distinct periods. In each period, however, slavery, plantations, and staple crops all conspired to limit urban development.

The Colonial Period: Staples and Their Institutions. In the colonial and revolutionary periods, most urban growth resulted from agricultural processing (such as milling grains) and mercantile activities. In Virginia, the relatively light processing requirements of tobacco discouraged the centralization of settlement, thus slowing the development of towns and cities. Laws such as the Navigation Acts, which required Virginians to ship their tobacco to Britain, strongly discouraged the growth of an indigenous mercantile community. Philadelphia's vibrant hinterland produced wheat and other grains that not only required heavy processing, but also escaped the heavy hand of the Navigation Acts. With the opportunity to market their region's staples to a wide range of destinations, Philadelphia merchants transformed the Quaker City into a mercantile headquarters, setting the stage for future growth.

Rural Markets in the Early Republic. From 1800 to 1840, Philadelphia made the transition from a mercantile center to a manufacturing city. The dense markets of Philadelphia's hinterland, filled with tens of thousands of prosperous family farmers, encouraged entrepreneurs in the Quaker City to produce a wide array of consumer goods. In contrast, Virginia's thinly populated countryside failed to provide the same markets that promoted industrialization in the Philadelphia area. Virginians, rationally responding to the incentives that their slave economy generated, continued to invest in plantation agriculture rather than manufacturing enterprises that could spur urban growth. "[T]he restraints on the extent of markets imposed by the institutions of slavery and plantation agriculture," as economist Viken Tchakerian puts it, accounted for inability to develop a thriving manufacturing sector.[5]

The Advantages of Agglomeration in the Antebellum Decades. By the 1840s, Philadelphia's mercantile and industrial heritage had led to

---

[5] Tchakerian, "Productivity, Extent of Markets, and Manufacturing," p. 520.

the accumulation of a large reservoir of skilled workers, technological know-how, and marketing expertise that allowed Quaker City firms to compete in national markets. The agglomeration of firms in the Philadelphia region created labor networks that provided both skilled and unskilled labor, while a variety of institutions encouraged the dissemination of technical knowledge. Most Virginia manufacturing firms – far removed from networks of specialized suppliers, without access to pools of skilled workers, and unable to benefit from decades of practical experience – found themselves at a disadvantage even when competing in markets close to home.

One theme that ties together this narrative is the cumulative nature of urban development. Each stage of Virginia's development intensi-fied the disadvantages it would face in the next period. Virginia's dependence on slavery and staples in the colonial period contributed to the lack of markets in the early national era, which then denied its manufacturers the advantages of agglomeration in the antebellum decades. As we have seen, many Virginians vigorously supported urban and industrial growth to achieve economic independence from northern financiers and manufacturers. The advocates of diversifica-tion and modernization found, however, that it was far easier to stay on the old path of plantation agriculture and slave labor rather than blaze a new one leading to large cities and development. In stark con-trast, Philadelphia already possessed the ingredients for sustained development in the early nineteenth century, including a vigorous mercantile community, a supply of skilled mechanics, and dense mar-kets of eager consumers. Even determined efforts by Virginia entre-preneurs could not overcome the initial advantages that Philadelphia industrialists enjoyed.

It should be noted from the outset that these explanations have sig-nificant limitations when applied to America as a whole. Emphasizing the presence of thick rural markets and the advantages of agglomera-tion works well to explain urbanization and industrialization in the middle Atlantic states, where large cities such as Philadelphia, New York, and Baltimore became engines of market development. The argument does not work as well for New England, where networks of small cities and towns (as opposed to large cities) often accounted for technological change. Nor did agglomeration necessarily lead to industrialization. New Orleans, for example, was one of the largest cities in the antebellum period, but the trade of the Mississippi Valley never turned the Crescent City into an industrial dynamo on the order of New York or Philadelphia. Suffice it to say that urbanization and industrialization, despite decades of intense scholarly research, are still mysterious enough to undermine almost any generalized model. This exploratory analysis is only a starting point for other comparisons of urban development.[6]

"Nature *Has Said There Shall Not*"

The inability of Virginians to build large towns was apparent almost from the colony's founding. Influential leaders such as Governor William Berkeley implemented diversification schemes—including bounties for manufacturing enterprises—as early as 1661, and the colonial legislature periodically passed legislation to encourage town building.[7] Thomas Jefferson aptly summarized the failure of these efforts when he wrote that "the *laws* have said there shall be towns; but *Nature* has said there shall not, and they remain unworthy of enumeration."[8] By 1720, Virginia's tobacco economy had produced three villages (Williamsburg, Yorktown, and Norfolk) with no more than 500 residents apiece, and two hamlets (West Point and Hampton) with somewhere between 100 and 250 residents.[9] In contrast, Philadelphia in 1720 was already home to 5,000 residents.[10]

Virginians frequently blamed tobacco, the source of their considerable wealth, for the colony's lack of towns and cities. An impressive array of evidence indicates that they were right. Historians and economists have long recognized that tobacco had few "forward linkages" – the activities necessary to convert the raw crop into a marketable commodity – that promoted urban growth. Tobacco required relatively little processing before the crop was exported. Planters cured, stripped, and packed the tobacco themselves on the plantation, eliminating the need for towns. In the seventeenth and early eighteenth centuries, colonists often bypassed towns altogether, relying instead on ships and boats to pick up the crop on one of the many rivers and creeks that penetrated the Tidewater region. Even the need for horses and wagons was minimal, as planters and farmers packed their tobacco in huge hogsheads that could be rolled to the nearest

---

[6] It should be noted from the outset that ideological opposition did little to hinder the growth of Virginia's cities. Ideological opposition to urban growth, often based on Jeffersonian fears that city life undermined republican virtue, certainly existed in the Old Dominion. Such sentiments, however, rarely interfered with the practical politics of the state legislature. Conflict among cities, as historian David Goldfield has argued, was much more pronounced than conflict between urban boosters and planters. See Goldfield, "Urban-Rural Relations," pp. 146–48. The analysis of Virginia's state economic policy presented in the last chapter seems to confirm Goldfield's point.

[7] Morgan, *American Slavery*, pp. 186-92; O'Mara, *Historical Geography*, pp. 55-59, 61-62.

[8] Jefferson, *Notes on the State of Virginia*, pp. 233-34.

[9] Nash, *Urban Crucible*, p. 407; Kulikoff, *Tobacco and Slaves*, p. 106.

[10] Earle and Hoffman, "Urban Development"; Kulikoff, *Tobacco and Slaves*, pp. 123-27.

dock.[11] As for manufactured goods and other services that towns might provide, Virginians relied on roving merchants, itinerant artisans, and skilled slaves. Jefferson was right: Nature, through its emissary of tobacco, had decreed that colonial Virginia would have few towns and cities.

Nature, however, was not fixed. The search for fresh land took many Virginia planters beyond the fall line, making the direct loading of ships impossible. On the falls separating the Tidewater from the Piedmont, a series of towns arose that would become some of Virginia's most important cities: Alexandria (on the Potomac River), Richmond (on the James), and Petersburg (on the Appomattox). These towns, located at natural transshipment points, serviced the growing backcountry economy. They received a helping hand from the Virginia Inspection Act of 1730, which required public inspectors to ensure that tobacco was "good, sound, well-conditioned, and merchantable, and free from trash, sand, and dirt."[12] Designed to limit production and improve the reputation of Virginia's tobacco, the law also promoted the centralization of trade in towns that finagled permission from the colonial legislature to build inspection warehouses. The James River town of Richmond, for example, inspected almost a fifth of the state's tobacco crop by the early 1780s, growing into a flourishing city of 1,800 residents.[13] Yet the tobacco trade, even if more centralized, did little to promote subsidiary producers and services. Noting the pronounced absence of shops and other urban amenities, the daughter of one Virginia politician remarked in 1779 that Richmond "may at some future period be a great city, but at present it will scarce afford one comfort in life."[14]

Wheat, on the other hand, needed towns and cities. Processing wheat into flour – an operation done most cheaply on a scale transcending the individual farm – was a boon for Philadelphia. Farmers often found it profitable to send their grain to large mills in a central location, which could better utilize water power than smaller and less efficient local mills.[15] Minimizing transportation costs was

---

[11] The tobacco production process is outlined in Breen, *Tobacco Culture*, pp. 46–53. On the use of water transportation to ship tobacco directly from plantations to England, see Morgan, *American Slavery*, pp. 223–24.

[12] Kulikoff, *Tobacco and Slaves*, pp. 108–16, quotation p. 109.

[13] Kulikoff, *Tobacco and Slaves*, p. 124.

[14] Quoted in Ward and Greer, *Richmond During the Revolution*, p. 41.

[15] Earle and Hoffman have calculated that farmers could receive higher prices for their wheat in Philadelphia rather than converting it to flour first (thereby absorbing the milling charges themselves). This holds true even when the lower transportation cost of flour is taken into account. While they do not speculate on the economic dynamics underlying these relative prices, it seems plausible to assume the millers in the Philadelphia area could achieve substantial economies of scale in the milling of flour. See "Urban Development," pp. 74–76.

important, for grain was a bulky commodity that required expensive wagon carriage for overland journeys. Here Philadelphia's location, snugly positioned between the Delaware and Schuylkill Rivers, enhanced its advantages as a milling and shipping headquarters. Farmers from all over eastern Pennsylvania, southern New Jersey, and the northern Chesapeake sent their surpluses to the Philadelphia region. Philadelphia quickly became an important marketing center as well. Farmers visiting the Quaker City could purchase needed supplies and have their wagons repaired and horses shod.[16]

A dramatic increase in grain prices around the middle of the eighteenth century greatly stimulated Philadelphia's growth. Population growth in Europe, combined with a series of poor harvests, caused the price of wheat to double between 1740 and the early 1770s.[17] American colonists found lucrative new markets in the Wine Islands, the West Indies, and southern Europe. Settlers from all over Europe flooded Philadelphia's hinterland. Specialized flour merchants sent agents and contacts scurrying about the countryside, contracting with farmers to fill ships with flour and wheat. Between 1750 and 1775, Philadelphia's population nearly doubled to become the largest city in colonial America, with the flour trade (accounting for more than half of the value of Philadelphia's exports) leading the way.[18] The prosperity of Philadelphia and its hinterland farmers inspired Thomas Paine to remark that America would flourish as long as "eating is the custom of Europe."[19] A few years later Lord John Sheffield called Philadelphia "the capital of the corn country."[20]

Rising grain prices generated significant urban development in the Chesapeake as well. As grain prices rose, planters and farmers in the Tidewater increasingly converted their tired tobacco land into fields of wheat and corn. In 1733 Virginia's grain exports were worth only 10,000 pounds sterling, or about 6 percent of the value of the colony's total exports; 40 years later Virginia's grain exports were worth 145,000 pounds sterling, or about 25 percent of total exports.[21] Chesapeake cities such as Baltimore and Norfolk become important mercantile and milling centers. Shipping primarily corn and hogs to the West Indies, Norfolk's population grew to around 6,000 residents

---

[16] Price, "Economic Function," pp. 151–52; Doerflinger, "Farmers and Dry Goods," pp. 188–89.

[17] Bezanson, Gray, and Hussey, *Prices in Colonial Pennsylvania*, p. 50.

[18] Doerflinger, *A Vigorous Spirit*, pp. 123–24; Jensen, *Maritime Commerce*, p. 7-8; Nash, *Urban Crucible*, 407–8.

[19] Paine is quoted in Appleby, *Capitalism and a New Social Order*, p. 42. Appleby outlines how the explosive growth of the grain trade created a spirit of optimism that provided the foundations of Jeffersonian political economy in the early republic.

[20] Jensen, *Maritime Commerce*, p. 8.

[21] McCusker and Menard, *Economy of British North America*, p. 132.

in 1774. Baltimore's growth was similarly impressive.[22] As McCusker and Menard suggest, the growth of Norfolk and Baltimore dramatically highlighted the developmental differences between wheat and tobacco. "[T]he relatively small trade in the foodstuffs of the region's periphery had induced a much greater degree of urbanization and an economy more developed and less 'colonial' than that of the plantation belt."[23]

The Navigation Acts and the Export of Tobacco

Colonial cities grew not merely through milling grain, but from shipping it to distant locales. In colonial Philadelphia, for example, mariners and merchants composed 29 percent of the workforce, and many others provided goods and services for the mercantile community.[24] This mercantile community not only created jobs and opportunities that spurred urban growth, but reaped important "invisible earnings" through shipping services that financed new ventures to open new markets. Virginia and Maryland, on the other hand, generally lacked an indigenous mercantile community until the late colonial period, when Baltimore and Norfolk began their ascent. The slow growth of an indigenous mercantile community – and hence the slow growth of mercantile seaports – reflected the importance of British merchants in the tobacco trade. While colonial seaports dominated the grain trade, London and Glasgow exerted an iron grip on tobacco that did not loosen until well after the American Revolution. The ownership of vessels clearing ports reveals much about the differences between the tobacco and grain trades: British merchants owned only a quarter of the ships clearing Pennsylvania waters in the early 1770s, but controlled three-quarters of the ships clearing Chesapeake ports during the same period.[25]

Pennsylvania's staple produced mercantile growth and Virginia's staple retarded it largely because of the differing "rules of the game" that producers, merchants, middlemen, and retailers had to follow in order to turn a raw material into a marketable commodity. The Virginia Tobacco Inspection Act of 1730, as we have already seen, was

[22] Earle and Hoffman, "Urban Development," pp. 48–51; Hoffman, *Spirit of Dissension*, pp. 76–80; and Doerflinger, *A Vigorous Spirit*, pp. 113–15. Earle and Hoffman argue that a number of smaller towns in the backcountry also developed to help service the growing grain trade. From Maryland to South Carolina, towns such as Winchester, Strasburg, Staunton, Charlotte, and Salisbury grew rapidly during the later colonial period.

[23] McCusker and Menard, *Economy of British North America*, p. 133.

[24] Nash, *Urban Crucible*, pp. 387–90.

[25] McCusker and Menard, *Economy of British North America*, p. 192.

one legal change that encouraged the growth of towns. For the most part, however, the rules that governed tobacco marketing served to discourage urban growth. The most important of these were the Navigation Acts of 1660 and subsequent legislation that forced Virginians to export their crops directly to Britain or one of its colonies.[26] These acts mandated that Virginians send their tobacco crop to London, Glasgow, and other British ports, where it was then reexported to various European markets. The Navigation Acts gave Britain a near monopoly in the Chesapeake's lucrative tobacco trade – about 80 percent of Virginia's exports were sent to the mother country (Table 6.1).

The Navigation Acts seriously impeded urban growth. Because almost all of Virginia's tobacco had to be exported to Britain first, it made sense for the tobacco trade's marketing and commercial infrastructure to locate in British ports, where merchants had intimate knowledge of European markets, special contacts with state-sponsored monopolies on the Continent, and greater experience with Europe's arcane duty systems. A Virginia planter or merchant trying to market tobacco himself, as historian Jacob Price has argued, would have been "uncomfortably dependent upon one's correspondent." As Price points out, tobacco merchants had to deposit bonds to guarantee heavy import duties, which was "a rather technical business and required finding others to sign one's bonds as sureties. All this created cash-flow and credit problems for new firms in the trade."[27] Intense trade regulation and high customs duties led to what Jacob Price and Paul Clemens have called "a revolution of scale in overseas trade" within London and other British ports. By 1775, 12 large firms accounted for 71 percent of all tobacco imported into London.[28] The high start-up costs for the tobacco trade, both in terms of specialized expertise and financial capital, exerted a strong influence well after the Revolution ended America's participation in the Navigation Acts.[29] The ships, sailors, and counting houses that made the tobacco trade possible were therefore located in London and Glasgow rather than in Alexandria and Norfolk.

[26] McCusker and Menard, *Economy of British North America*, pp. 47–49. Smuggling may have undermined the Navigation Acts somewhat, but additional enforcement limited its significance. According to McCusker and Menard, "By the end of the War of Spanish Succession in 1713 colonial trade conformed in almost every particular to the navigation system; it continued to do so until the American Revolution" (p. 49).

[27] Price, "Economic Function," p. 167.

[28] Price and Clemens, "Revolution of Scale in Overseas Trade," p. 24.

[29] Jensen, *Maritime Commerce*, p. 78 and Doerflinger, *A Vigorous Spirit*, pp. 287–91. Doerflinger attributes the continued British dominance to the sluggish response of Virginia's planters, who were supposedly too cautious to invest their capital in risky mercantile ventures, but his own example seems to suggest that even Philadelphia's entrepreneurial merchants failed to capture this trade.

Table 6.1. *Explaining the Differences in Mercantile Development: The Greater Variety of International Destinations for Middle Colony Goods, 1768–1772*

Destination	Value of Chesapeake Exports in Pounds Sterling (percentage of regional total)	Value of Middle Colony Exports in Pounds Sterling (percentage of regional total)
Great Britain	827,052 (79)	68,369 (13)
Ireland	28,850 (3)	51,730 (10)
Southern Europe	99,163 (9)	181,759 (35)
West Indies	91,818 (9)	223,610 (43)
Africa	0	1,077 (<1)
Total	1,046,883	526,545

Notes and Sources: McCusker and Menard, *Economy*, pp. 130, 199.

London and Glasgow had no corresponding advantages in grains or other exports from colonial Philadelphia. The Navigation Acts excluded wheat, corn, meat, and lumber from its list of regulated commodities, which meant that these products could be exported to a wide variety of markets. Philadelphia merchants took full advantage of their opportunities, sending the produce of the surrounding hinterland to Ireland, the Wine Islands, the West Indies, Southern Europe, and Britain itself (Table 6.1). The diversified portfolio of destinations made it imperative for merchants to establish North American centers where they could buy and store their goods, secure insurance and other financial services, trade information about distant markets with trusted friends, repair and outfit their ships, and combine cargoes for full loads.[30] Philadelphia's superior location and rich hinterland made it a logical choice for such an entrepreneurial headquarters. British businessmen often provided credit and financing for many Philadelphia ventures, but they never secured the lucrative middleman position they enjoyed in the tobacco trade.[31] Quaker City merchants used their profits to buy more ships, so that by the early 1770s, the city's mercantile fleet was worth about 500,000 pounds sterling. The growth of the Philadelphia mercantile community also created a small but growing number of artisans who formed the core of a skilled, flexible workforce.[32]

[30] Price, "Economic Function," p. 143 and Earle and Hoffman, "Urban Development," pp. 9–11.

[31] Britain modified its corn laws in 1766 so that American grains entered duty free. Some grain shipped from Britain to America was used by British merchants to satisfy foreign demand, but the amount was never significant. See Sachs, "Agricultural Conditions," pp. 284–85.

[32] Price, "Economic Function," pp. 153–54.

If the grain trade led to Philadelphia's colonial growth, then what happened to Virginia cities such as Norfolk that also based their trade on grains? The main problem was one that will be addressed in the following section: sparsely-populated hinterlands. Even Virginia cities that shipped mostly wheat and corn served hinterlands with relatively small populations, thus limiting the markets for both merchants and manufacturers.[33] The situation in the Quaker City was far different. As Alice Hanson Jones argues, colonial Philadelphia had already established the foundation for its industrialization.[34] Andrew Burnaby, an English traveler, put it more vividly when visiting Philadelphia in 1760. "Can the mind have a greater pleasure in contemplating the rise and progress of cities and kingdoms," he asked, "than in perceiving a rich and opulent state arising out of a small settlement or colony?"[35] Just how rich and opulent Philadelphia would become would have surprised even this prophetic observer.

Rural Demand and Philadelphia's Transition to a Manufacturing City

Philadelphia grew in the colonial period because of its vigorous mercantile community. The Quaker City's maritime commerce continued to prosper in the post-Revolutionary period, but a long list of geographic and marketing problems clouded its mercantile future. Its location on the Delaware River made the port vulnerable to freezes that disrupted shipping during the winter months. Philadelphia's specialization in the West Indies trade also proved far less remunerative than New York's flourishing trade with Britain and Ireland, while the continued growth of Baltimore drew away a substantial part of the Quaker City's hinterland trade.[36] Philadelphia lost its status as America's leading city to New York in the early nineteenth century, and appeared headed for further decline.

Yet Philadelphia grew at an impressive rate during the first half of the nineteenth century, especially compared to Virginia's laggard urbanization. The initial advantage of Philadelphia over Virginia's cities was important – even if the Old Dominion's cities had grown at the same rate as Philadelphia in the nineteenth century, the Quaker city would have been far larger (Table 6.2). But Philadelphia grew faster in percentage terms as well. With the single exception of the 1850s, when Henrico County (home of Richmond) grew slightly faster,

---

[33] Earle and Hoffman, "Urban Development," pp. 42–46.
[34] Jones, Wealth of a Nation to Be, p. 311.
[35] Quoted in Ernst and Merrens, "Camden's Turrets," p. 554.
[36] These factors are outlined in Lindstrom, Economic Development, pp. 32–35 and Doerflinger, A Vigorous Spirit, pp. 341–42.

Table 6.2. *Achieving Urban Dominance:*
The Growth of Philadelphia County versus Richmond and Norfolk

Year	Philadelphia	Henrico (Richmond)	Norfolk
1790	54,391	12,000	14,524
1800	81,009 (49%)	14,836 (24%)	19,419 (34%)
1810	111,210 (37%)	19,680 (33%)	22,872 (18%)
1820	137,097 (23%)	23,667 (20%)	23,943 (5%)
1830	188,797 (38%)	28,797 (22%)	24,806 (4%)
1840	258,037 (37%)	33,076 (15%)	27,569 (11%)
1850	408,762 (58%)	43,572 (32%)	33,036 (20%)
1860	565,529 (38%)	61,616 (41%)	36,277 (10%)

Notes and Sources: Growth rates are beside absolute population statistics. All statistics from Andriot, *Population Abstract*, pp. 673, 823–24.

Philadelphia had higher growth rates before the Civil War than these three Virginia cities. Philadelphia's substantial lead in the colonial era had widened into a yawning gap.

An impressive expansion of Philadelphia's manufacturing sector accounted for Philadelphia's heady population increases. In the colonial and revolutionary periods, Philadelphia's manufacturers focused on processing industries (milling, tanning, sugar refining) or artisanal trades (shipbuilding, construction) that supported the city's mercantile community. In the early nineteenth century, the city's manufacturers became the tail that wagged the dog of international commerce.[37] By 1840, the value of Philadelphia's manufacturing output ($22.2 million) exceeded that of the entire state of Virginia ($16.8 million). Moreover, Philadelphia achieved this significant manufacturing growth without dependable access to western markets; the city's industrialization began four decades before the completion of trunk railroads.

Philadelphia's wealthy and populous hinterland provided the impetus for the city's industrial growth. In the colonial period, prosperous farm families in Philadelphia's hinterland purchased a wide variety of imported goods. Scholars carefully scrutinizing account books, probate inventories, and trade records have shown the growing prominence of ovens and stoves, feather beds and bed linen, fancy fabrics and table cloths within rural households.[38] The trend continued

[37] Historical geographer Allan Pred has argued that large American cities had a decided mercantile orientation until the 1840s. Lindstrom and Sharpless, however, provide an effective refutation of his argument. See Pred, "Manufacturing," p. 308 and Lindstrom and Sharpless, "Urban Growth," pp. 165–71.

[38] Doerflinger, "Farmers and Dry Goods"; Tully, "Economic Opportunity"; and Jones, *Wealth of a Nation to Be*, pp. 309–11. According to Jones, the Middle Colonies already had a substantial lead over the South in the acquisition of consumer goods. The

in the early nineteenth century, when ordinary farmers and artisans desired to appear tasteful and genteel. Historian Richard Bushman has described this cultural impulse as the "refinement of America." The impulse to appear respectable and refined led even isolated farmers to dress up their ramshackle log cabins with new consumer goods. Bushman's sample of probate inventories from Kent County, Delaware (part of Philadelphia's hinterland) in the 1770s and 1840s reveals that in the early period not a single household owned a carpet or a clock. By the 1840s, 31 percent of the poorest households and 56 percent of the total sample owned such items.[39]

Philadelphia entrepreneurs strove to satisfy the refined tastes of these ordinary farm families. Philadelphia manufacturers, emboldened by the disruption of British trade between 1806 and 1816, produced more goods for the surrounding countryside, thereby increasing the size and buying power of Philadelphia's own population. Philadelphia's additional demand for foodstuffs and other raw materials spurred more production and specialization within the hinterland, raising rural incomes and consumer purchases. The upward spiral continued in the 1820s and 1830s, making residents of both the hinterland and the city increasingly wealthy. Diane Lindstrom calls this dynamic, interactive process the "Eastern demand model" to underscore that southern or western demand for manufactured goods had little bearing on this stage of industrialization. Her painstaking statistical analysis concludes that demand from the Quaker City's surrounding countryside "was sufficient to explain the transformation of Philadelphia."[40] Other studies documenting a strong correlation between hinterland size and urban growth in the early republic provide additional support for Lindstrom's conclusions.[41]

The connection between Philadelphia's hinterland and early industrialization was part of a process that economic historians have called "Smithian" growth, after the famous author of the *Wealth of Nations*. Smith argued that economic growth arose not from revolutionary new

average value of consumer goods per capita in the South was 3.1 pounds sterling; the value of consumer goods per capita in the Middle Colonies was 4 pounds sterling. Sachs makes an important point to explain this difference: Grain prices were rising faster than the price of imported manufactured goods. See Sachs, "Agricultural Conditions," p. 281.

[39] Bushman, *Refinement of America*, pp. 227–31. Other recent studies showing the popularity of new consumer goods in the countryside include Perkins, "Consumer Frontier," and Jaffee, "Peddlers of Progress."

[40] Lindstrom, *Economic Development*, p. 112. Lindstrom notes that trade between large eastern seaboard centers rapidly expanded after the mid-1830s, foreshadowing the 1850s when interregional commerce became especially important. Nevertheless she makes clear that Philadelphia's rich hinterland initially sparked the city's development.

[41] See, for example, Crowther, "Urban Growth," pp. 628–30 and Lindstrom and Sharpless, "Urban Growth."

inventions or the exploitation of key natural resources, but from the steady application of the division of labor in response to expanding markets. Economic historians of nineteenth century America have made "the extent of markets" one of their central organizing principles. Entrepreneurs with access to large markets, encouraged to produce more goods as efficiently as possible, transformed small artisan enterprises into workshops organized around a greater division of labor. Inventors near large markets – many of them of quite modest wealth – patented technological advances that complemented the organizational changes underway. As productivity rose, so too did wages, giving Smithian growth a self-sustaining character in which large markets created even larger ones.[42]

The Smithian model helps explain how transportation improvements furthered Philadelphia's early industrialization. The early turnpikes, canals, and railroads strengthened the mutual dependence of city and hinterland, enlarging the market for manufacturers and encouraging more market production from farmers. In the late eighteenth and early nineteenth centuries, turnpikes solidified links between Philadelphia and outlying market towns. As noted in the last chapter, the state's canals proved even more important. They not only increased the flow of wheat, corn, and other agricultural commodities coming into Philadelphia, but they also opened central Pennsylvania's vast deposits of anthracite coal and iron for Philadelphia capitalists. Local railroads built in the 1830s and 1840s (the Cumberland Valley Railroad being a good example) broadened and intensified the already strong relationship between Philadelphia and its hinterland.

A brief examination of the textile industry clarifies the relationship between hinterland demand and Philadelphia's industrialization. Between 1810 and 1840, the value added by Philadelphia textile firms grew seven-fold.[43] The imposing textile mills of Lowell dominate most history textbooks, but in Philadelphia small firms were the norm. As late as 1850 the average textile firm employed only 38 workers. The combination of small mills and workshops has led historian Philip Scranton to classify Philadelphia's textile industry as "proprietary capitalism" in which individual enterprises and family

---

[42] Kenneth Sokoloff has been the leading proponent of the Smithian growth framework. His most important articles include Sokoloff, "Invention, Innovation and Manufacturing Productivity"; Sokoloff, "Was the Transition"; Sokoloff, "Productivity Growth in Manufacturing"; Lamoreaux and Sokoloff, "Long-term Change"; and Engerman and Sokoloff, "Factor Endowments." The argument that Smithian growth increased real wages is controversial, but the econometric evidence strongly suggests that the real wages of most workers rose. See, for example, Sokoloff and Villaflor, "Market for Manufacturing Workers."

[43] Lindstrom, *Economic Development*, p. 43.

partnerships flourished. The small size of Philadelphia's firms allowed the production of specialty goods – finely colored cottons, complex cotton and wool mixtures, carpets and hosiery – that created niche markets that the monotonous output of Lowell could not fill.[44]

The cultural emphasis on refinement that swept Philadelphia's hinterland created a demand that Philadelphia's industrial structure was well suited to meet. Newspaper advertisements in Cumberland County made clear the relationship between refinement on the countryside and demand for Philadelphia textiles. In 1835, one Carlisle newspaper noted that "two or three new Stores have been opened in this borough." It especially praised a new ladies shop, noting that goods sold there included "the most beautiful selections of Silks, Calicoes, and Ginghams."[45] Philadelphia manufacturers, one can safely assume, produced most of these fancy textiles.

The resulting boom in textiles, in turn, helped foster the growth of the machinery and chemicals industry. The value added by Philadelphia's machine industry rose almost ninefold between 1810 and 1840, a remarkable accomplishment given that 1840 was the heart of a general business depression.[46] The small, sophisticated firms of the textile industry often demanded new looms and mills that machinery firms produced.[47] Moreover, the scarcity of water power in the city often encouraged textile firms and other manufacturers to use steam engines. Philadelphia became a leader in the use of industrial steam engines, and by 1838 the city's flour mills, textile firms, and metals industry collectively used 126 steam engines.[48] Textiles also contributed to the growth of the chemical industry, which flourished as manufacturers demanded dyes and nitrates for cotton goods and other prints. Chemicals, in fact, became the city's fastest growing industry.[49] By 1840 the Quaker City, to borrow the terminology of Jane Jacobs, had developed "the symbiotic nests of producers' goods and services" essential for future growth.[50]

The emergence of Philadelphia's locomotive industry demonstrates how these symbiotic nests encouraged new industries. The founder of

---

[44] Scranton, *Proprietary Capitalism* and Freedley, *Philadelphia and Its Manufacturers*, pp. 232–64.
[45] *American Volunteer*, 14 May 1835, p. 3.
[46] Lindstrom, *Economic Development*, p. 43. The unfortunate absence of records has led Lindstrom to rely on Coxe's *A Statement of Arts and Manufacturers* (1810) and the 1840 census. These dates introduce a downward bias, since 1840 was part of a general business depression.
[47] Scranton, *Proprietary Capitalism*, p. 71.
[48] Cochran, *Frontiers of Change*, p. 78.
[49] Lindstrom, *Economic Development*, p. 43.
[50] Jacobs, *Cities and the Wealth of Nations*, p. 62. For another excellent example of such "symbiotic nests" and their relation to expanding markets, see Remer, *Printers and Men of Capital*, pp. 125–48.

Philadelphia's first locomotive was Mathias W. Baldwin, who began his business career producing bookbinding tools, and in 1822 diversified into engraving rolls used to print cotton goods. Books and cotton textiles – two consumer goods eagerly demanded by Philadelphia's hinterland – thus gave Baldwin his start. Baldwin then established a general machine firm that produced hydraulic presses and steam engines. His experience with steam engines made him an excellent candidate to enter the new field of locomotive production. After building a model locomotive for the Philadelphia Museum in 1830, Baldwin designed and constructed the real thing for the Philadelphia and Germantown Railroad Company. Producing locomotives on a large scale, the Baldwin Works became one of the most important firms in Philadelphia, employing 600 in 1857.[51] The link between consumer markets and producers' goods had led to the creation of a thriving new sector. Without a flourishing machine industry, Baldwin would never have built his locomotive works in Philadelphia; without a demand for books, textiles, and other consumer goods, the machine industry would never have flourished.

Opportunities for Philadelphia manufacturers increased dramatically in the 1850s, when the Pennsylvania Railroad expanded the market for Philadelphia's goods well beyond its hinterland. The entire Midwest was now a possible market for Philadelphia goods, converting Lindstrom's "Eastern demand model" into something more akin to a "national demand model." The Quaker City solidified the transition from mercantile to industrial center, achieving even more remarkable dominance over Virginia in the 1840s and 1850s. By 1860, Philadelphia produced $136 million worth of manufacturing goods, while the Old Dominion produced only $50.7 million.[52] It may appear strange to compare a single county to an entire state, but Philadelphia so dwarfed Virginia's manufacturing centers that any other comparison is almost meaningless. Here indeed was a house dividing.

The agglomeration of skilled labor, technological expertise, specialized suppliers, and marketing know-how allowed Philadelphia manufacturers to succeed in highly competitive markets. Economists call the advantages resulting from agglomeration "external economies" because they exist outside individual firms. Beginning with the British economist Alfred Marshall, economists have postulated that agglomeration results in a variety of advantages, including a deep market for high-skilled workers, a pool of specialty suppliers and subcontractors, and the possibility of "technological spillovers" (an innovation in

[51] Cochran, *Frontiers of Change*, p. 95; Freedley, *Philadelphia and Its Manufactures*, pp. 306–11.

[52] *Manufacturers* (1860 Manufacturing Census), pp. 527, 637.

one firm quickly reaching its neighbors).[53] These advantages of agglomeration, as economist Paul Krugman notes, depended on establishing a strong initial foothold in an industry so that a city "will attract still more population, at the expense of regions with smaller initial production."[54]

Qualitative evidence strongly suggests that the benefits of agglomeration exerted a powerful influence over Philadelphia's industrialization. Labor markets are a case in point. Skilled workers – whether in textiles, machinery, or iron and steel – found it advantageous to locate in an area with hundreds of potential employers. The numerous opportunities in Philadelphia, in fact, gave the Quaker City an enviable reputation as "the paradise of the skilled workman."[55] The agglomeration of manufacturing firms made Philadelphia an especially attractive place for immigrants, who provided the bulk of the skilled workforce, especially in the crucial textile sector. One might go so far as to argue that the immigration of skilled workers was the single most important "supply" factor that fueled the rapid rise of the textile industry in the early nineteenth century. These immigrants, many of them highly skilled handloom weavers from the British Isles, quickly established networks that provided reliable information flows about new opportunities, helped raise capital for aspiring immigrant entrepreneurs, and eased the cultural transition to the New World. The formation of immigrant networks thus added to the external economies resulting from agglomeration: The networks made Philadelphia a prime destination for immigrants, thus making the city more attractive to firms utilizing immigrant labor.[56]

The Philadelphia labor market, rich in skilled workers, allowed small firms to flourish through flexible labor arrangements. The textile industry is once again a good example of the interactive relationships between suppliers, producers, and skilled workers. Philadelphia's textile industry gave small firms great flexibility in reacting to

---

[53] Hoover and Vernon argue that small firms benefit most from agglomeration, since they depend heavily upon suppliers and contracting out certain work. See *Anatomy of a Metropolis*, pp. 45–51.

[54] Krugman, "Increasing Returns," p. 487.

[55] Scranton, *Proprietary Capitalism*, p. 53.

[56] Scranton, *Proprietary Capitalism*, pp. 177–95; Shelton, *Mills of Manayunk*, pp. 33–35; and Freedley, *Philadelphia and Its Manufacturers*, p. 249. Freedley's remarks concerning immigrants and the print and dye textile trade are worth quoting at length: "In the operation of Printing and Dyeing Textile Fabrics, the manufacturers of the United States have, without doubt, been greatly aided by the emigration of artisans from Europe. The attractions of Philadelphia, as a place of residence, have drawn hither the most skillful of these artisans – many of whom bring with them experience gained by almost unremitting attention to these departments of industry during the past half century in England, France, and Germany" (p. 249).

fashion trends that could dramatically alter demand. A firm that suddenly hit upon a popular style, for example, could turn to numerous subcontractors and independent weavers to meet the sudden surge in sales. As Scranton has documented, the "urban milieu" of the industry "allowed crosstown links between producers of yarn and weavers, each sustaining the other's growth or viability."[57] Historian Thomas Cochran found the same dynamics at work in Philadelphia's machine tool industry, that benefited from the "continuous interchange of information, special equipment, routine subcontracting for parts or operations, and in-house manufacture of machines by goods producers" that resulted from agglomeration.[58]

On a broader level, agglomeration contributed to a "cultural system" that encouraged technological advance.[59] The interchange between suppliers, producers, and workers led to the creation of more formal institutions to disseminate scientific and engineering information. The best-known example, the Franklin Institute, provided lectures on mechanical and scientific subjects, published a scientific journal, displayed engineering and mineral models, and sponsored an annual exhibition to promote the "Useful Arts." Neighborhood versions of the Franklin Institute offered lectures and sponsored libraries on the same subjects. These institutes made Philadelphia a particularly attractive environment for inventors, designers, and engineers who could benefit from the constant interchange of knowledge, thus bringing new technologies and production methods to the attention of manufacturers and mechanics.[60]

One might argue that emphasizing agglomeration undervalues the importance of natural resources to Philadelphia's industrialization. The rich reserves of anthracite coal in eastern Pennsylvania, after all, provided the primary fuel for most of the city's furnaces and steam engines. It would be more accurate, however, to reverse the causality between natural resources and Philadelphia's industrialization: Quaker City manufacturers "created" anthracite, not vice versa. Many residents of anthracite counties had long considered the "stone coal," composed largely of carbon, economically worthless because it was difficult to ignite. During the War of 1812, Philadelphia iron manufacturers, desperate for a dependable supply of fuel after sources of foreign bituminous coal had been cut off, began successful experiments with

---

[57] Scranton, *Proprietary Capitalism*, p. 270.
[58] Cochran, *Frontiers of Change*, p. 73.
[59] Meinig, *The Shaping of America*, pp. 389–90.
[60] The *Journal of the Franklin Institute*, for example, outlined the possibilities of anthracite coal in 1826, helping manufacturers adapt their furnaces and steam engines to the new fuel. See Scharf, *History of Philadelphia*, p. 2272.

anthracite. After the war, Philadelphia businessmen invested in anthracite fields while simultaneously experimenting with new grates and furnaces that could use the smokeless, long-burning coal. By the late 1820s, anthracite was a proven, low-cost fuel. At every step of the way, Philadelphia entrepreneurs, responding to the incentives of a large market, provided the capital and conducted the experiments that converted anthracite into one of antebellum America's most important energy sources.[61]

Plantation Slavery and the Lack of Market Demand

While Philadelphia's economy benefited from agglomeration, urban growth in Virginia stagnated because slavery discouraged rural population growth, thereby limiting the size of potential markets. To show the impact of slavery on market size, consider the following experiment. Imagine that Virginia's rivers and waterways led to one central city that dominated the entire Tidewater region. What sort of rural markets would entrepreneurs in our imaginary city find? Compared to Philadelphia, markets would be sparse. In 1810, the Tidewater region had only 32.5 residents per square mile versus 43 for the Philadelphia region (Table 6.3). Over the next decade, the disparity became even more pronounced: 53.6 residents per square mile for Philadelphia's hinterland, versus 34 for Virginia. One imagines that potential manufacturers in our imaginary Tidewater society would have packed their bags and headed north to denser and more lucrative markets.

What accounted for the slow population growth of the Tidewater region? Staple-crop theories, however important in the colonial period, cannot account for this difference. Wheat, after all, was the main crop of the Tidewater region by the Revolutionary War. The main reason for Virginia's low population density was that slavery removed the constraint on how much acreage a single family could work, creating much larger farms. Everything else being equal, larger farms meant fewer farms per square mile of land and hence fewer people. According to the 1850 census, the 21 counties in Philadelphia's immediate hinterland contained 51,694 farms (4.3 farms per square mile). The entire Tidewater region of Virginia had only 16,241 farms and plantations (1.6 per square mile).[62] The difference might have been somewhat smaller in the earlier decades, but the evidence

---

[61] This paragraph draws heavily on Chandler, "Anthracite Coal," pp. 149–53. Philadelphia capital also played a vital role in building the canals and railroads that allowed the wide-scale exploitation of anthracite. See, for example, Davis, *Anthracite Aristocracy*, pp. 4–5, 19, 108.

[62] The areas are the same used in Table 6.4, with the farms in Philadelphia County also counted.

Table 6.3. *The Impact of Slavery on Market Size:*
Population Densities of Philadelphia's Hinterland and Tidewater Virginia

Year	Immediate Hinterland of Philadelphia (total population)	Hinterland of "Imaginary Tidewater City" (total population)	Hinterland of "Imaginary Tidewater City" (free population only)
1800	404,959 (35.3 per square mile)	338,833 (30.2 per square mile)	129,424 (12.4 per square mile)
1810	493,223 (43.0 per square mile)	340,161 (32.5 per square mile)	127,551 (12.2 per square mile)
1820	614,682 (53.6 per square mile)	356,159 (34.0 per square mile)	147,297 (14.1 per square mile)

Notes and Sources: Figures include both slave and free populations. Many counties that might have been included in the Philadelphia hinterland were excluded to keep each hinterland approximately the same size (10,000–11,000 square miles). The calculations for Philadelphia are therefore biased downward. Philadelphia hinterland includes Berks, Bucks, Chester, Delaware, Lancaster, Montgomery, and Philadelphia counties in Pennsylvania; Burlington, Cape May, Cumberland, Gloucester, Hunterdon, Monmouth, Salem, and Sussex counties in New Jersey; and all counties in Delaware. The Tidewater hinterland includes the Tidewater counties – taken from Freehling's *Drift toward Dissolution* – listed in the appendix.

suggests that small family farms meant that the Philadelphia region had more people and hence more potential consumers.[63]

Distinguishing between slave and free populations made Tidewater Virginia's potential market even smaller. More than half of the Tidewater's population consisted of slaves, which dramatically reduced the buying power of the region as a whole. Although historians have found that masters sometimes gave slaves cash rewards to encourage good work, these small allowances added little to consumer demand.[64]

[63] Emphasizing the relationship between slavery and market size is hardly novel. Eugene Genovese's famous essay "The Significance of the Slave Plantation for Southern Economic Development" argued that "the retardation of the home market for both industrial and agricultural commodities" accounted for the South's inability to industrialize. My argument differs somewhat from Genovese's. Whereas Genovese emphasized that small markets prevented southern firms from achieving economies of scale, I stress the advantages of agglomeration that Philadelphia manufacturers enjoyed. Economic historians have generally found economies of scale to be of only limited importance in early American industrialization, opening up Genovese to considerable criticism. See, for example, Fogel and Engerman, "Economics of Slavery," p. 337.

[64] The large literature on cash rewards and independent production includes Fogel, *Without Consent or Contract*, pp. 188-94; Fogel and Engerman, *Time on the Cross*, pp. 151-52; McDonald, "Independent Economic Production"; Campbell, "As 'A Kind of Freeman?'"; and Walsh, "Slave Life."

Charles Dew's detailed research into slave life at Buffalo Forge ironworks reveals that the most a highly skilled slave could hope to earn in
a given year was $100; in most years, their earnings fell somewhere
between $30 and $50.[65] The typical field hand would make far less.
The cheap textiles and shoes supplied by masters hardly measured up
to the quality and variety of goods that Philadelphia consumers
demanded. No wonder that abolitionists such as Cassius M. Clay
declared that "A home market cannot exist in a slave state."[66]

Slavery also discouraged the development of towns, thus putting
an additional brake on the growth of consumer demand. Because
slaveholders had an economic incentive to keep their workers busy
all year around, many plantations were often diversified enterprises
that grew their own food, employed their own carpenters, and owned
their own mills. Smaller farmers needing such services often turned to
their wealthier neighbors to hire out a skilled artisan or utilize the
plantation's blacksmith.[67] Virginia's towns, therefore, had relatively
little to do with the day-to-day operations of a plantation outside of
marketing its crops. The relative underdevelopment of small towns in
the Old Dominion – recall that even thriving Charlottesville fell well
behind Carlisle in population growth – translated into another missing layer of consumer demand.[68]

Geography only made things worse. The confluence of the Delaware and Schuylkill Rivers encouraged the growth of one large city
to dominate eastern Pennsylvania, but the parallel rivers in Virginia
led to the formation of many smaller cities, each serving its own ripar-
ian hinterland. With a rural population spread over a wide area, transportation costs to a central city would have been high. It therefore
made economic sense to have a number of smaller cities to service
Virginia's plantation economy. Alexandria, Norfolk, Lynchburg,
Petersburg, and Richmond thus divided the Old Dominion's potential market – which was already small to begin with – into a number of
smaller markets. The dynamic interplay of population density and
geography helps explain not only the low overall rate of urbanization

<hr/>

[65] Dew, *Bond of Iron*, pp. 171-203.
[66] Quoted in Genovese, *Political Economy*, p. 173. David R. Meyer's comparison of southern and Midwestern industrialization also stresses the South's lack of markets. See
"Emergence of the American Manufacturing Belt," pp. 164-68 and "Industrial
Retardation."
[67] On the relative self-sufficiency of the plantation, see Anderson and Gallman's classic
"Slaves as Fixed Capital" as well as Fogel, *Without Consent or Contract*, pp. 109-10. Fogel
adds an interesting twist to this argument. By limiting the number of millers, merchants, and other rural entrepreneurs, slavery might well have also limited the
growth of entrepreneurial talent that could transfer resources out of agriculture and
into industry.
[68] The relative absence of small towns within the South is documented in Elkins and
McKitrick, "A Meaning for Turner's Frontier," pp. 341-42.

in Virginia, but also why the state's small urban population was divided into small cities instead of one large one.

One important question remains to be answered. If slavery stunted the growth of Virginia's cities, then how did Baltimore grow so rapidly in the nineteenth century? Baltimore became one of the largest cities in antebellum America because it had a special resource that Virginia's cities lacked: excellent access to markets in free-labor areas. The Susquehanna River, although often treacherous to navigate, allowed Baltimore's merchants to tap central and southern Pennsylvania, while a network of turnpikes connected the city to western Maryland, where slavery was relatively weak.[69] In the 1830s and 1840s, the city's most important transportation projects, including the Chesapeake and Ohio Canal and the Baltimore and Ohio Railroad, increased the size of the city's free-labor hinterland. Baltimore's growth provides an instructive lesson: A large city could develop in a slave state as long as it had a free-labor hinterland.

Richmond and the Limitations of Virginia's Industrialization

Without a hinterland similar to Philadelphia or Baltimore, industrial and urban growth proceeded slowly in the Old Dominion. Yet even if potential markets were small in Virginia, what prevented Old Dominion's manufacturers from at least supplying their own markets? The question is important because some historians have argued that by 1860 the South had large enough home markets to support a large textile industry.[70] What this static analysis ignores is that the southern population, spread out over a wide area, was not large enough to encourage the *concentration* of industry with its attendant advantages. Virginia firms, even with lower transportation costs, had trouble competing in their own state without access to the same agglomerated pools of supplies, workers, and technology available in Philadelphia and other northern cities.

The example of Richmond highlights the disadvantages of Virginia manufacturers. In the 1850s, Richmond had earned its reputation as the "Lowell of the South." Railroads significantly strengthened ties to central and southwestern Virginia, thereby increasing trade and the potential market for manufactured goods. Especially impressive was the massive Tredegar Iron Works, which produced railroad tracks, large cannons, and other iron goods. Under the aggressive leadership of Joseph Anderson, the company grew from a fledgling enterprise in

---

[69] Fields, *Slavery and Freedom on the Middle Ground*, p. 42.
[70] Fogel and Engerman, "Economics of Slavery," p. 337.

the 1840s to one of the most impressive factories of the South. By 1860, Tredegar was capitalized at $1,000,000 and employed 800 men. Another widely reported success was the Gallego Mills, the largest wheat-milling complex in the United States. The superior flour of the Gallego Mills could survive the lengthy journey to South America and Australia, allowing the firm to carve out a lucrative niche in world markets.[71] One should not exaggerate the success of Richmond – in 1860 the number of employees in Philadelphia's textile and clothing sectors exceeded Richmond's entire population – but nevertheless the city's success suggested that Virginia might someday achieve commercial and industrial independence from the North.

Richmond manufacturers, however, rarely competed against Philadelphia's agglomeration of firms and skilled workers. Examining the number of firms and employees in each city's major industries reveals that manufacturers in Richmond and Philadelphia rarely overlapped (Table 6.4). Philadelphia had particularly strong advantages in textile production and chemicals, while Richmond entrepreneurs concentrated in processing industries, where the tobacco and wheat production of its hinterland could provide important advantages. The tobacco industry alone employed 45 percent of the city's manufacturing workforce. Unfortunately for Richmond's boosters, tobacco and wheat did not fundamentally transform the city's economy. These processing industries created a local market for steam engines, but Richmond's machine industry remained quite small in comparison to Philadelphia's.

Richmond's tobacco manufacturers deserve special comment, for they highlight the conditions under which Virginia entrepreneurs could succeed. Whereas most tobacco consumption in the eighteenth century was in the form of snuff and cigars, in the early 1800s chewing tobacco became increasingly popular among American workers. Since manufacturing cigars and snuff differed dramatically from producing plugs of chewing tobacco, Virginians entering this industry faced little northern competition. Indeed, Virginians had a decided advantage because the main skill in producing chewing tobacco was picking the best tasting leaf. Historian Frederick Siegel found that "[A]n intimate knowledge of the crop [was] a prerequisite for success. In his capacity as a buyer, the manufacturer had to choose a leaf wrapper that would appeal to fickle consumers. This required an ability to make small distinctions between the seemingly similar masses of loose tobacco brought before him."[72] Using hired slaves as a flexible workforce, the Old Dominion's tobacco manufacturers expanded

---

[71] Goldfield, *Urban Growth*, p. 193 and Goldfield, "Pursuing the Urban Dream," p. 58.
[72] Siegel, *Roots of Southern Distinctiveness*, p. 126.

production dramatically in the 1840s and 1850s.[73] For once, Virginia's entrepreneurs enjoyed the advantages of being the first to serve a market.

Richmond's flourishing tobacco manufacturers suggest that slavery did not *directly* deter the growth of Virginia industry. Some historians have argued that slavery inhibited urban and industrial growth because white Virginians feared that slaves concentrated in cities were inherently more dangerous than slaves diffused throughout the countryside. The influx of slaves into Richmond's tobacco factories, for instance, created a storm of protest from newspaper editors, local politicians and other concerned citizens.[74] Although many in Richmond distrusted the slaves working in tobacco factories, little direct evidence suggests that these attitudes prevented the growth of tobacco manufacturing and other industrial enterprises. The very presence of industrial slaves in Richmond, in fact, indicates that Virginians readily ignored the strictures of newspaper editorialists and political speeches when sizeable profits could be had. Dreams of growth and prosperity overcame more distant fears of slave revolts and political upheaval. To put it another way, the fundamental problem for Virginia's manufacturers revolved around the structure of the state's economy, not ideological opposition to urban slavery.

The structural defects of Virginia's economy made new market niches hard to find. Philadelphia's advantages – derived from a rich home market, decades of accumulated experience, and readily available skilled labor – limited the ability of Virginia firms to compete directly with northern rivals. The Tredegar Works was a case in point. Tredegar, in the words of one historian, was "inherently uncompetitive."[75] The firm survived only through a combination of government contracts, liberal credit to financially suspect railroads, and regional goodwill that "Buy Southern" campaigns generated.[76] Part of the problem for Tredegar was an undependable supply of pig iron. The Old Dominion once had a flourishing pig iron industry that utilized the iron and timber reserves of the Shenandoah Valley. Technologically advanced Pennsylvania producers, however, undercut the isolated and obsolescent valley furnaces, forcing Anderson to import most of his pig iron from the Keystone State.[77] To make matters worse, Anderson had to acquire northern machinery and parts because of the absence

---

[73] For an overview of the growth of Virginia's tobacco industry, see Siegel, *Roots of Southern Distinctiveness*, pp. 120–35 and Robert, *Tobacco Kingdom*, pp. 161–96.
[74] Ashworth, *Slavery, Capitalism, and Politics*, pp. 108–12. For a summary of the debate from a "cliometric" perspective, see Fogel, *Without Consent or Contract*, pp. 107–8.
[75] Meinig, *The Shaping of America*, p. 389.
[76] Lewis, *Coal, Iron, and Slaves*, pp. 195–98.
[77] Dew, *Ironmaker of the Confederacy*, pp. 32–34. Dew reports that pig iron production in Virginia plummeted from 22,163 tons in 1850 to 11,396 tons in 1860.

Table 6.4. *Regional Specialization and Manufacturing: A Comparison of Selected Industries in Philadelphia and Richmond, 1860*

Industry	Philadelphia			Richmond		
	Firms	Number Employed	Percent of U.S. Workforce	Firms	Number Employed	Percent of U.S. Workforce
Textile Related	1,192	42,523	13.19	23	233	0.07
Calico printing	6	801	20.57	0	0	0.00
Carpets	120	2,370	35.46	0	0	0.00
Caps & hats	74	1,325	11.26	3	10	0.09
Clothing (Ready-made)	464	18,260	15.15	16	89	0.07
Cotton goods	119	13,010	10.75	1	20	0.02
Dyeing	46	357	11.15	0	0	0.00
Hosiery	97	2,613	28.70	0	0	0.00
Millinery	209	928	19.55	2	14	0.29
Woolens	57	2,859	6.91	1	100	0.24
Iron & Steel Products	227	3,671	5.91	19	984	1.97
Machinery	78	4,104	10.05	9	475	1.04
Locomotives	2	1,255	30.07	0	0	0.00
Machinist tools	1	190	41.76	0	0	0.00
Misc. machines	13	311	13.23	0	0	0.00
Steam engines	62	2,111	5.83	9	475	1.31
Textile machines	13	548	11.38	0	0	0.00

Processing	484	4,110	2.40	80	3,780	2.20
Cigars	231	1,307	16.34	2	6	0.08
Flour	29	191	0.69	12	276	1.00
Leather	83	1,292	5.09	1	3	0.01
Liquors	113	705	5.60	2	42	0.33
Lumber	17	115	0.15	11	83	0.11
Sugar refining	8	478	13.72	0	0	0.00
Tobacco	3	22	0.12	52	3,370	17.87
Boots & Shoes	715	8,487	6.90	20	159	0.13
Chemicals	90	1,701	37.00	0	0	0.00

Notes and Sources: Calculated from *Manufacturers* (1860 manufacturing census), pp. 522–27, 616–17.

of specialized suppliers in the Richmond area. Anderson also had great difficulty finding skilled workers. Dew reports that "When Anderson needed to replace a foreman or add skilled labor, he almost invariably addressed his inquires to Northern business acquaintances."[78]

The Limitations of Virginia's Economic Success

The inability of Tredegar to compete effectively with northern producers suggests that Virginians were quite rational to invest in plantations and slaves rather than industrial enterprises. If Tredegar could survive only because of comfortable government contracts and regional goodwill, then what would happen to other large enterprises? Plantation agriculture, especially with the particularly high grain and tobacco prices of the 1850s, made better sense. Fogel and Engerman, as well as other economic historians, are therefore correct to stress that Virginians and other Southerners followed their "comparative advantage" in staple agriculture. Comparative advantage, however, is not so much an explanation of the problem as a restatement of the question. Why were Virginians stuck with a "comparative advantage" that left them with far lower per capita incomes than the industrializing Northeast? As early as 1840, after all, income per (free) person was $96 in the South Atlantic region (including Virginia) and $130 for the Northeast (including Pennsylvania).[79]

Virginia's reliance on plantations and slaves had its roots in the colonial era, when tobacco's lack of forward linkages and the Navigation Acts conspired to limit city growth. These disadvantages were significant, but hardly insurmountable. Baltimore, for example, grew dramatically during the antebellum decades after a slow start in the colonial period. Baltimore, however, could draw upon the trade of a dense network of free-labor farms in western Maryland and southern Pennsylvania. In Virginia, slavery limited rural population growth to create small hinterlands for the state's cities. Virginia's system of

---

[78] Dew, *Ironmaker of the Confederacy*, p. 28. Berlin and Gutman ("Natives and Immigrants") report that Richmond and other southern cities attracted thousands of immigrants during the 1840s and 1850s. Could these immigrants have provided the same network of skilled mechanics that existed in the Philadelphia region? On limited scale, perhaps, but not on a level that could have provided local manufacturers with highly specialized workmen at a moment's notice.

[79] Fogel, *Without Consent or Contract*, p. 85. Gavin Wright's analysis of the comparative advantage concept is useful here: "As frequently used, the term comparative advantage is no more than a tautology: goods would not be produced unless it were profitable to do so, and if it was profitable to produce these goods, the region must have had a comparative advantage in those goods. If economists can speak so loosely, then the parrot who became an economist by learning to say 'supply and demand' will become an international economist by learning only one more term." *Political Economy*, pp. 111–12.

parallel rivers further subdivided local markets. The absence of large, nearby markets doused the economic incentives to move resources out of agriculture and into manufacturing.

Once the Old Dominion had fallen behind in manufacturing by the 1840s, it proved exceedingly difficult to catch up without a concentration of specialized suppliers and skilled labor. While Richmond grew significantly during the antebellum decades, most of the city's industries revolved around processing tobacco and wheat. As the example of the Tredegar Iron Works suggests, Virginia entrepreneurs could not profitably compete against northern rivals in iron manufacturing, textiles, and a host of other major industries. The Old Dominion's plantation economy thus perpetuated itself, producing considerable profits but only limited development.

The situation in Philadelphia was much different. In the colonial period, Philadelphia was blessed with a number of important advantages: excellent access to water transportation; booming markets for the products of its hinterlands; and the legal right to participate in the international grain trade. Philadelphia's substantial growth in the colonial period, however, did not guarantee that it would become a great manufacturing center. Entrepreneurs in Philadelphia expanded manufacturing output in the early nineteenth century because their city's hinterland provided excellent markets close to home. A snowball effect then ensued. The presence of manufacturing opportunities encouraged skilled laborers and specialized firms to move to Philadelphia, encouraging more growth. Utilizing the advantages of agglomeration, Philadelphia turned its substantial head start into an advantage that even the most determined industrialists in Virginia could not overcome.

Epilogue
Railroad Networks
and the Civil War

Virginia's railroads on the eve of the Civil War – a collection of local lines that failed to reach the Midwest – typified the southern network as a whole. While the South and the North were about equal in per capita mileage, the northern network almost tripled the South's on a square-mile basis.[1] Moreover, southern railroads generally had fewer stations, fewer employees, and less rolling stock than their northern counterparts.[2] Southern inferiority largely stemmed from the region's lack of integrated trunk lines. Historian Tony A. Freyer, for example, has compared the "centralized private managerial power" of northern railroads with the South's failure to "consolidate the region's roads into unified systems."[3] Even Robert William Fogel, who depicts a growing and prosperous southern economy, contrasts "the great railroad trunk lines connecting the cities of the Midwest and the East" with the conspicuous absence of "railroad links between the Midwest and the South."[4]

Southerners would pay a high price for their lack of trunk lines. Economically, manufacturers along the South Atlantic coast would have only limited access to midwestern markets. Economic isolation, in turn, had profound cultural significance. Historian Ronald J. Zboray argues that as northern railroad systems grew more integrated, book publishing became concentrated in a few northern cities such as New York and Boston. Literature hostile to slavery – including the runaway bestseller *Uncle Tom's Cabin* – emanated from these commercial centers to an increasingly large number of northern towns, hamlets, and villages.[5] Remote from the national centers of culture, Southerners were increasingly portrayed as unrefined and illiterate – "a bowie-knife style of civilization," according to one northern critic – in

---

[1] Wright, *Old South, New South*, p. 22. See especially Table 2.2.
[2] Stover, *Railroads of the South*, pp. 13–14.
[3] Freyer, "Law and the Antebellum Southern Economy," p. 54. Eugene Alvarez adds that "the Southern railway system by 1861 left much to be desired. The network was severely handicapped by the failure to develop any real system of trunk lines." See *Travel on Southern Antebellum Railroads*, p. 164.
[4] Fogel, *Without Consent or Contract*, p. 304.
[5] Zboray, *Fictive People*, p. 66.

national magazines and novels.[6] Southern intellectuals felt their isolation all too keenly. "It would scarcely be too extravagant," one Charleston poet wrote, "to entitle the Southern author the Pariah of modern literature."[7] Railroads and internal improvements, heralded for decades as a way to "bind the republic together," contributed to the alienation of the South from the national mainstream.[8]

The railroads that tied together the Northeast and Midwest also contributed to the South's political isolation. In the early nineteenth century, the fundamental economic and political orientation of the Midwest remained unsettled. Slavery was largely absent in the region, but large areas of Ohio, Indiana, and Illinois still had strong ties with the South. Many settlers in the region hailed from slave states. The trade of the Midwest, flowing down the Ohio and Mississippi Rivers, created a thriving southern commerce dominated by St. Louis and New Orleans. The "natural" relationship between the South and Midwest, however, diminished in significance during the 1840s and 1850s. The Erie Canal and the trunk railroads encouraged Midwesterners to ship their products to northern cities, purchase their manufactured goods from northern factories, finance their railroads and banks with northern capital, and buy their books and magazines from northern presses.[9] Midwestern towns competing for capital and migrants promoted their prospects in Philadelphia, New York, and Boston, not Richmond, Norfolk, or Charleston.[10] Far more than economic interest, of course, accounted for the complex political alignment of the West and North in the 1840s and 1850s. Nevertheless, trunk line railroads helped insure that most of the Midwest stood on the northern side of the house divided during the sectional crisis of the 1850s.

When the Civil War came, the southern railroad network was ill-prepared for the challenges confronting it. The Confederacy had only one east – west rail route that connected the Mississippi to the eastern seaboard. Under the management of a number of separate companies – some with differing gauges – the meandering line from Memphis to Richmond was "lightly constructed and poorly equipped for the

[6] Bushman, *Refinement of America*, pp. 390–98. Quote from Horace Bushnell in *Refinement*, p. 393.
[7] Quoted in Faust, *A Sacred Circle*, p. 10.
[8] Larson, "Bind the Republic Together," pp. 363–87. Richard John perceptively notes that "Between 1792 and 1835, the expansion of the facilities of communication had worked to strengthen the bonds of Union. Between 1835 and 1861, however, the same facilities worked no less inexorably to drive the Union apart." See *Spreading the News*, p. 260.
[9] Taylor, for example, notes that even as the absolute value of trade along the Mississippi expanded in the 1850s in response to the rapid settlement of the West, its relative importance had declined dramatically. *Transportation Revolution*, pp. 163–69.
[10] Adler, *Yankee Merchants*, p. 43.

enormous load it was called on to carry"[11] Southern railroads took weeks to transport supplies and raw materials between eastern and western theaters, especially when Union troops in eastern Tennessee cut the Confederacy's "direct" rail connection. In September of 1863, southern railroads took several weeks to transport 12,000 men from Virginia to Georgia. Half of those troops arrived too late to participate in the crucial battle of Chickamauga, while artillery units assigned to the units arrived five days after the battle was over.[12] Perhaps those 6,000 men and acompanying artillery might have turned an indecisive victory into an important strategic success.

Northerners, on the other hand, excelled at the movement of resources and troops along trunk lines such as the Pennsylvania Railroad and the Baltimore and Ohio. When the Confederates had almost cut off the Union army at Chattanooga, northern railroads moved two entire corps from the Potomac to Tennessee. The movement of 20,000 men with accompanying artillery, horses, and equipment in 11 days constituted "the longest and fastest movement of such a large body of troops before the twentieth century."[13] Even more importantly, northern trunk railroads helped insure that Midwestern grain and livestock would feed the North when the Confederacy cut off the Mississippi River. In the South, meanwhile, the lack of adequate transportation meant hardship in a land of plenty. Historian Emory Thomas notes that "People went hungry in the midst of full cribs, barns, and smokehouses. A bountiful harvest counted for little if local railroad tracks were destroyed by foes or cannibalized by friends, if the road to town were a quagmire, or if wagons and mules were impressed to serve the army."[14]

The failure of the South's transportation network is all the more ironic given the great enthusiasm that Southerners displayed for internal improvements. The evidence from Albemarle, in particular, shows that spirited rivalries for turnpikes, canals, and railroads animated local politics. The county's enthusiasm for internal improvements undermines a common assumption that the South's vibrant networks of kinship groups and rural communities were hostile to economic development. Communities and neighborhoods encouraged developmental projects partly because residents believed that higher land values, greater town growth, and increased commercial activity deterred migration to the frontier. Developmental projects frequently harnessed traditional southern values such as honor and loyalty in the name of economic modernization. Aspiring politicians

[11] Turner, *Victory Rides the Rails*, p. 31.
[12] Turner, *Victory Rides the Rails*, pp. 282–86.
[13] McPherson, *Battle Cry of Freedom*, p. 675.
[14] Quoted in Beringer, et al., *Why the South Lost*, p. 12.

frequently displayed their patriotism and honor through the support of a canal or railroad.

Given such enthusiasm for internal improvements, one wonders why Virginia kept losing ground to Pennsylvania and other northern states. Perhaps a more enlightened legislative policy – such as focusing the state's resources to speedily complete a single trunk line – would have saved the Old Dominion and the rest of the South from disaster. This reasoning overlooks the intimate relationship between economic structure and economic policy. A polity composed of small, evenly matched cities encouraged legislative intrigue antithetical to rational planning. Assuming that a single trunk line would have transformed Virginia's economy confuses the symptoms of the state's economic failures with its underlying causes. The inability to build a trunk line had grievous consequences for the Old Dominion, but it was also symptomatic of deeper problems that left Virginians unable to generate a sufficient concentration of traffic, capital, and people to finish such a venture.

No government policy, however wise or farsighted, could have replicated the tremendous advantages of a large commercial city. In the early nineteenth century, the impact of urban capital was limited; residents of Cumberland County, for example, financed almost all of their turnpikes and toll bridges with local resources. But the turnpikes and bridges built in Cumberland and other hinterland localities increased trade with Philadelphia. By the 1830s, the interaction of Philadelphia with its hinterland had set into motion a dizzying spiral of development. The prosperity of the countryside encouraged the growth of Philadelphia, which then allowed the Quaker City to improve transportation and expand its potential market. By the 1850s, Philadelphia had the wealth, population, and political power to anchor an impressive railroad network that linked the city's merchants and manufacturers to Chicago and points beyond.

The root cause of Philadelphia's economic success was a densely populated hinterland that provided the city's entrepreneurs with a large market for manufactured goods in the early nineteenth century. Emphasizing population size as an explanation for industrialization might strike some as a case of putting the cart before the horse. Population growth, after all, is usually considered a result, not a cause, of economic development. To a certain extent, this claim is true. Philadelphia's industrialization, which made the city an attractive destination for thousands of immigrants, did indeed promote rapid population growth. The population density of Philadelphia's hinterland, however, was far ahead of Virginia's well *before* the Quaker City began its industrial ascent. The initial concentration of people in Philadelphia's hinterland created the necessary incentives to encourage manufacturers.

Readily available water transportation and excellent access to anthracite coal were also important, but these favorable conditions would have been moot if tens of thousands of farm families had not provided a market for Philadelphia's factories and workshops.

Slavery stunted the growth of markets that had done so much to encourage Philadelphia's development. Slavery encouraged the growth of largely self-sufficient plantations that limited population density and town growth. Virginia's sparse population created its own self-reinforcing cycle: The lack of markets discouraged manufacturing and urbanization, which led to more investment in slaves and plantations that further stifled market development. Without a city of the size and scale of Philadelphia, Virginians had to rely on local enterprise and state investment. The result was a fragmented transportation network that did little to encourage Virginia's industrialization.

Virginians tried mightily to overcome their lack of adequate markets that left them without a large urban center. Yet political exhortation, government investment, and local boosterism never reversed slavery's smothering impact on urban development. For all the hopes of rejuvenating their economy, Virginians never quite understood that the chains of slavery also shackled the invisible hand of the market. Left without a true commercial center, Virginian's economy would remain fettered to staple agriculture.

Appendix on
Sources and Methods

Most statistical appendixes serve as a refuge for tables and to⟩ dull for the main text. The reason for their lackluster state is nc to surmise. Historians eagerly devote page after page to the lates oretical concepts, but often gloss over the nuts and bolts of arch research and statistical methods. This appendix tries to be a bit different. Although arranged topically, it narrates the many mistakes and occasional discoveries that I made in the seven years of researching and writing this book. Much of what follows will strike many as pedestrian and commonsensical. But however simple-minded this discussion may be, it at least highlights a question that often receives little attention: How do historians produce new knowledge? The emphasis on the mundane and the practical, I hope, will not only save fellow researchers the many hours that I wasted following dead-end leads and wrong-headed techniques, but also help demystify social science history.

Let us begin with the very basics: computer programs. After spending hundreds of hours entering in names and numbers, I began to see the computer as an essential tool for accomplishing my task. The program that I used most often for entering data and performing computations was Microsoft Excel. I stumbled onto Excel by accident, but the program has proven effective for my needs, especially as it improved over the years. As a spreadsheet, Excel allows one to sort a large number of records alphabetically, a particularly useful function when linking names from census records and tax lists to business records. Excel also comes with a surprisingly complete package of statistical tools (including regression analysis) that ended my short and unhappy relationship with powerful mainframe programs. More sophisticated quantitative historians will undoubtedly sneer at my single-minded devotion to a mere spreadsheet program, but I happily acknowledge my limitations.

What made Excel particularly useful was its "portability" – it could be used on a laptop computer, even the relatively primitive 386 IBM models of the early 1990s. This meant that a great deal of data from archival sources – especially hard-to-copy business ledgers – could be entered directly into the program. Microfilmed material, especially tax and census manuscripts, proved to be a different story. I found the combination of blurry microfilm and a small computer screen too much for my eyes. Making handwritten notes thus became an essential intermediate step for microfilm which is too expensive or unwieldy to copy. I eventually discovered that photocopied worksheets with appropriate spaces for each variable made the handwritten collection of data faster and more accurate. My files became stuffed with such worksheets, which I could then enter into the computer in the comfort of home and office.

I. Calculating the Distribution of Wealth for Each County

One of my first tasks was entering data from county tax lists and census manuscripts into Excel. I knew that whatever direction my research took me, the distribution of wealth in each county would be an important statistic to calculate. And the tax lists and census records necessary for these calculations were readily available at the Los Angeles Family History Center or through interlibrary loan.[1] In my initial flush of enthusiasm, I began to enter every name from the 1800 Albemarle tax list. There was no substitute for scholarly thoroughness, I reasoned. After weeks of tedious labor, I had yet to finish this one list, learning the hard way why social and economic historians use samples.

My particular sampling method was somewhat unorthodox. I took all of the last names beginning with "B" and "W" from the tax records and census records of each county. This method has some important potential biases, especially in ethnically diverse localities. Would the surnames in the "Bs" and "Ws" overrepresent certain ethnic groups and hence give a misleading picture of each county's economy? The answer appears to be no. Judith Ridner, using 1808 tax data for *all* Carlisle residents, calculated that the top 10 percent owned 51.9 percent of the town's wealth and that the top 50 percent owned 96.5 percent of the town's wealth.[2] A sample based on surnames with "Bs" and "Ws" in 1808 Carlisle tax records shows that the top 10 percent owned 47.4 percent and the top 50 percent owned 97.6 percent of wealth. Not perfect, to be sure, but close enough for general assessments of how wealth was distributed. The "Bs" and "Ws" samples for the two counties as a whole – which were far larger than the Carlisle 1808 sample – should be even more accurate.

Even with accurate samples, tax and census records are hardly ideal for calculating the distribution of wealth. As noted in the text,

[1] I thank Holly Brewer for introducing me to the Family History Center.
[2] Ridner, "A Handsomely Improved Place" (Ph. D. diss.), p. 375.

tax assessors frequently undervalued property. This bias may have been particularly severe for larger land holdings, as politically well-connected owners could have exerted pressure for lower assessments. An even more serious problem is that the assessments usually ignored wealth not in the form of land and slaves. Pennsylvania and Virginia, for example, only intermittently taxed government and corporate securities. The same problem exists for the 1850 census, which only recorded the value of a household's real property. The only exception to the omission of paper wealth were the Cumberland tax lists for 1838, which recorded "money at interest." In Carlisle, the top 10 percent owned 67 percent of real property and 75 percent of total wealth (including the "money at interest" variable). The following tables, based on real property holdings, thus tend to *underestimate* the concentration of overall wealth.

For Cumberland County, I separated Carlisle from the rural townships. One disadvantage of the "Bs" and "Ws" sample was that for Carlisle itself, the number of households proved too small to accurately estimate the wealth of the top 5 percent. For 1838 and 1850, I took all of the household heads with an occupation, so these two samples are much larger. (The data for 1838 and 1850 were also used to chart changes in Carlisle's occupational structure, as outlined in the following table.) Comparing these samples shows that inequality in Carlisle grew substantially over time, especially between 1838 and 1850. Those who owned property (including artisans) reaped big benefits from rising land values, while the influx of immigrants and wage workers created a growing class of households with little or no real property.

Table 1. *Distribution of Real Property in Carlisle*

Year (source)	Number of Sample Households	Percentage of Real Property Owned by Top 5 Percent	Percentage of Real Property Owned by Top 10 Percent
1808 (tax lists)	43	not calculated	47
1820 (tax lists)	70	not calculated	61
1838 (tax lists)	395	41	67
1850 (census)	574	59	74

Notes and Sources: For 1808 and 1820, the sample includes all households in Carlisle with surnames beginning with "B" or "W" appearing on microfilmed tax lists at the Los Angeles Family History Center. For 1838 and 1850, the sample includes all households with a listed occupation appearing in the 1838 tax lists or the 1850 census (both available on microfilm at the Los Angeles Family History Center). Farmers and farm land were excluded from the calculations.

Wealth was more evenly distributed in Cumberland's rural townships. The "Bs" and "Ws" samples for three rural townships show that the top decile owned about half of real property and the top 5 percent owned about a third. These calculations should be taken as lower-bound estimates. Although the three rural townships represent farmers from the fertile central valley (South Middleton and Southampton) as well as those from the hilly areas on the county's fringes (Mifflin), the sample cannot account for property owners who owned farms and mills across township lines. I found it extremely difficult to rectify this problem, especially given that Cumberland's numerous farm families were divided into townships that had their own tax lists. Was the John Wood that owned a farm in Middleton township the same John Wood that owned a mill in Southampton township? I could never be sure. On the other hand, anecdotal evidence suggests the ownership of multiple properties seemed concentrated among Carlisle's elite; lawyers such as Charles B. Penrose invested quite heavily in rural real estate and industrial enterprises throughout the county. Correcting the bias, in other words, would do little to increase the visibility of inequality *within* the rural townships.

In any case, accounting for multiple farm ownership in Cumberland would probably not raise inequality to the level of Albemarle's slave society. The top 10 percent of the Albemarle distribution owned around 70 percent of the value of all real estate throughout the nineteenth century.[3] Two factors accounted for the greater inequality in Albemarle. The richest Albemarle planters owned multiple farms and plantations that the county's tax lists (unlike those of Cumberland County) clearly documented. For example, Nelson Barksdale, the wealthiest landowner in the 1850 sample, owned ten separate tracts of land collectively valued at $48,049. Each individual farm in Albemarle was also far larger than individual farms in Cumberland, as slavery removed the labor constraint that generally prevented large-scale farms in free-labor states. Northern charges that southern slaveholders constituted a "landed aristocracy" thus had at least a vague ring of truth.

Slaves, ironically enough, were distributed more equally than land in Albemarle. The top 10 percent owned "only" between 52–58 percent of the county's slaves (a distribution similar to that of land ownership in Cumberland County). A large number of small slaveholders accounted for the relatively even distribution. In 1850, for example,

---

[3] The concentration of land in Albemarle was much greater than Gavin Wright has found for other southern piedmont counties, where the top 10 percent held only 48 percent of all wealth. The difference, though, is easily explainable. As Wright notes, his census samples recorded only owner–operators of farms. The Albemarle tax records, on the other hand, recorded all households, including landless laborers'. Moreover, Wright's census sample did not capture those who own multiple farms, which occurred quite frequently among Albemarle's economic elite. See Wright, *Political Economy of the Cotton South*, p. 26.

Table 2. *Distribution of Rural Property in Selected Cumberland Townships*

Year (source)	Number of Sample Households	Percentage of Real Property Owned by Top 5 Percent	Percentage of Real Property Owned by Top 10 Percent
1808 (tax lists)	129	34	52
1820 (tax lists)	135	33	49
1838 (tax lists)	185	30	51

Notes and Sources: Calculated from a "Bs" and "Ws" sample of Southampton, South Middleton, and Mifflin townships, microfilm, Los Angeles Family History Center. All rural real estate was included in the calculations, including mills, distilleries, and land.

Table 3. *Distribution of Slaves and Real Property in Albemarle*

Year	Sample Households	Percentage of Slaves Owned by Top 5 Percent	Percentage of Slaves Owned by Top 10 Percent	Percentage of Real Property Owned by Top 5 Percent	Percentage of Real Property Owned by Top 10 Percent
1800	349	36	52	55	69
1830	439	36	54	—	—
1840	453	36	53	54	72
1850	547	38	58	54	73

Notes and Sources: Calculated from a "Bs" and "Ws" sample from microfilmed tax lists at the VSLA (ordered through inter-library loan). Only slaves above the age of eleven were recorded in the tax records. The "real property" figures include the value of all rural land and buildings, but do not include urban real estate.

19 percent of the county's free households in the sample owned 1 or 2 slaves. More Albemarle residents owned slaves than land, suggesting that staple production using slave labor was the easiest way of climbing the economic ladder. The large number of discrete farms owned by the largest landowners made sense: The wealthy landowners, one might assume, rented farms to yeomen families, at least some of whom owned a slave or two.

II. Weak Links?
The Perils of Charting Individuals Over Time

The "Bs" and "Ws" sampling method has the crucial advantage of allowing one to trace particular individuals from one set of records to the next, making it possible to calculate persistence rates. In theory, tracing somebody from one set of tax records to the next is a straight-forward process, but practical details such as slight spelling changes, the use of initials, and illegible handwriting made the calculation of persistence rates arduous and uncertain.

A small change in method minimized these problems. When I first calculated persistence rates, I printed hard copies of the two lists that I wanted to compare. (Since I tended to take samples during census years, the interval between the two lists was usually ten years.) I then eyeballed the two lists, circling names that appeared on both. Double-and triple-checking my work, however, revealed that merely eyeball-ing data on two separate lists was inaccurate, as my eyes tended to skip over names that were similar but not exact. It was hard going, for example, to link "Saml. Webster" in the 1830 tax list to the "Samuel Webster" who appeared in the 1840 tax list. I eventually solved the problem through merging the two tax lists on Excel to create one large list. I then sorted the large list alphabetically, so that "Saml. Web-ster" appeared right above "Samuel Webster." Persistence rates that once hovered between 35 to 40 percent now jumped to around 50 percent. And since I had wealth-holding data already entered, it was relatively easy to see the impact of slave ownership on persistence. As discussed in Chapter 2, wealthy slaveholders persisted at a signifi-cantly higher rate than Albemarle's other residents.

For the 1850s, I used the same basic method, except that I used a "Bs" and "Ws" sample taken from census manuscripts rather than tax data. In theory, the census manuscripts ought to have made it easier to

Table 4. *Persistence Rates in Albemarle, 1830–1860*

Decade (record type)	Number of Households in Sample	Persistence Rates of Planters Owning >15 Slaves	Persistence Rates of Planters Owning >10 Slaves	Overall Persistence Rates
1830s (tax lists)	439	70 %	70 %	46 %
1840s (tax lists)	453	70 %	60 %	50 %
1850s (census records)	399	not calculated	not calculated	36 %

Notes and Sources: Calculated from a "Bs" and "Ws" sample taken from microfilmed tax lists at the VSLA (ordered through interlibrary loan) and microfilmed census manuscripts at the Los Angles Family History Center. Because the slaves schedules were kept separately from the population manuscripts, no attempt was made to calculate the persistence rates of wealthy slaveholders in the 1850s.

link names from 1850 to 1860. The census records, after all, provided important cues such as age and occupation that should have made it easier to trace individuals over time. Alas, the laziness of the 1860 census taker, who often recorded initials instead of first names, made linking a nightmare. The drop in persistence rates over the 1850s might well be an artifact of this defect in the records. Having ages made the job somewhat easier, but not much. A great many Albemarle residents lied or were uncertain about their age. Samuel Bennington the wheelwright, for example, miraculously aged only five years between 1850 and 1860.

For Cumberland's artisans and farmers, I did not attempt to link individuals over time, largely because the best tax and census records were too dispersed over time to calculate ten-year persistence rates. I did, however, record all of the names, occupations, and real property holdings for all of Carlisle's household heads who had a listed occupation in the 1838 tax records and the 1850 census records. This allowed me to chart how Carlisle's occupational structure changed in response to the Cumberland Valley Railroad. One important complication entered this task. A number of Cumberland men were listed as "freemen" in the 1838 tax records, which generally designated unmarried males. Since the tax assessor provided no other information about these presumably young males, I excluded them from the sample.

III. Linking Stockholders to Tax and Census Records

I thought linking stockholders of various corporations to tax and census records would be easy. Simply enter the names of the stockholders into Excel, sort alphabetically, and scroll down the microfilmed manuscripts of the tax and census records. This method proved disastrous. Eyeballing census and tax records was laborious, particularly for populous Cumberland County. I suspected that I was missing many matches. This suspicion was confirmed when I matched the stockholder lists to my "Bs" and "Ws" samples that I already had entered into Excel. I invariably found a much higher percentage of the stockholders than when I eyeballed the microfilm records. I needed to do more than match the "Bs" and "Ws" in the shareholder lists, however, while avoiding the unappealing task of checking and rechecking microfilmed manuscript records for the approximately 2,500 names that I needed to link.

Census indices, compiled by genealogists, eventually solved my problem. The indices, which exist for almost every state between 1790 to 1860, alphabetically list all heads of households recorded in the census. The census indices also provide the precise page number of the census manuscript on which a particular person appears, as well as the township or parish in which the person lived. By matching all of the names on my stockholders lists to the census indices, I could then use the township data or census page numbers to locate the names that I needed to link. Moreover, this method allowed me to determine the location of stockholders who lived outside of either Albemarle or Cumberland, which was particularly important for improvements that ran through more than one county.

Although a great improvement, this method was hardly perfect. Some names could not be located in the census indices – a local farmer who purchased stock in a turnpike in 1815 could have died or moved by the time of the 1820 census. The earliest census indices, usually compiled by volunteer genealogists, also have gaps and transcription errors. The worst problem, however, was that it became impossible to link names that were too common. Scores of John Smiths and Henry Millers lived in Pennsylvania – how could I know what John or Henry was the one that invested in the Harrisburg Toll Bridge or the Cumberland Valley Railroad? My solution was to match definitively only those names that appeared once or twice in the census indices. If two "George Washburns" appeared in the census index, for example, I considered the one living closest to Cumberland County the more likely to be the true investor. If three "George Washburns" appeared in the census index, I considered the name impossible to link. This meant that I threw out many potential matches, but at least I could be confident about the matches that I did make. I sometimes kept matches that violated this protocol when local histories and company records made clear the identity and location of investors.[4]

IV. Calculating State Investment for Virginia's Counties

Calculating state investment in each Virginia county was one of the few tasks that proved easier than expected. Each county was given credit for any railroad or canal that crossed or touched its borders. The state investment in the Rivanna Navigation Company, for example, was divided between Albemarle and Fluvanna, the two counties through which the company passed. Albemarle also received $\frac{1}{9}$ credit for the state investment in the Orange and Alexandria Railroad (which passed through nine counties), $\frac{1}{9}$ credit for the Virginia Central (which also passed through nine counties), and $\frac{1}{14}$ credit for the James River and Kanawha Company (which passed through 14 counties).

<hr>

[4] Some of the shareholder lists – including one for the James River and Kanawha Company and the Cumberland Valley Railroad – identified the county of the investor, or at least the town where he purchased shares.

Three possible problems arise from this method, but none of them seems overly serious. First, the state investment totals are cumulative, accounting for the total investment a county received until 1860. This prevents any analysis of how the distribution of state investment changed over time. This problem should not interfere with any of the substantive conclusions, since the main improvement in the West – the Ohio and Covington Railroad – was not funded until 1853 and not finished until after the Civil War. A second problem is that mileage was not scaled for each county. The result is that a county which an improvement barely skirted received the same credit as a county which contained 15 or 20 miles of the same improvement. The substantive impact of this defect is not clear. Even when a canal or railroad skirted a county's borders, it could have profound developmental consequences, as the James River and Kanawha Canal had for Scottsville and the rest of Albemarle.

Finally, the data excludes state investment in turnpikes, plank roads, and toll bridges. These improvements received more than $5 million in state investment. Because turnpike mileage was more evenly distributed throughout the state, this could mean that the railroad and canal data overstate the unequal distribution of state funds. This is unlikely, however, to undermine any of the previously stated conclusions. From an economic standpoint, the impact of turnpikes and plank roads was more limited than that of railroads and canals, providing some justification for their exclusion. Even though the West received somewhere between 45 and 55 percent of the state's turnpike investment, on a per-mile basis eastern Virginia did much better, receiving more than $1,000 for every mile of turnpike built compared to the West's $300.

As for the regressions, a number of different specifications were tried, only two of which were reported in Chapter 5. In these trial runs, three interrelated variables performed well: per capita taxes that a county paid, per capita tobacco production, and the percentage of the total population enslaved. Unfortunately, including all three variables in a regression is fraught with difficulty because they were all highly correlated. Counties with lots of slaves generally paid high state taxes, and counties that grew lots of tobacco generally had many slaves.

In a straight statistical sense, taxes and tobacco production actually explain more of the variation in state investment, but there is good reason to be suspicious of the causal relationships. Taxes were correlated not only with slaves, but also higher property values and town development. Hence, it is very likely that railroads and canals increased the per capita tax rate, rather than the per capita tax rate influencing state investment. The same problem of causality also muddles the interpretation of the per capita tobacco production variable:

Counties with railroads and canals were more likely to grow tobacco, especially in the late 1850s when tobacco prices were extremely high. Given these interpretative problems, it makes sense to stress the interaction of slavery and geography as the main determinants of state investment.

A number of other independent variables were tried, including wheat production, urbanization, and free population. The free population variable was included to test whether state investment tried to take advantage of economies of scale. The poor performance of this variable suggests that such economies played little role in state investment decisions. Urbanization – as measured by a dummy variable for each county with a city that had more than 5,000 people – was also insignificant. While many urbanized counties ranked high in absolute investment, their higher population lowered their per capita ranking. Another problem was that Wheeling, located in the West, received little in the way of state funding for internal improvements. The statistical insignificance of the wheat variable is not surprising since much of the wheat production was concentrated in the trans-Allegheny region.

One missing variable is per capita manufacturing output. Unfortunately, the 1860 manufacturing census for Virginia excluded 11 counties. The urban dummy, however, effectively acts as a proxy since a good portion of Virginia's manufacturing was in its cities, especially Richmond, Petersburg, Wheeling, and Danville. Given the poor performance of the urban dummy, it is likely that the manufacturing variable would also have been insignificant.

The regional divisions used in Tables 5.4 and 5.5 were taken from Alison Goodyear Freehling's *Drift Toward Dissolution*. While certain counties crossed geographical boundaries, Freehling's classifications generally agree with other sources. The exact divisions are as follows:

Tidewater: Accomack, Alexandria, Caroline, Charles City, Chesterfield, Elizabeth City, Essex, Fairfax, Gloucester, Greensville, Hanover, Henrico, Isle of Wight, James City, King and Queen, King George, King William, Lancaster, Mathews, Middlesex, Nansemond, New Kent, Norfolk, Northampton, Northumberland, Prince George, Prince William, Princess Anne, Rappahannock, Richmond, Southampton, Spotsylvania, Stafford, Surry, Sussex, Warwick, Westmoreland, and York.

Piedmont: Albemarle, Amelia, Amherst, Appomattox, Bedford, Brunswick, Buckingham, Campbell, Charlotte, Culpeper, Cumberland, Dinwiddie, Fauquier, Fluvanna, Franklin, Goochland, Greene, Halifax, Henry, Loudoun, Louisa, Lunenburg, Madison, Mecklenburg, Nelson, Nottoway, Orange, Patrick, Pittsylvania, Powhatan, and Prince Edward.

Valley: Allegheny, Augusta, Bath, Berkeley, Botetourt, Clarke, Frederick, Hampshire, Hardy, Highland, Jefferson, Morgan, Page, Pendleton, Roanoke, Rockbridge, Rockingham, Shenandoah, and Warren.

Trans-Allegheny: Barbour, Boone, Braxton, Brooke, Buchanan, Cabell, Calhoun, Carroll, Clay, Craig, Doddridge, Fayette, Floyd, Giles, Gilmer, Grayson, Greenbrier, Hancock, Harrison, Jackson, Kanawha, Lee, Lewis, Logan, Marion, Marshall, Mason, McDowell, Mercer, Monongalia, Monroe, Montgomery, Nicholas, Ohio, Pocahontas, Pleasants, Preston, Pulaski, Putnam, Raleigh, Randolph, Ritchie, Roane, Russell, Scott, Smyth, Taylor, Tazewell, Tucker, Tyler, Upshur, Washington, Wayne, Webster, Wetzel, Wirt, Wise, Wood, Wyoming, and Wythe.

Bibliography

I. Manuscript Sources

Carlisle, Pennsylvania
Cumberland County Historical Society
  Cumberland Valley Railroad Stockholders List
  John Lefever Diary, edited and transcribed by Robert J. Smith
  Robert Whitehill, Jr. Papers
Charlottesville, Virginia
Alderman Library, University of Virginia
  Albemarle Agricultural Society, Minute Book
  Brady Papers
  Brown Family Papers
  George Carr Papers
  John Hartwell Cocke Papers
  Dade Family Papers
  James L. Kemper Papers
  Wilson Carey Nicholas Papers
  Thomas Jefferson Randolph Papers
  Rivanna Navigation Company, Minute Book
  Streeter Railway Collection
  V. W. Southall Broadsides
  Charles B. Shaw Papers
Harrisburg, Pennsylvania
Pennsylvania State Archives
  John Bear Papers
  Cumberland Valley Railroad, Balance Sheets and List of Subscribers
  Cumberland Valley Railroad, Minutes of the Board of Managers
  Harrisburg, Carlisle, and Chambersburg Turnpike Ledgers
  Pennsylvania Railroad Collection
Philadelphia, Pennsylvania
Historical Society of Pennsylvania
  Cadwalader Collection
Richmond, Virginia
Virginia Historical Society
  Coles Family Papers

Minor Family Papers
Virginia State Library and Archives
    Albemarle County Court Papers, Ended Chancery Case 429
    Albemarle County Legislative Petitions
    Fund for Internal Improvement Journals, Archives of the Second
      Auditor
    James River and Kanawha Company Papers, Archives of the Board
      of Public Works
    Rivanna Navigation Company Papers, Archives of the Board of
      Public Works
    Staunton and James River Turnpike Papers, Archives of the Board
      of Public Works
    Virginia Central Railroad Papers, Archives of the Board of Public
      Works

II. Newspapers and Magazines

American Farmer
American Railroad Journal
American Volunteer
Carlisle Republican
Charlottesville Advocate
Farmer's Register
Lynchburg Daily Republican
Lynchburg Daily Virginian
Richmond Enquirer
Southern Argus
Southern Planter
Virginia Advocate

III. Government Records

Albemarle County Deed Book, microfilm. Virginia State Library and
    Archives, 1830.
Albemarle County Personal Property Tax Lists, microfilm. Virginia
    State Library and Archives.
Albemarle County Real Property Tax Lists, microfilm. Virginia State
    Library and Archives.
Annual Reports on Rail Road Companies of the State of Virginia. Richmond,
    various years.
Board of Public Works. *Annual Reports of the Board of Public Works.* Rich-
    mond, various years.
Cumberland County Tax Lists, microfilm. Family History Library, Los
    Angeles.

DeBow, J. D. B. (ed.). *Statistical View of the United States.* Washington: Superintendent of the United States Census, 1854; reprint, New York: Gordon and Breach, 1970.

Journal of the Senate of the Commonwealth of Virginia. Richmond, various years.

Journal of the House of Delegates of the Commonwealth of Virginia. Richmond, various years.

Laws of Pennsylvania. Harrisburg, various years.

Laws of Virginia. Richmond, various years.

Pennsylvania House Journal. Harrisburg, various years.

Revised Code of Virginia. Richmond, 1819.

United States Bureau of the Census. *Abstract of the Returns of the Fifth Census.* Washington, D.C., 1832.

United States Bureau of the Census. *The Seventh Census of the United States.* Washington, D.C., 1853.

United States Bureau of the Census. *Agriculture of the United States in 1860.* Washington, D.C., 1864.

United States Bureau of the Census. *Manuscript Returns for Albemarle County, Virginia, and Cumberland County, Pennsylvania,* microfilm. Family History Library, Los Angeles.

United States Bureau of the Census. *Population of the United States in 1860.* Washington, D.C., 1864.

United States Bureau of the Census. *Manufacturers of the United States in 1860.* Washington, D.C., 1865.

United States Bureau of the Census. *Historical Statistics of the United States, Colonial Times to 1970,* Bicentennial Edition, Part 1. Washington, D.C., 1975.

IV. Published Primary Sources

Blake, John Lauris. *The Farmer's Every-Day Book: Or, Sketches of Social Life in the Country.* Auburn, N.Y.: Derby Miller, 1850.

Bruce, Charles. *Speech of Charles Bruce.* Richmond: Hammersley and Co., 1858.

Burrowes, Thomas Henry. *State-Book of Pennsylvania . . .* Philadelphia: U. Hunt & Son, 1846.

Coxe, Tench. *A Statement of the Arts and Manufactures of the United States of America for the Year 1810.* Philadelphia: A. Cornman, Jr., 1814.

Crozet, Claudius. *Outline of Improvements in the State of Virginia.* Philadelphia: C. Sherman, 1848.

Cuming, Fortesque. *Sketches of a Tour to the Western Country.* Pittsburgh: Cramer, Spear, and Eichbaum, 1810.

Dwight, Margaret Van Horn. "A Traveller in the County, 1810." *Cumberland County History* 13 (Winter 1996): 114–18.

Edwards, Richard. *Statistical Gazetteer of the States of Virginia and North Carolina.* Richmond: Richard Edwards, 1856.

Fitzhugh, George. *Sociology for the South: or, The Failure of Free Society.* Richmond: A. Morris, 1854.

Freedley, Edwin T. *Philadelphia and Its Manufactures: A Hand-book.* Philadelphia: Edward Young, 1859.

Gilpin, Joshua. "A Traveller in the County, 1809." *Cumberland County History* 12 (Winter 1995): 112–18.

Gordon, Thomas F. *A Gazetteer of the State of Pennsylvania.* Philadelphia: T. Belknap, 1832.

Gynn, Walter. *Report of the Chief Engineer to the President and Directors of the James River and Kanawha Company.* n. p., 1848.

James River and Kanawha Company. *Collections of All Acts of the General Assembly Relating to the James River and Kanawha Company.* Richmond: Samuel Shepherd, 1835.

Jefferson, Thomas. "A Memorandum (Services to My Country)." In *Jefferson: Private and Public Papers.* New York: Vintage Books, 1990.

———. *Notes on the State of Virginia* [1787]. In *Thomas Jefferson: Writings,* edited by Merrill D. Peterson, 124–325. New York: Library of America, 1994.

Jones, T. L. "Journal" [1862–1869]. In *Records of the Antebellum Southern Plantations from the Revolution Through the Civil War.* Series J, Part 9, edited by Kenneth M. Stampp. Bethesda, Md.: microfilm, University Publications of America, 1989–1997.

Lincoln, Abraham. "A House Divided: Speech Delivered At Springfield, Illinois, At the Close of the Republican State Convention, June 16, 1858." In *Abraham Lincoln: His Speeches and Writings,* edited by Roy P. Basler, 372–81. Cleveland: World Publishing Co., 1946.

MacKinney, Gertrude, ed. *Pennsylvania Archives.* Ninth Series. Harrisburg: Bureau of Publications, 1931.

Manning, William. *The Key of Liberty: The Life and Democratic Writings of William Manning, "A Laborer," 1747–1814.* Edited and with an introduction by Michael Merrill and Sean Wilentz. Cambridge: Harvard University Press, 1993.

Martin, Joseph. *A New and Comprehensive Gazetteer of Virginia and the District of Columbia.* Charlottesville: Moseley and Tompkins, 1835.

"Newville in 1859: Extracts from its Newspaper." *Cumberland County History* 14 (Summer 1997): 50–67.

Pennsylvania Railroad Company. *First Annual Report of the Directors of the Pennsylvania Rail-Road Company.* Philadelphia, 1847.

———. *Second Annual Report of the Directors of the Pennsylvania Rail-Road Company . . .* Oct. 31, 1848. Philadelphia, 1848.

———. *Fourth Annual Report of the Directors of the Pennsylvania Rail-Road Company . . .* December 31, 1850. Philadelphia, 1851.

Penrose, Charles B. *Speech of Charles B. Penrose, Senator from Cumberland and Perry on the Subject of the Re-charter of the Bank of the United States and the Restoration of Deposits*, microfilm. Harrisburg: Henry Welsh, 1834.

Poulson, Zachariah. *An Historical Account of the Rise, Progress and Present State of Canal Navigation in Pennsylvania.* Philadelphia: Zachariah Poulson, 1795.

Richmond, City Council. *Reports and Resolutions Adopted by the Council of the City of Richmond.* Richmond: Colin, Baptist, and Nowlan, 1850.

Rutherfoord, John C. *Speech of John C. Rutherfoord of Goochland.* n. p., 1858.

Scharf, Thomas J. and Thompson Westcott. *History of Philadelphia, 1609–1884.* Volume III. Philadelphia: L. H. Everts & Co., 1884.

Segar, Joseph. "Speech of Joseph Segar, Esq. of Elizabeth City County on the Covington and Ohio Railroad." In *Proceedings of the Internal Improvement Convention Held at the White Sulphur Springs.* Richmond: The Dispatch, 1855.

Shaw, Charles B. *Letters of Charles B. Shaw, Engineer, Comparing the Projected Railroad from Covington to the Ohio.* Richmond: Colin and Nowlan, 1851.

———. *Letters of Charles B. Shaw . . . on the Subject of a Connection between Richmond and the Valley of the Ohio.* n. p., 1851.

———. *Remarks on the Gauge of the Covington and Ohio Railroad.* n. p., 1853.

Tocqueville, Alexis de. *Democracy in America* [1835 and 1840]. Abridged with an introduction by Thomas Bender. New York: Modern Libary College Editions, 1981.

Tucker, George, *Political Economy for the People.* Philadelphia: C. Sherman & Son, 1859; reprint, New York: Augustus M. Kelley, 1970.

V. Dissertations and Unpublished Manuscripts

Coleman, Elizabeth Dabney. "The Story of the Virginia Central Railroad, 1850–1860." Ph.D. Dissertation, University of Virginia, 1957.

Coyner, M. Boyd., Jr. "John Hartwell Cocke of Bremo: Agriculture and Slavery in the Antebellum South." Ph.D. Dissertation, University of Virginia, 1961.

Dabney, William Minor. "Jefferson's Albemarle: A History of Albemarle County, Virginia, 1727–1819." Ph.D. Dissertation, University of Virginia, 1951.

Golladay, Victor Dennis. "The Nicholas Family of Virginia, 1722–1820." Ph.D. Dissertation, University of Virginia, 1973.

Grinath, Arthur, John Wallis, and Richard Sylla. "Debt, Default, and Revenue Structure: The American State Debt Crisis of the Early 1840s." Unpublished Manuscript, University of Maryland, 1995.

Hess, Karl. "Four Decades of Social Change: Scottsville, Virginia, 1820–1860." M. A. Thesis, University of Virginia, 1973.

Hunter, Robert F. "The Turnpike Movement in Virginia, 1816–1860." Ph.D Dissertation, Columbia University, 1957.

Koons, Kenneth E. "Families and Farms in the Lower-Cumberland Valley of Southcentral Pennsylvania, 1800–1850." Ph.D. Dissertation, Carnegie-Mellon University, 1986.

Majewski, John D. "Commerce and Community: Economic Culture and Internal Improvements in Pennsylvania and Virginia, 1790–1860." Ph.D. Dissertation, University of California, Los Angeles, 1994.

Plummer, Wilbur C. "The Road Policy of Pennsylvania." Ph.D. Dissertation, University of Pennsylvania, 1925.

Ridner, Judith Anne. "A Handsomely Improved Place: Economic, Social, and Gender-Role Development in a Backcountry Town, Carlisle, Pennsylvania, 1750–1810." Ph.D. Dissertation, College of William and Mary, 1994.

Turner, Charles W. "The Virginia Railroads, 1828–1860." Ph.D. Dissertation, University of Minnesota, 1946.

Watts, Charles Wider. "Colonial Albemarle: The Social and Economic History of a Piedmont Virginia County, 1725–1775." M. A. Thesis, University of Virginia, 1948.

VI. Published Secondary Sources

Adams, Sean Patrick. "Different Charters, Different Paths: Corporations and Coal in Antebellum Pennsylvania and Virginia." *Business and Economic History* 27 (Fall 1998): 78–90.

Adler, Dorothy R. *British Investment in American Railways, 1834–1898*, edited by Muriel E. Hidy. Charlottesville: University of Virginia, 1970.

Adler, Jeffrey S. *Yankee Merchants and the Making of the Urban West: The Rise and Fall of Antebellum St. Louis.* New York: Cambridge University Press, 1991.

Alvarez, Eugene. *Travel on Southern Antebellum Railroads, 1828–1860.* University, Al.: University of Alabama Press, 1974.

Anderson, Ralph V., and Robert E. Gallman, " Slaves as Fixed Capital: Slave Labor and Southern Economic Development." *Journal of American History* 64 (1977): 24–46.

Androit, John L. *Population Abstract of the United States.* Volume I. McLean, Va.: Andriot Associates, 1983.

Appleby, Joyce. *Capitalism and a New Social Order: The Republican Vision of the 1790s.* New York: New York University Press, 1984.
———. "Republicanism in Old and New Contexts." *William and Mary Quarterly* 43 (1986): 20–34.
Ashworth, John. *Slavery, Capitalism, and Politics in the Antebellum Republic: Volume I: Commerce and Compromise, 1820–1850.* New York: Cambridge University Press, 1995.
Atack, Jeremy. "Returns to Scale in Antebellum United States Manufacturing." *Explorations in Economic History* 14 (1977): 337–59.
Atack, Jeremy, and Fred Bateman. *To Their Own Soil: Agriculture in the Antebellum North.* Ames: Iowa State University Press, 1987.
Baer, Christopher T. *Canals and Railroads of the Mid-Atlantic States, 1800–1860.* Wilmington, Delaware: Regional Economic History Research Center, Eleutherian Mills-Hagley Foundation, 1981.
Bailyn, Bernard. *The Ideological Origins of the American Revolution.* Cambridge: Belknap Press of Harvard University Press, 1967.
Ball, D. E., and G. M. Walton. "Agricultural Productivity in Eighteenth-Century Pennsylvania." *Journal of Economic History* 34 (1976): 102–17.
Banning, Lance. "Jeffersonian Ideology Revisited: Liberal and Classical Ideas in the New American Republic." *William and Mary Quarterly* 43 (1986): 3–19.
Bateman, Fred, and Thomas Weiss. *A Deplorable Scarcity: The Failure of Industrialization in the Slave Economy.* Chapel Hill: University of North Carolina Press, 1981.
Beeman, Richard R. *The Evolution of the Southern Backcountry: A Case Study of Lunenburg County, Virginia, 1746–1832.* Philadelphia: University of Pennsylvania Press, 1984.
Berlin, Ira, and Herbert G. Gutman. "Natives and Immigrants, Free Men and Slaves: Urban Workingmen in the Antebellum American South." *American Historical Review* 88 (December 1983): 1175–1200.
Bernstein, Michael A., and Sean Wilentz. "Marketing, Commerce, and Capitalism." *Journal of Economic History* 44 (1984): 171–73.
Bezanson, Anne, Robert D. Gray, and Mirian Hussey. *Prices in Colonial Pennsylvania.* Philadelphia: University of Pennsylvania Press, 1935.
Bezis-Selfa, John. "Planter Industrialists and Iron Oligarchs: A Comparative Prosopography of Early Anglo-American Ironmasters." *Business and Economic History* 22 (Fall 1993): 62–70.
Black, Robert C. *The Railroads of the Confederacy.* Chapel Hill: University of North Carolina Press, 1952.
Blumin, Stuart M. *The Urban Threshold: Growth and Change in a Nineteenth-Century American Community.* Chicago: University of Chicago Press, 1976.

Bowman, Shearer Davis. *Masters and Lords: Mid-19th Century U.S. Planters and Prussian Junkers.* New York: Oxford University Press, 1993.

Breen, T. H. *Tobacco Culture: The Mentality of the Great Tidewater Planters on the Eve of the Revolution.* Princeton: Princeton University Press, 1985.

Bushman, Richard L. *The Refinement of America: Persons, Houses, Cities.* New York: Vintage Books, 1993.

Campbell, John. "As 'A Kind of Freeman'?: Slaves' Market-Related Activities in the South Carolina Up Country, 1800–1860." In *Cultivation and Culture: Labor and the Shaping of Slave Life in the Americas,* edited by Ira Berlin and Philip D. Morgan, 243–74. Charlottesville: University Press of Virginia, 1993.

Cashin, Joan E. *A Family Venture: Men and Women on the Southern Frontier.* New York: Oxford University Press, 1991.

Censer, Jane Turner. *North Carolina Planters and Their Children, 1800–1860.* Baton Rouge: Louisiana State University Press, 1984.

Chandler, Alfred D., Jr. "Anthracite Coal and the Beginnings of the Industrial Revolution in the United States." *Business History Review* 46 (1972): 141–80.

———. *The Visible Hand: The Managerial Revolution in American Business.* Cambridge: Harvard University Press, 1977.

Clark, Christopher. "Household Economy, Market Exchange, and the Rise of Capitalism in the Connecticut Valley." *Journal of Social History* 13 (1979): 169–89.

———. *The Roots of Rural Capitalism: Western Massachusetts, 1780–1860.* Ithaca: Cornell University Press, 1992.

Clarke, Robert Joseph. *The Tobacco Kingdom: Plantation, Market, and Factory in Virginia and North Carolina, 1800–1860.* Durham: Duke University Press, 1938.

Clemens, Paul G. E. *The Atlantic Economy and Colonial Maryland's Eastern Shore: From Tobacco to Grain.* Ithaca: Cornell University Press, 1980.

Clemens, Paul G. E., and Lucy Simler. "Rural Labor and the Farm Household in Chester County, Pennsylvania, 1750–1820." In *Work and Labour in Early America,* edited by Stephen Innes, 106–43. Chapel Hill: University of North Carolina Press, 1988.

Cochran, Thomas C. *Frontiers of Change: Early Industrialization in America.* New York: Oxford University Press, 1981.

Coleman, Elizabeth Dabney. "Edmund Fontaine and the Virginia Central Railroad." In *America in the Middle Period: Essays in Honor of Bernard Mayo,* edited by John B. Boles. Charlottesville: University of Virginia Press, 1973.

Coleman, James. *Foundations of Social Theory.* Cambridge: Belknap Press of Harvard University Press, 1990.

Conkin, Paul Keith. *Prophets of Prosperity: America's First Political Economists.* Bloomington: Indiana University Press, 1980.

Couper, William. *Claudius Crozet.* Charlottesville: The Historical Publishing Company, 1936.

Craven, Avery Odelle. *Edmund Ruffin, Southerner: A Study of Secession.* Baton Rouge: Louisiana State University Press, 1966.

Cronon, William. *Nature's Metropolis: Chicago and the Great West.* Chicago: W. W. Norton & Company, 1991.

Crowther, Simeon J. "Urban Growth in the Mid-Atlantic States, 1785–1850." *Journal of Economic History* 36 (1976): 624–44.

Davis, Edward J. *The Anthracite Aristocracy: Leadership and Social Change in the Hard Coal Regions of Northeastern Pennsylvania, 1800–1930.* DeKalb: Northern Illinois University Press, 1985.

Davis, Lance E. "Capital Mobility and American Growth." In *The Reinterpretation of American Economic History*, edited by Robert W. Fogel and Stanley L. Engerman, 285–300. New York: Harper and Row, 1971.

Davis, Lance E., and Douglass C. North. *Institutional Change and American Growth.* New York: Cambridge University Press, 1971.

Degler, Carl N. *Neither Black Nor White: Slavery and Race Relations in Brazil and the United States.* New York: Macmillan, 1971.

Demaree, Albert Lowther. *The American Agricultural Press, 1819–1860.* New York: Columbia University Press, 1941; reprint, Philadelphia: Porcupine Press, 1974.

Dew, Charles B. *Bond of Iron: Master and Slave at Buffalo Forge.* New York: W. W. Norton, 1994.

———. *Ironmaker of the Confederacy: Joseph R. Anderson and the Tredegar Iron Works.* New Haven: Yale University Press, 1966.

Doerflinger, Thomas M. "Farmers and Dry Goods in the Philadelphia Market Area, 1750–1800." In *The Economy of Early America: The Revoluntionary Period, 1763–1790*, edited by Ronald Hoffman, John J. McCusker, Russell R. Menard, and Peter J. Albert, 166–95. Charlottesville: University Press of Virginia, 1988.

———. *A Vigorous Spirit of Enterprise: Merchants and Economic Development in Revolutionary Philadelphia.* Chapel Hill: University of North Carolina Press, 1986.

Dunaway, Wayland Fuller. *A History of the James River and Kanawha Company.* New York: Columbia University Press, 1922.

Dunlavy, Colleen A. *Politics and Industrialization: Early Railroads in the United States and Prussia.* Princeton: Princeton University Press, 1994.

Durrenberger, Joseph Austin. *Turnpikes: A Study of the Toll Road Movement in the Middle Atlantic States and Maryland.* Valdosta, Ga.: Southern Stationery & Printing Company, 1931.

Dusinberre, William. *Them Dark Days: Slavery in the American Rice Swamps.* New York: Oxford University Press, 1996.

Earle, Carville, and Ronald Hoffman. "Urban Development in the Eighteenth-Century South." *Perspectives in American History* 10 (1976): 7–80.

Easterlin, Richard A. "Will Raising the Incomes of All Increase the Happiness of All?" *Journal of Economic Behavior and Organization* 27 (1995): 35–47.

Egerton, Douglas R. "Markets Without a Market Revolution: Southern Planters and Capitalism." *Journal of the Early Republic* 16 (Summer, 1996): 207–21.

Elkins, Stanley. *Slavery: A Problem in American Institutional and Intellectual Life.* Chicago: University of Chicago Press, 1959.

Elkins, Stanley, and McKitrick, Eric. "A Meaning for Turner's Frontier: Part I: Democracy in the Old Northwest." *Political Science Quarterly* 69 (1954): 321–53.

Engerman, Stanley L. "The Antebellum South: What Probably Was and What Should Have Been." *Agricultural History* 44 (January 1970): 127–42.

———. "A Reconsideration of Southern Economic Growth, 1770–1860." *Agricultural History* 49 (April 1975): 343–61.

Engerman, Stanley L., and Kenneth L. Sokoloff. "Factor Endowments, Institutions, and Differential Paths of Growth Among New World Economies: A View from Economic Historians of the United States." In *How Latin America Fell Behind: Essays on the Economic Histories of Brazil and Mexico, 1800–1914,* edited by Stephen Haber, 260–304. Stanford: Stanford University Press, 1997.

Ernst, Joseph A., and H. Roy Merrens. "Camden's Turrets Pierce the Skies! The Urban Process in the Southern Colonies during the Eighteenth Century." *William and Mary Quarterly* 30 (1973): 549–74.

Faust, Drew Gilpin. *James Henry Hammond and the Old South: A Design for Mastery.* Baton Rouge: Louisiana State University Press, 1982.

———. *A Sacred Circle: The Dilemma of the Intellectual in the Old South, 1840–1860.* Baltimore: The Johns Hopkins University Press, 1977.

Feller, Daniel. "The Market Revolution Ate My Homework." *Reviews in American History* 25 (1997): 408–15.

Fields, Barbara Jeanne. *Slavery and Freedom on the Middle Ground: Maryland during the Nineteenth Century.* New Haven: Yale University Press, 1985.

Fischbaum, Marvin, and Julius Rubin. "Slavery and the Economic Development of the American South." *Explorations in Economic History* 6 (1968): 116–27.

Fishlow, Albert. *American Railroads and the Transformation of the Antebellum Economy.* Cambridge: Harvard University Press, 1965.

Fleisig, Heywood. "Slavery, the Supply of Agricultural Labor, and the Industrialization of the South." *Journal of Economic History* 36 (1976): 572–95.

Fogel, Robert William, and Stanley L. Engerman. *Time on the Cross: The Economics of American Negro Slavery.* New Edition. New York: W. W. Norton and Company, 1989.

———. "The Economics of Slavery." In *The Reinterpretation of American Economic History,* edited by Robert W. Fogel and Stanley L. Engerman, 311–41. New York: Harper and Row, 1971.

Fogel, Robert William. "Notes on the Social Saving Controversy." *Journal of Economic History* 39 (1979): 1–54.

———. *Railroads and American Economic Growth.* Baltimore: The Johns Hopkins University Press, 1964.

———. *Without Consent or Contract: The Rise and Fall of American Slavery.* New York: W. W. Norton and Company, 1989.

Foner, Eric. *Free Soil, Free Labor, Free Men: The Ideology of the Republican Party before the Civil War.* New York: Oxford University Press, 1970.

Ford, Lacy K., Jr. *Origins of Southern Radicalism: The South Carolina Upcountry, 1800–1860.* New York: Oxford University Press, 1988.

Fox-Genovese, Elizabeth. *Within the Plantation Household: Black and White Women in the Old South.* Chapel Hill: University of North Carolina Press, 1988.

Fredrickson, George M. *The Comparative Imagination: On the History of Racism, Nationalism, and Social Movements.* Berkeley: University of California Press, 1997.

Freehling, Alison Goodyear. *Drift Toward Dissolution: The Virginia Slavery Debate of 1831–1832.* Baton Rouge: Louisiana State University Press, 1982.

Freyer, Tony A. "Law and the Antebellum Southern Economy: An Interpretation." In *Ambivalent Legacy: A Legal History of the South,* edited by David J. Bodenhamer and James W. Ely, Jr. Jackson: University of Mississippi Press, 1984.

———. *Producers Versus Capitalists: Constitutional Conflict in Antebellum America.* Charlottesville: University Press of Virginia, 1994.

Genovese, Eugene D. *The Political Economy of Slavery: Studies in the Economy and Society of the Slave South.* Second Edition. Middletown, Conn.: Wesleyan University Press, 1989.

———. *From Rebellion to Revolution: Afro-American Slave Revolts in the Making of the Modern World.* Baton Rouge: Louisiana State University Press, 1979.

———. *The World the Slaveholders Made: Two Essays in Interpretation.* Second Edition. Middletown, Conn.: Wesleyan University Press, 1988.

Gilmore, Grant. "From Tort to Contract: Industrialization and the Law." *Yale Law Journal* 86 (1977): 788–97.

Gilmore, William. *Reading Becomes a Necessity of Life: Material and Cultural Life in Rural New England, 1780–1835.* Knoxville: University of Tennessee Press, 1989.

Glickstein, Jonathan A. *Concepts of Free Labor in Antebellum America.* New Haven: Yale University Press, 1991.

Goldfield, David R. "Pursuing the American Dream: Cities in the Old South." In *The City in Southern History: The Growth of Urban Civilization in the South,* edited by Blaine A. Brownell and David R. Goldfield, 52–91. Port Washington, N.Y.: Kennikat Press, 1977.

———. *Urban Growth in the Age of Sectionalism: Virginia, 1847–1861.* Baton Rouge: Louisiana State University Press, 1977.

———. "Urban-Rural Relations in the Old South: The Example of Virginia." *Journal of Urban History* 2 (1976): 146–68.

Goldin, Claudia, and Kenneth Sokoloff. "Women, Children, and Industrialization in the Early Republic: Evidence from the Manufacturing Censuses." *Journal of Economic History* 42 (1982): 741–74.

Goodrich, Carter. "American Development Policy: The Case of Internal Improvements." *Journal of Economic History* 14 (1956): 449–60.

———. *Canals and American Economic Development.* New York: Columbia University Press, 1961.

———. *Government Promotion of American Canals and Railroads, 1800–1890.* New York: Columbia University Press, 1960.

———. "Internal Improvements Reconsidered." *Journal of Economic History* 30 (1970): 289–311.

———. "National Planning of Internal Improvements." *Political Science Quarterly* 63 (1948): 16–44.

———. "Public Spirit and American Improvements." *Proceedings of the American Philosophical Society* 92 (1948): 305–09.

———. "The Virginia System of Mixed Enterprise: A Study of State Planning of Internal Improvements." *Political Science Quarterly* 64 (1949): 355–87.

Greenberg, Kenneth S. *Masters and Statesmen: The Political Culture of American Slavery.* Baltimore: The Johns Hopkins University Press, 1985.

Gunn, L. Ray. *The Decline of Authority: Public Economic Policy and Political Development in New York, 1800–1860.* Ithaca: Cornell University Press, 1988.

Hahn, Steven. *The Roots of Southern Populism: Yeoman Farmers and the Transformation of the Georgia Upcountry, 1850–1890.* New York: Oxford University Press, 1983.

———. "The Yeomanry of the Nonplantation South: Upper Piedmont

Georgia, 1850–1860." In *Class, Conflict, and Consensus: Antebellum Southern Community Studies*, edited by Orville Vernon Burton and Robert C. McMath, Jr. 29–52. Westport, Conn.: Greenwood Press, 1982.

Handlin, Oscar, and Mary Flug Handlin. *Commonwealth: A Study in the Role of Government in the American Economy*. Revised Edition. Cambridge: Harvard University Press, 1969.

———. "Origins of the American Business Corporation." *Journal of Economic History* 5 (1945): 1–23.

Harris, J. William. *Plain Folk and Gentry in a Slave Society: White Liberty and Black Slavery in Augusta's Hinterlands*. Middletown, Conn.: Wesleyan University Press, 1985.

Hartog, Hendrik. *Public Property and Private Power: The Corporation of the City of New York in American Law, 1730–1870*. Chapel Hill: University of North Carolina Press, 1983.

Hartz, Louis. *Economic Policy and Democratic Thought: Pennsylvania, 1776–1860*. Cambridge: Harvard University Press, 1948.

Heath, Milton. *Constructive Liberalism: The Role of the State in Economic Development in Georgia to 1860*. Cambridge: Harvard University Press, 1954.

———. "Public Railroad Construction and the Development of Private Enterprise in the South before 1861." *Journal of Economic History* 10 (1950): 40–53.

Henretta, James A. "Families and Farms: *Mentalite* in Pre-Industrial America." *William and Mary Quarterly* 35 (1978): 3–32.

———. *The Origins of American Capitalism: Collected Essays*. Boston: Northeastern University Press, 1991.

Heyrman, Christine Leigh. *Commerce and Culture: The Maritime Communities of Colonial Massachusetts, 1690–1750*. New York: W. W. Norton and Company, 1984.

Higginbotham, Sanford Wilson. *The Keystone in the Democratic Arch: Pennsylvania Politics, 1800–1816*. Harrisburg: Pennsylvania Historical and Museum Commission, 1952.

Hoffman, Ronald. *A Spirit of Dissension: Economics, Politics, and the Revolution in Maryland*. Baltimore: The Johns Hopkins University Press, 1973.

Hoover, Edgar M., and Raymond Vernon. *Anatomy of a Metropolis: The Changing Distribution of People and Jobs Within the New York Metropolitan Region*. Cambridge: Harvard University Press, 1959.

Horwitz, Morton. *The Transformation of American Law, 1780–1860*. Cambridge: Harvard University Press, 1977.

Howe, Daniel Walker. "The Market Revolution and the Shaping of Identity in Whig-Jacksonian America." In *The Market Revolution in America: Social, Political, and Religious Expressions, 1800–1880*, edited by Melvyn Stokes and Stephen Conway, 259–81. Charlottesville: University Press of Virginia, 1996.

Hurst, James Willard. *Law and the Conditions of Freedom in the Nineteenth-Century United States.* Madison: University of Wisconsin Press, 1964.

———. *Law and Markets in U.S. History.* Madison: University of Wisconsin Press, 1977.

Innes, Stephen. *Creating the Commonwealth: The Economic Culture of Puritan New England.* New York: W. W. Norton and Company, 1995.

———. "Fullfilling John Smith's Vision: Work and Labor in Early America." In *Work and Labor in Early America,* edited by Stephen Innes, 3–47. Chapel Hill: University of North Carolina Press, 1988.

Irwin, James R. "Exploring the Affinity of Wheat and Slavery in the Virginia Piedmont." *Explorations in Economic History* 25 (1988): 295–322.

Jacobs, Jane. *Cities and the Wealth of Nations: Principles of Economic Life.* New York: Random House, 1984.

Jaffee, David. "Peddlers of Progress and the Transformation of the Rural North, 1760–1820." *Journal of American History* 78 (1991): 511–35.

Jensen, Arthur L. *The Maritime Commerce of Colonial Philadelphia.* Madison: State Historical Society of Wisconsin, 1963.

Jensen, Joan M. *Loosening the Bonds: Mid-Atlantic Farm Women, 1750–1850.* New Haven: Yale University Press, 1986.

John, Richard R. *Spreading the News: The American Postal System from Franklin to Morse.* Cambridge: Harvard University Press, 1995.

Johnson, Arthur M., and Barry E. Supple. *Boston Capitalists and Western Railroads: A Study in the Nineteenth-Century Railroad Investment Process.* Cambridge: Harvard University Press, 1967.

Johnston, Angus James II. *Virginia Railroads in the Civil War.* Chapel Hill: University of North Carolina Press, 1961.

Jones, Alice Hanson. *Wealth of a Nation to Be: The American Colonies on the Eve of the Revolution.* New York: Columbia University Press, 1980.

Jones, Daniel P. *The Economic and Social Transformation of Rural Rhode Island.* Boston: Northeastern University Press, 1992.

Kahn, Zorina B., and Kenneth L. Sokoloff. "Schemes of Practical Utility: Entrepreneurship and Innovation Among 'Great Inventors' in the United States, 1790–1865." *Journal of Economic History* 48 (1993): 289–307.

Kasson, John F. *Civilizing the Machine: Technology and Republican Values in America, 1776–1900.* New York: Penguin Books, 1976.

Kenzer, Robert C. *Kinship and Neighborhood in a Southern Community:*

Orange County, North Carolina, 1849–1881. Knoxville: University
of Tennessee Press, 1987.

Klein, Daniel B. "The Voluntary Provision of Public Goods? The Turnpike Companies of Early America." *Economic Inquiry 28* (October
1990): 788–812.

Klein, Daniel B., and John Majewski. "Economy, Community, and
Law: The Turnpike Movement in New York, 1797–1845." *Law &
Society Review* 26 (1992): 469–512.

Klein, Daniel B., and Chi Yin. "Use, Esteem, and Profit in Voluntary
Provision: Toll Roads in California, 1850–1902." *Economic Inquiry*
34 (October 1996): 678–92.

Klein, Maury. *The Great Richmond Terminal: A Study of Businessmen and
Business Strategy.* Charlottesville: University Press of Virginia, 1970.

Klein, Philip Shriver. *Pennsylvania Politics, 1817–1832: A Game Without
Rules.* Philadelphia: Historical Society of Pennsylvania, 1940.

Klein, Theodore B. *The Canals of Pennsylvania and the System of Internal
Improvement.* Bethlehem, Pa.: Canal Press, 1973.

Kloppenberg, James T. "The Virtues of Liberalism: Christianity,
Republicanism, and Ethics in Early American Political Discourse." *Journal of American History* 74 (1987): 9–33.

Kolchin, Peter. *American Slavery, 1619–1877.* New York: Hill and Wang,
1993.

———. *Unfree Labor: American Slavery and Russian Serfdom.* Cambridge:
Harvard University Press, 1987.

Krugman, Paul. "Increasing Returns and Economic Geography." *Journal of Political Economy* 99 (June 1991): 483–99.

———. *Geography and Trade.* Cambridge: MIT Press, 1986.

Kulik, Gary. "Dams, Fish, and Farmers: Defense of Public Rights in
Eighteenth-Century Rhode Island." In *The Countryside in the Age of
Capitalist Transformation: Essays in the Social History of Rural Amer-
ica,* edited by Steven Hahn and Jonathan Prude, 25–50. Chapel
Hill: University of North Carolina Press, 1985.

Kulikoff, Allan. *The Agrarian Origins of American Capitalism.* Charlottesville: University Press of Virginia, 1992.

———. *Tobacco and Slaves: The Development of Southern Cultures in the
Chesapeake, 1680–1800.* Chapel Hill: University of North Carolina
Press, 1986.

———. "The Transition to Capitalism in Rural America." *William and
Mary Quarterly* 46 (1989): 120–44.

Lamoreaux, Naomi R. "Banks, Kinship, and Economic Development:
The New England Case." *Journal of Economic History* 46 (1986):
647–67.

———. *Insider Lending: Banks, Personal Connections, and Economic Development in Industrial New England.* New York: Cambridge University
Press, 1994.

Lamoreaux, Naomi R., and Kenneth L. Sokoloff. "Long-term Change in the Organization of Inventive Activity." *Proceedings of the Academy of Science* 93 (1996): 12686–92.

Larson, John Lauritz. "Bind the Republic Together: The National Union and the Struggle of Internal Improvements." *Journal of American History* 74 (1987): 363–87.

———. *Bonds of Enterprise: John Murray Forbes and Western Development in America's Railway Age.* Cambridge: Harvard University Press, 1984.

Laurie, Bruce. *Artisans into Workers: Labor in Nineteenth-Century America.* New York: Noonday Press, 1989.

Lemon, James T. *The Best Poor Man's Country: A Geographical Study of Southeastern Pennsylvania.* Baltimore: The Johns Hopkins University Press, 1972.

Lewis, Ronald L. *Coal, Iron, and Slaves: Industrial Slavery in Maryland and Virginia, 1715–1865.* Westport, Conn.: Greenwood Press, 1979.

Lindstrom, Diane. *Economic Development in the Philadelphia Region, 1810–1850.* New York: Columbia University Press, 1978.

Lindstrom, Diane, and John Sharpless. "Urban Growth and Economic Structure in Antebellum America." *Research in Economic History* 3 (1978): 161–216.

Lively, Robert A. "The American System: A Review Article." *Business History Review* 29 (1955): 81–96.

Livingood, James Weston. *The Philadelphia-Baltimore Trade Rivalry, 1780–1860.* Harrisburg: The Pennsylvania Historical and Museum Commission, 1947.

Macpherson, C. B. *The Political Theory of Possessive Individualism: Hobbes to Locke.* Oxford: Clarendon Press, 1962.

Maier, Pauline. "The Revolutionary Origins of the American Corporation." *William and Mary Quarterly* 50 (January 1993): 51–84.

Majewski, John. "Who Financed the Transportation Revolution? Regional Divergence and Internal Improvements in Antebellum Pennsylvania and Virginia." *Journal of Economic History* 56 (1996): 763–88.

———. "A Revolution Too Many?" *Journal of Economic History* 57 (1997): 476–80.

Majewski, John, Christopher T. Baer, and Daniel B. Klein. "Responding to Relative Decline: The Plank Road Boom of Antebellum New York." *Journal of Economic History* 53 (1993): 106–22.

Malone, Dumas. *Jefferson the Virginian.* Boston: Little, Brown, and Company, 1948.

McCollough, Robert, and Walter Leuba. *The Pennsylvania Main Line Canal.* Martinsburg, Pa.: Morrisons Cove Herald, 1962.

McCoy, Drew R. *The Elusive Republic: Political Economy in Jeffersonian America.* New York. W. W. Norton and Company, 1980.

McCusker, John J., and Russel R. Menard. *The Economy of British America, 1607–1789, with Supplementary Bibliography.* Chapel Hill: University of North Carolina Press, 1985.

McDonald, Roderick A. "Independent Economic Production by Slaves on Antebellum Louisiana Sugar Plantations." In *Cultivation and Culture: Labor and the Shaping of Slave Life in the Americas,* edited by Ira Berlin and Philip D. Morgan, 275–99. Charlottesville: University Press of Virginia, 1993.

McGehee, Minnie Lee. "The Rivanna Navigation Company." *The Bulletin of the Fluvanna County Historical Society* 5 (1967): 1–20.

McGrane, Reginald C. *The Correspondence of Nicholas Biddle.* Boston and New York: Houghton Mifflin and Company, 1919.

McPherson, James M. *Battle Cry of Freedom: The Civil War Era.* New York: Oxford University Press, 1988.

———. *Ordeal by Fire: The Civil War and Reconstruction.* Second Edition. New York: McGraw-Hill, 1992.

Meinig, D. W. *The Shaping of America: A Geographical Perspective on 500 Years of History: Volume 2: Continental America, 1800–1867.* New Haven: Yale University Press, 1993.

Merrill, Boynton, Jr. *Jefferson's Nephews: A Frontier Tragedy.* Second Edition. Lexington: University of Kentucky Press, 1987.

Merrill, Michael. "The Anticapitalist Origins of the United States." *Review* 8 (1990): 465–97.

———. "Cash is Good to Eat: Self-Sufficiency and Exchange in the Rural Economy of the United States." *Radical History Review* 3 (1977): 42–71.

Meyer, David R. "Emergence of the American Manufacturing Belt: An Interpretation." *Journal of Historical Geography* 9 (1983): 145–74.

———. "The Industrial Retardation of Southern Cities, 1860–1880." *Explorations in Economic History* 25 (1988): 366–86.

Miller, Nathan. *The Enterprise of the Free: Aspects of Economic Development in New York State during the Canal Period, 1792–1838.* Ithaca: Cornell University Press, 1962.

Mitchell, Robert D. *Commercialism and Frontier: Perspectives on the Early Shenandoah Valley.* Charlottesville: University Press of Virginia, 1977.

Moore, John Hammond. *Albemarle: Jefferson's County, 1727–1976.* Charlottesville: University Press of Virginia, 1976.

Moore, Virginia. *Scottsville on the James: An Informal History.* Charlottesville: Jarman Press, 1969.

Mordecia, John Brooke. *A Brief History of the Richmond, Fredericksburg and Potomac Railroad.* Richmond: Old Dominion Press, 1941.

Morgan, Edmund S. *American Slavery, American Freedom: The Ordeal of Colonial Virginia.* New York: W. W. Norton and Company, 1975.

Morgan, Phillip D., and Michael L. Nicholls. "Slaves in Piedmont Virginia, 1720–1790." *William and Mary Quarterly* 46 (1989): 211–51.

Morriss, R. G. "Speech of R. G. Morriss, of Richmond, Delivered at the Convention." In *Proceedings of the Internal Improvement Convention Held at the White Sulphur Springs.* Richmond: The Dispatch, 1855.

Morton, Richard L. "The Virginia State Debt and Internal Improvements, 1820–1838." *Journal of Political Economy* 25 (1917): 339–73.

Nash, Gary B. *The Urban Crucible: Social Change, Political Consciousness, and the Origins of the American Revolution.* Cambridge: Harvard University Press, 1979.

Nevin, Alfred. *Men of Mark: Cumberland Valley, PA, 1776–1876.* Philadelphia: Fulton Publishing Company, 1876.

Nicholls, Michael L. "Piedmont Plantations and Farms: Transplanting Tidewater Traditions?" *The Magazine of Albemarle County History* 49 (1991): 1–17.

Noe, Kenneth W. *Southwest Virginia's Railroad: Modernization and the Sectional Crisis.* Urbana: University of Illinois Press, 1994.

O'Mara, James. *An Historical Geography of Urban System Development: Tidewater Virginia in the Eighteenth Century.* York, Ontario: Geographical Monographs, 1983.

Oakes, James. "The Politics of Economic Development in the Antebellum South." *Journal of Interdisciplinary History* 15 (1984): 305–16.

Olson, Mancur. *The Logic of Collective Action.* Cambridge: Harvard University Press, 1965.

Parker, William N. "Slavery and Southern Economic Development: A Hypothesis and Some Evidence." In *The Structure of the Cotton Economy of the Antebellum South,* edited by William N. Parker, 115–25. Washington, D.C.: Agricultural History Society, 1970.

Pawson, Eric. *Transport and Economy: The Turnpike Roads of Eighteenth Century Britain.* London: Academic Press, 1977.

Pease, William H., and Jane H. Pease. *The Web of Progress: Private Values and Public Styles in Boston and Charleston, 1828–1843.* New York: Oxford University Press, 1985.

Perkins, Elizabeth A. "The Consumer Frontier: Household Consumption in Early Kentucky." *Journal of American History* 78 (1991): 486–510.

Persky, Joseph. *The Burden of Dependency: Colonial Themes in Southern Economic Thought.* Baltimore: The Johns Hopkins University Press, 1992.

Pessen, Edward. "How Different From Each Other Were the Antebellum North and South?" *American Historical Review* 85 (1980): 1119–49.

Phillips, Ulrich Bonnell. *A History of Transportation of the Eastern Cotton Belt to 1860.* New York; Columbia University Press, 1908; reprint, Octagon Books, 1968.

Poor, Henry Varnum. *History of the Railroads and Canals of the United States of America.* New York: John H. Schulz, 1860.

Pred, Allan. "Manufacturing in the American Mercantile City: 1800–1840." *Annals of the Association of American Geographers* 56 (1966): 307–38.

———. *Urban Growth and City-Systems in the United States, 1840–1860.* Cambridge: Harvard University Press, 1980.

Price, Jacob M. "Economic Function and the Growth of American Port Towns in the Eighteenth Century." *Perspectives in American History* 8 (1974): 123–88.

Price, Jacob M., and Paul G. E. Clemens. "A Revolution in Scale in Overseas Trade: British Firms in the Chesapeake Trade, 1675–1775." *Journal of Economic History* 47 (1987): 1–43.

Pruitt, Bettye Hobbs. "Self-Sufficiency and the Agricultural Economy of Eighteenth-Century Massachusetts." *William and Mary Quarterly* 41 (1984): 333–64.

Ransom, Roger L. "Canals and Development: A Discussion of the Issues," *American Economic Review* 54 (1964): 365–89.

———. *Conflict and Compromise: The Political Economy of Slavery, Emancipation, and the American Civil War.* New York: Cambridge University Press, 1989.

Reidy, Joseph P. *From Slavery to Agrarian Capitalism in the Cotton Plantation South: Central Georgia, 1800–1880.* Chapel Hill: University of North Carolina Press, 1992.

Reiser, Catherine Elizabeth. *Pittsburgh's Commercial Development, 1800–1850.* Harrisburg: Pennsylvania Historical and Museum Commission, 1951.

Remer, Rosalind. *Printers and Men of Capital: Philadelphia Book Publishers in the New Republic.* Philadelphia: University of Pennsylvania Press, 1996.

Robert, Joseph Clarke. *The Tobacco Kingdom: Plantations, Market, and Factory in Virginia and North Carolina, 1800–1860.* Durham: Duke University Press, 1938.

Rodgers, Daniel T. "Republicanism: The Career of a Concept." *Journal of American History* 79 (June 1992): 11–38.

Rothenberg, Winifred B. "The Emergence of a Capital Market in Rural Massachusetts, 1780–1838." *Journal of Economic History* 45 (1985): 781–808.

———. "The Emergence of Farm Labor Markets and the Transformation of the Rural Economy: Massachusetts, 1750–1855." *Journal of Economic History* 48 (1988): 537–66.

———. The Market and Massachusetts Farmers, 1750–1855." *Journal of Economic History* 41 (1981): 283–324.

———. "The Market and Massachusetts Farmers: Reply." *Journal of Economic History* 43 (1983): 479–80.

———. *From Market-Places to a Market Economy: The Transformation of Rural Massachusetts, 1750–1850.* Chicago: University of Chicago Press, 1992.

Royal, William L. *A History of Virginia Banks and Banking Prior to the Civil War.* New York: Neale Publishing Company, 1907.

Rubin, Julius. "Canal or Railroad? Imitation and Innovation in the Response to Philadelphia, Baltimore, and Boston." *Transactions of the American Philosophical Society* 51, Part 7 (1961).

———. "The Limits of Agricultural Progress in the Nineteenth-Century South." *Agricultural History* 49 (1975): 362–75.

Rupp, I. Daniel. *The History and Topography of Dauphin, Cumberland, Franklin, Adams, and Perry Counties.* Lancaster City, Pa.: Gilbert Hills, 1846.

Ryan, Mary P. *Cradle of the Middle Class: The Family in Oneida County, New York, 1790–1865.* New York: Cambridge University Press, 1981.

Sachs, William S. "Agricultural Conditions in the Northern Colonies before the American Revolution." *Journal of Economic History* 8 (1953): 274–90.

Scheiber, Harry N. "At the Borderlands of Law and Economic History: The Contributions of Willard Hurst." *American Historical Review* 75 (1970): 744–56.

———. "Back to The Legal Mind? Doctrinal Analysis and the History of Law." *Reviews in American History* 5 (1977): 458–66.

———. "Federalism and the American Economic Order, 1789–1910." *Law and Society Review* 10 (1975): 57–118.

———. "Government and the Economy: Studies of the 'Commonwealth' Policy in Nineteenth-Century America." *Journal of Interdisciplinary History* 3 (1972): 135–51.

———. *Ohio Canal Era: A Case Study of Government and the Economy, 1820–1861.* Athens, Ohio: The Ohio University Press, 1969.

———. "Property Law, Expropriation, and Resource Allocation by Government: The United States, 1789–1910." *Journal of Economic History* 33 (1973): 232–51.

———. "Regulation, Property Rights, and Definition of 'The Market': Law and the American Economy." *Journal of Economic History* 41 (1981): 103–09.

———. "State Policy and the Public Domain: The Ohio Canal Lands." *Journal of Economic History* 25 (1965): 86–113.

Scheiber, Harry N., and Stephen Salsbury. "Reflections on George Rogers Taylor's *The Transportation Revolution, 1815–1860*: A

Twenty-five Year Retrospect." *Business History Review* 51 (1977): 79–89.

Schotter, H. W. *The Growth and Development of the Pennsylvania Railroad Company.* Philadelphia: Allen, Lane, and Scott, 1927.

Schwartz, Gary T. "Tort Law and the Economy in Nineteenth-Century America: A Reinterpretation." *Yale Law Journal* 90 (July 1981): 1717–75.

Schweikart, Larry. *Banking in the American South from the Age of Jackson to Reconstruction.* Baton Rouge: Louisiana State University Press, 1987.

Schweitzer, Mary M. *Custom and Contract: Household, Government, and the Economy in Colonial Pennsylvania.* New York: Columbia University Press, 1987.

Scranton, Philip. *Proprietary Capitalism: The Textile Manufacture at Philadelphia, 1800–1885.* Philadelphia: Temple University Press, 1983.

Sellers, Charles. *The Market Revolution: Jacksonian America, 1815–1846.* New York: Oxford University Press, 1991.

Shade, William G. *Democratizing the Old Dominion: Virginia and the Second Party System, 1824–1861.* Charlottesville: University Press of Virginia, 1996.

Shaefer, Donald F. "A Statistical Profile of Frontier and New South Migration: 1850–1860. *Agricultural History* 59 (1985): 563–78.

Shaw, Ronald E. "Canals in the Early Republic: A Review of Recent Literature." *Journal of the Early Republic* 4 (1984): 119–42.

Shelton, Cynthia J. *The Mills of Manayunk: Industrialization and Social Conflict in the Philadelphia Region, 1787–1837.* Baltimore: The Johns Hopkins University Press, 1986.

Siegel, Frederick F. *The Roots of Southern Distinctiveness: Tobacco and Society in Danville, Virginia, 1780–1865.* Chapel Hill: University of North Carolina Press, 1987.

Simler, Lucy, and Paul G. E. Clemens. "The Best Poor Man's Country in 1783: The Population Structure of Rural Society in Late 18th-Century Southeastern Pennsylvania." *Proceedings of the American Philosophical Society* 133 (1989): 234–61.

Simon, Julian. *The Ultimate Resource.* Princeton: Princeton University Press, 1981.

Slaughter, Thomas P. *The Whiskey Rebellion: Frontier Epilogue to the American Revolution.* New York: Oxford University Press, 1986.

Sloan, Herbert E. *Principle and Interest: Thomas Jefferson and the Problem of Debt.* New York: Oxford University Press, 1995.

Snyder, Charles McCool. *The Jacksonian Heritage: Pennsylvania Politics, 1833–1848.* Harrisburg, Pa.: Pennsylvania Historical and Museum Commission, 1958.

Sokoloff, Kenneth L. "Inventive Activity in Early Industrial America: Evidence from Patent Records, 1790–1846." *Journal of Economic History* 48 (1988): 813–50.

———. "Invention, Innovation, and Manufacturing Productivity Growth in the Antebellum Northeast." In *American Economic Growth and Standards of Living before the Civil War*, edited by Robert E. Gallman and John Joseph Wallis, 345–78. Chicago: University of Chicago Press, 1992.

———. "Productivity Growth in Manufacturing during Early Industrialization: Evidence from the American Northeast, 1820–1860." In *Long-Term Factors in American Economic Growth*, edited by Stanley L. Engerman and Robert E. Gallman, 679–736. Chicago: University of Chicago Press, 1986.

———. "Was the Transition from the Artisanal Shop to the Non-Mechanized Factory Associated with Gains in Efficiency? Evidence from the U.S. Manufacturing Censuses of 1820 and 1850." *Explorations in Economic History* 21 (1984): 351–82.

Sokoloff, Kenneth L., and Georgia C. Villaflor. "The Market for Manufacturing Workers During Early Industrialization: The American Northeast, 1820 to 1860." In *Strategic Factors in Nineteenth Century American History*, edited by Claudia Goldin and Hugh Rockoff, 29–65. Chicago: University of Chicago Press, 1992.

Steckel, Richard H. "Household Migration and Rural Settlement in the United States, 1850–1860." *Explorations in Economic History* 26 (1989): 190–218.

Stewart, Peter C. "Railroads and Urban Rivalries in Antebellum Eastern Virginia." *Virginia Magazine of History and Biography* 81 (1973): 3–22.

Stover, John F. *The Railroads of the South, 1865–1900*. Chapel Hill: University of North Carolina Press, 1955.

Stokes, Melvyn, and Stephen Conway, eds. *The Market Revolution in America: Social, Political, and Religious Expressions, 1800–1880*. Charlottesville: University Press of Virginia, 1996.

Stott, Richard. "Artisans and Capitalist Development." *Journal of the Early Republic* 16 (Summer 1996): 257–71.

Sutherland, Stella Helen. *Population Distribution in Colonial America*. New York: Columbia University Press, 1936.

Swanson, Donald F. "Bank Notes Will Be But as Oak Leaves: Thomas Jefferson on Paper Money." *Virginia Magazine of History and Biography* 101 (January 1993): 37–52.

"A Symposium on Charles Sellers, *The Market Revolution: Jacksonian America, 1815–1846*." *Journal of the Early Republic* 12 (1992): 445–76.

Taylor, George Rogers. *The Transportation Revolution, 1815–1860*. New York: Holt, Rinehart, and Winston, 1951.

Taylor, George Rogers, and Irene D. Neu. *The American Railroad Network, 1861–1890.* Cambridge: Harvard University Press, 1956.

Tchakerian, Viken. "Productivity, Extent of Markets, and Manufacturing in the Late Antebellum South and Midwest," *Journal of Economic History* 54 (1994): 497–525.

Trelease, Allen W. *The North Carolina Railroad, 1849–1871, and the Modernization of North Carolina.* Chapel Hill: North Carolina University Press, 1991.

Tully, Alan. "Economic Opportunity in Mid-Eighteenth Century Rural Pennsylvania." *Historie Sociale — Social History* 9 (1976): 111–28.

Turner, George Edgar. *Victory Rode the Rails: The Strategic Place of Railroads in the Civil War.* Indianapolis: Bobbs-Merrill Company, 1953.

Van Dolsen, Nancy. "Transportation, Competition, and the Growth of a Town: Carlisle, 1750–1860." *Cumberland County History* 14 (Summer 1997): 19–31.

Vickers, Daniel. "Competency and Competition: Economic Culture in Early America." *William and Mary Quarterly* 47 (1990): 3–29.

———. "The Northern Colonies: Economy and Society, 1600–1775." In *The Cambridge Economic History of the United States,* Vol. 1, edited by Stanley L. Engerman and Robert E. Gallman, 209–48. New York: Cambridge University Press, 1996.

Wade, Richard C. *Slavery in the Cities: The South, 1820–1860.* New York: Oxford University Press, 1964.

Wallis, John Joseph, Richard Sylla, and John B. Legler. "Interaction of Taxation and Regulation of Banks in Early Nineteenth Century America." In *The Regulated Economy: A Historical Approach to Political Economy,* edited by Claudia Goldin and Gary D. Libecap, 121–44. Chicago: University of Chicago Press, 1994.

Walsh, Lorena S. "Slave Life, Slave Society, and Tobacco Production in the Tidewater Chesapeake, 1620–1820." In *Cultivation and Culture: Labor and the Shaping of Slave Life in the Americas,* edited by Ira Berlin and Philip D. Morgan, 170–99. Charlottesville: University Press of Virginia, 1993.

Ward, Harry M., and Harold E. Greer, Jr. *Richmond During the Revolution, 1755–1783.* Charlottesville: University Press of Virginia, 1977.

Ward, James A. *J. Edgar Thompson: Master of the Pennsylvania.* Westport, Conn.: Greenwood Press, 1980.

Watson, Harry L. *Liberty and Power: The Politics of Jacksonian America.* New York: Hill and Wang, 1990.

———. "Slavery and Development in a Dual Economy: The South and the Market Revolution." In *The Market Revolution in America: Social, Political, and Religious Expressions, 1800–1880,* edited by Melvyn Stokes and Stephen Conway, 43–73. Charlottesville: University Press of Virginia, 1996.

———. "Squire Oldway and His Friends: Opposition to Internal Improvements in Antebellum North Carolina." *North Carolina Historical Review* 54 (1977): 106–19.

Watts, Charles Wilder. "Land Grants and Aristocracy in Albemarle County, 1727–1755." *Papers of the Albemarle County Historical Society* 8 (1947–1948): 1–26.

Watts, Randy. *Mainline Railroads, 1828 to 1993.* Carlisle: Keystone Computer Services, 1993.

Weiss, Rona S. "The Market and Massachusetts Farmers, 1750–1850: Comment." *Journal of Economic History* 43 (1983): 475–78.

Wertenbaker, Thomas Jefferson. "The Rivanna." *Magazine of Albemarle County History* 14 (1954–55): 1–8.

Westhaeffer, Paul J. *History of the Cumberland Valley Railroad, 1835–1919.* Washington, D.C.: D.C. Chapter of the National Railway Historical Society, 1979.

Wilentz, Sean. *Chants Democratic: New York City and the Rise of the American Working Class, 1788–1850.* New York: Oxford University Press, 1984.

———. "Society, Politics, and the Market Revolution, 1815–1848." In *The New American History*, edited by Eric Foner, 51–71. Philadelphia: Temple University Press, 1991.

Wiley, Samuel T., Esq. *Biographical and Portrait Cyclopedia of the Nineteenth Congressional District, Pennsylvania.* Philadelphia: C. A. Ruoff Company, 1897.

Wing, Conway P. *History of Cumberland County, Pennsylvania.* Philadelphia: James D. Scott, 1879.

Wood, Gordon S. *The Creation of the American Republic, 1776–1787.* Chapel Hill: University of North Carolina Press, 1969.

———. "The Enemy is Us: Democratic Capitalism in the Early Republic." *Journal of the Early Republic* 16 (Summer 1996): 293–308.

———. *The Radicalism of the American Revolution.* New York: Knopf, 1992.

Woodruff, Nan Elizabeth. "The Transition to Capitalism in America." *Reviews in American History* 20 (1992): 168–74.

Woods, Edgar. *Albemarle County in Virginia.* Bridgewater, Va.: C. J. Carrier, 1900.

Wright, Gavin. *Old South, New South: Revolutions in the Southern Economy Since the Civil War.* New York: Basic Books, 1986.

———. *The Political Economy of the Cotton South: Households, Markets, and Wealth in the Nineteenth Century.* New York: W. W. Norton and Company, 1978.

Wyatt-Brown, Bertram. *Honor and Violence in the Old South.* New York: Oxford University Press, 1986.

Young, Douglas. *A Brief History of the Staunton and James River Turnpike.*

Second Revised Edition. Charlottesville: Virginia Highway and
Research Transportation Council, 1975.

Zboray, Ronald J. *A Fictive People: Antebellum Economic Development and
the American Reading Public.* New York: Oxford University Press,
1993.

Index

With the exception of the Cumberland Valley Railroad, the Pennsylvania Railroad, and the Virginia Central Railroad, all individual railroad companies are listed under the heading "railroads (companies)."

abolitionism, 136
Agricultural Society of Albemarle, 21, 31–32
Albemarle County (VA), 170, 180, 181; agricultural reform in, 21–25; agricultural specialization in, 43, 68, 69t; colonial settlement of, 14–15; distribution of land in, 15, 176–77; kinship networks in, 17, 20, 70–71; land values in, 29–30, 44; manufacturing in, 42–43; migration patterns in, 20–21, 177–78; political power in, 16–17; population of, 17–18, 42, 65; prosperity of, 67–71; slavery in, 4, 15–16, 71–72, 176–77; stagnation of, 17–21; town rivalry in, 25–28, 97–102; see also Charlottesville, Scottsville
Albemarle Hole and Corner Club, 22
Albemarle Insurance Company, 66
Alexandria (VA), 127, 145, 160
Allegheny County, see Pittsburgh
American Farmer, 22, 44–45n28
American Revolution, 147, 148
American Volunteer, 72–73, 103–4, 105, 107–8
Anderson, Joseph, 161–62, 163–64
anthracite coal, 157–58, 172
Appalachian Mountains, 4, 115, 122
Appomattox River, 145
artisans: economic attitudes of, 81–84; investment in corporations by, 51t, 64t
Ashworth, John, 1
Augusta County (VA), 28, 63, 66, 101

Bailey, Thomas R., 98, 99
Baldwin, Mathias W., 155
Baltimore, 43, 46, 75, 115, 143, 146; hinterland of, 161, 166; trade of, 37, 48

Bank of the United States, 87, 94, 97, 100; political controversy over, 102–3, 104–5; railroad investments of, 74, 75t, 76; see also Biddle, Nicholas
banks (state): investment in, 50–52; political conflict over, 97–102, 107
Barley, Thomas P., 48
Bennington, Samuel, 179
Berkeley, William, 144
Biddle, Edward M., 78
Biddle, H. J., 77–78
Biddle, Nicholas, 9, 76, 77, 87, 99, 103, 115
Biddle, Thomas, 77
Biddle, Valeria Fullerton, 103
Biddle, William M., 103
Bolling, William, 34
Boston (MA), 127, 168, 169
Brady, James, 72
Branham, Robert, 16–17
Bristol (TE), 134
Brown, Bezaleel, 16–17
Brown, William T., 67
Bruce, Charles, 113, 141
Buchanan (VA), 126
Buckingham, John, 72
Buffalo Forge, 160
Burnaby, Andrew, 150
Burton, Thomas, 17
Bushman, Richard, 152
butter production, 80

Cadwalader, George, 77–78
California, 57
canals, 67, 133; see also Erie Canal, James River and Kanawha Company, Mainline Canal System, Rivanna Navigation Company
capitalism, 5–6, 138–39
Carey, Mathew, 115, 116

209